Broadcasting a Life

Broadcasting a Life
The Autobiography of Olive Shapley

in association with Christina Hart

Scarlet Press

Published by Scarlet Press
5 Montague Road, London E8 2HN

British Library Cataloguing-in-Publication Data
A catalogue record for this book is available from the British Library

ISBN 1 85727 038 X pb
ISBN 1 85727 083 5 hb

Designed and produced for Scarlet Press by
Chase Production Services, Chipping Norton, OX7 5QR
Typeset from the author's disk by
Stanford DTP Services, Milton Keynes
Printed in the EC by J.W. Arrowsmith Ltd, Bristol

To travel hopefully is a better thing than to arrive.

Robert Louis Stevenson, *Virginibus Puerisque: El Dorado*

Contents

	Foreword	ix
	Preface	xi
	Acknowledgements	xii
	Introduction	1
1	1910–20 – Family	2
2	1920–29 – Childhood	9
3	1929–34 – Oxford	23
4	1934–37 – Recruitment to the BBC	34
5	1937–39 – Radio documentaries	48
6	1939–41 – Outbreak of war	64
7	1942–45 – Letters from America	78
8	1942–45 – *Conversations in America*	94
9	1945–49 – Return to England	109
10	1949–53 – *Woman's Hour*	124
11	1953–59 – Rose Hill	139
12	1953–59 – *Something to Read*	156
13	1959–81 – The Rose Hill Trust	168
14	1981–92 – Stephens Terrace	182
15	1926–83 – Travel	188
16	1992–96 – Postscript	203
	References	210
	Index	211

Foreword

Barbara Castle

Olive Shapley has that elusive quality called personality. From the moment I bumped into her in the prim corridors of St Hugh's College, Oxford, as the 20s decade was merging into the tortured 30s, it was like a breath of fresh air from my Yorkshire moors. Yet Olive was technically a southerner, though with a spirit which reaches out to all regions, race and countries with an excited sense of discovery.

Olive fitted as uneasily as I did into an Oxford college which seemed to be exclusively peopled by young ladies from Roedean, Wycombe Abbey and Cheltenham Ladies' College. Her enthusiastic study of the Hindu philosopher Rabindranath Tagore stuck out as incongruously as my passion for the challenging politics of the Bradford Independent Labour Party which Keir Hardie had founded in 1903.

I found in Olive a fellow rebel worthy of the rough north from which I came and to which she instinctively responded. It was entirely appropriate that she should start her distinguished career in broadcasting with the BBC in Manchester.

I am delighted that Olive, with the help of her daughter, Christina, has at last written her autobiography. It is the story of one of the offshoots of British creative genius. Olive never reached – or aspired to – the top echelons of BBC management. She was content to delight and educate millions of listeners to the BBC's Northern radio with her new-style *Children's Hour* and *Woman's Hour* programmes and documentaries. She was one of the founts of inspiration without which national and international politics decline into aridity. It is typical of her that when her second husband died, she opened her Manchester home to unmarried mothers and then Vietnamese refugees.

Conventional epithets like 'brilliant innovator' do not suit her instinct for self-deprecation. She and I shared a deliciously

ix

liberating sense of irreverence about the values of all establishments, whether in broadcasting or politics. We neither of us believed in gesture politics or gesture rebellions. When we climbed that high gate at the end of St Hugh's garden in the middle of the night, risking dire punishment, it was not to prove anything, merely a simple desire to escape from our airless rooms to walk the river's bank in the misty moonlight because that seemed the natural thing to do.

In the years which have passed since our Oxford days I have seen Olive only occasionally, but every time I do it has been a refresher course in being ourselves. Even at her eightieth birthday party she had not really changed, holding court, propped on a high stool crinkling her nose and chuckling as she always did.

She has never, thank God, lost her sense of fun. When three or four years ago we were asked to take part in a *Woman's Hour* programme on growing old, we both instinctively recoiled. We finally agreed on condition that it was retitled *Growing Old Disgracefully*, and enjoyed ourselves. We were assured that the programme was a great success.

As I would have expected, Olive's account of her life is, as journalists like to say, a 'good read'. But it is also a valuable slice of social history of which we do not learn enough in our schools and universities.

Today a spiritual dehydration afflicts our market economy society. It is because Olive Shapley reaches those parts of the spirit that market economy values do not reach that I am proud to have known her and to write this foreword to her entertaining book.

Preface

'Why don't you just put a modem on your mother's PC?' said the young financial adviser. I had mentioned that I was to-ing and fro-ing between Yorkshire and mid Wales while collaborating with my mother on her autobiography, and he was appalled by our antiquated working methods. After some explanation Olive, already well into her eighties, found his remark amusing too. But my simple word processing and the scorned face-to-face communication got us there in the end.

Several people helped along the way and I want to acknowledge and thank them.

Richard Gallagher, as the original collaborator, got the project going. The Rt Hon Barbara Castle, now Baroness Castle of Blackburn, waited patiently to write the foreword. Dan Salt, Nicholas Salt, Brian Dyson, Gillian Hush and Gill Sargeant read the first draft and made valuable comments. Paddy Scannell gave permission to quote, as did Jacqueline Kavanagh of the BBC Written Archives Centre. Other Centre staff involved were Gwyniver Jones, Neil Somerville and Trevor White. The following offered advice and encouragement: Michael Barton, Michael Green, Gerald Hagan, Anne Karpf, Wendy Pye, Gillian Reynolds, Anthony Goff, Wallace Grevatt, and Diana Stenson. Ilkley Library and staff played their part, and Bridget Bennett and Gay Fullick helped in the photograph search. Ivy Doherty, Shelagh and Martin Herbert, and Laura and Andy Chapman provided domestic support. Finally, I now know why writers acknowledge their immediate households; in this case much gratitude goes to Tony and Adam Hart.

Christina Hart

Acknowledgements

The publishers and author wish to thank the following for the use of copyright material: the BBC Written Archives Centre for *First Steps in Learning*; *£.s.d: A Study in Shopping*; *Canal Journey*; *The Quiet House at Haworth*; *We have Been Evacuated*; *The Great Evacuation Question*; *Women in Wartime*; *Miners' Wives*; *Children in Wartime*; *Women in Europe*; *American Boys Calling Home*; *New York Speaks to London*; *A Wartime Thanksgiving Day*; *Meet the Ackermans*; *A Child Comes Home*, letter from Derek McCulloch; letter from Leslie G.D. Smith; *The Story of Saltaire*; *Family Affairs*. *Children's Hour* material: *Newsletter No. 1 – Letter from America*; *Newsletter No. 2 – Statue of Liberty*; *Newsletter No.11 – The White House*; *Newsletter No. 14 – Seeing the States by Railroad*; *Newsletter No. 29 – More Differences*; *Newsletter No. 36 – Thinking of Home*. *Woman's Hour* material: *Coronation Robes*; *To Travel Hopefully*; *Cohabiting People*. From the *Radio Times*: 'Coast and Country'; 'Something of a Handicap'; 'Fortnightly Newsletter for *Children's Hour*' and the *Listener* 'Critic on the Hearth'. Other written sources: *A Social History of British Broadcasting: Volume One, 1922–1939*, 1991, Paddy Scannell, Basil Blackwell Publishers and the BBC Written Archives; the *Daily Mail*; Paul Donovan, *The Radio Companion*, 1992, Harper Collins; 'Working Partners' in *Good Housekeeping*, National Magazine Company; the *Liverpool Daily Post* and *Echo*. For illustrations, the BBC Picture Archives for Olive Shapley portrait 1949, 'Something to Read', 'Miners' Wives' and the *Guardian* for the photograph accompanying article in 1989.

Every effort has been made to trace the copyright holders of the illustrations reproduced in this book; unfortunately, in some cases this has proved to be impossible. The author and publishers would be glad to hear from any copyright holders they have not been able to contact and to print due acknowledgements in the next edition.

Introduction

To write an autobiography is not the most arduous form of literary undertaking; it is done very successfully all the time. 'How delicious was the taste of nasturtium leaves between bread and butter in the long hot summers of our childhood,' is delightful to write and often delightful to read. My reason for starting the notes that led to this book was a grimmer one.

One day, when I was leaving Manchester for London in a great hurry in an under-serviced aged car, my daughter, whose father had died when she was seven months old, said to me rather sharply, 'I suppose you know that if you kill yourself in this car, we shall never know who we are.' This, I saw, was true. My three children would be left with a lot of family possessions, innumerable notes written in a kind of shorthand, but with no pointers. I was the only one who could tell them the way in which their father and their mother had been brought up and the ideas that lay behind their own upbringing. With me would go most of what remained of their father, the verbal memories of their grandparents. So, I determined to try and put some of this down. They will recognise the truth of it, but they could not possibly put this truth together for themselves.

As time went by this nucleus of private concerns spread to include my public life in the BBC. Broadcasting had brought together the children's father and me and was a passion we shared in the exciting early years of radio. For forty years my work in radio and television was always much more than just a job. It was a whole way of life for both me and my family. And so that also became an important part of the story that I wanted to tell.

1 1910–20 – Family

It all began with the compasses. One of my earliest memories is of my father telling me about his schooldays at Dulwich College. His family was poor but he had won a scholarship there. He walked five miles to school and back each day and sometimes there was only a slice of bread for his lunch. One day his class was told to bring in compasses for mathematics. My father was only able to take a home-made set, beautifully made by his father, but an object of great amusement to the schoolmaster and the rest of the class. My father told me this story without bitterness, but it struck a deep chord in me. In a matter of moments I became a socialist, a blood-and-thunder socialist.

My parents, William Gilbert Shapley and Kate Sophie Reimann, met at the small Unitarian church in Peckham. There was never any doubt in my mind that this was a very happy and successful marriage.

I never knew my father's parents. They came from Devon, where my grandfather had been a master carpenter in Exeter, going to work, I was told, in a long white coat and a silk hat. We still use some of the chests and walnut writing-desks he made, and through all our many removals I have kept his school exercise books, headed 'Francis Shapley, 1853' with words like 'Tempt None to Sin' and 'Impenitence Precludes Pardon' repeated nine times in faultless copper-plate writing.

My father had one sister, Alie. She was a deeply religious, upright spinster with very high standards and rather severe. I was always a little frightened of her. She was not lovable but she was certainly impressive. Aunt Alie was to play an important part in my childhood, being the only relative outside the immediate family circle with whom I had close contact. She was matron of a home for unmarried mothers in Great Portland Street, just around the corner from where the BBC would eventually be. At that time associating with unmarried mothers must have been something akin to Christ's associating with the lepers. Several decades later, I myself was to provide shelter at my house in Didsbury, Rose Hill, for women in a similar position. Perhaps Aunt Alie's ghost was watching over me even then. But also, unconventional as I was, I just felt that this was the right thing to do. I know that my attitudes conflict strongly with the moral restraints of so many others who experienced an Edwardian childhood. This is perhaps not surprising because, as I came to realise later, my family were remarkably ahead of their time, and I consider myself lucky in having had such liberal parents.

My maternal grandfather, Louis Ferdinand Augustus Emil Reimann, was German. His father had owned a bookshop in Frankfurt. Louis Ferdinand was a clever boy and was about to go to university when disaster struck. He came home one night and found that his father had set fire to the bookshop with himself inside, and his mother had come home and hanged herself behind a neighbour's door. My mother never had the least inkling of what lay behind this tragedy. Louis Ferdinand subsequently came to England, got a job as a clerk and married the daughter of a Norfolk farmer. They had six children very quickly and he died of pneumonia during the notorious winter when the Thames froze over. My mother, Kate Sophie, was the second child and was fifteen years old when she went out to work as a servant. Kate Sophie's mother turned the house into a servants' registry, taking in girls from the country who wanted to come to London and be trained. She was the only one of my grandparents whom I knew.

After leaving school my father joined the London County Council, training as what was, in those days, called a 'sanitary inspector' and became the chief inspector of the Public Health Department. He was eventually awarded the OBE for his services. As a child I took a great interest in his work and feel that the seeds of my social concern can be traced back to this. I remember him taking me out one night, when a census was made of London's homeless poor. I saw, under the arches, people sleeping wrapped in tattered blankets. It seemed unbelievable. On another occasion my father took me to visit the Chinese community in east London, which was a very small community in those days. There prevailed generally at that time a xenophobia which was totally absent from my family.

I had two older brothers. Frank was eleven years older than me and Bill five years older. When I was four, World War One broke out and in 1916 Frank joined up. He had been out one day with his scout troop and a woman had handed him a white feather and said, 'What's a big fellow like you doing playing at soldiers?' He had signed on for the navy even before he came home. He lied about his age, but at that stage in the war no one cared. Then, one day, a green envelope arrived on our doorstep. This was the only time that I remember seeing my mother cry. Frank had been drowned in the Battle of Jutland. It was my first experience of death. When I was older my mother told me that from this time she began to have frequent nightmares about drowning, and these continued thoughout her life.

I have a vivid memory of the outbreak of World War One. My father had helped me wash my hands before lunch. As he was drying them carefully with a towel, he said to me, 'Olive, I think I ought to tell you that we are at war with Germany.'

But apart from this and the great sadness of Frank's death, I have few memories of that war. Living in south London, we were very aware of air-raids and spent many nights in the cellar. My mother used to read to me, my father mended shoes on a sort of ironing board, my brother Bill slept, and somehow we all survived.

Bill and I were never very close. Five years is a big gap when you are growing up. I was regarded as 'kid sister' for a long time. However, for a few years we did become closer because of a mutual interest in music. Bill had a very impressive bass voice and had won a scholarship to a music school. Later he graduated from singing at Masonic affairs to a concert at the Queen's Hall in Langham Place and to one or two broadcasts. I had learnt the piano and enjoyed accompanying him. The possession of this voice gave Bill no pleasure and he finally abandoned singing and became a journalist.

When I was five I began attending Friern School. My first day there remains clear in my mind. Over twenty-five years later I wrote a short story about it, which was broadcast a number of times on radio, and translated into Swedish and published in an anthology. This is the true story, *First Steps in Learning*.

I had no presentiment of trouble when my mother took me to see the headmistress. It was not until the headmistress said in a kind voice, 'Of course, Olive musn't be separated from Gracie Munns,' that my heart sank. Gracie was a year older than myself and we had lived near to each other for as long as I could remember. Our parents and the neighbours had always liked to see us as devoted little friends and probably only Gracie and I knew the depths of our mutual dislike.

I could hardly explain all this to the headmistress at our first meeting. And so it happened that, on my first day at school, I was put not into the babies' class but into an older children's class, sharing a desk with Gracie.

'Fold your arms,' said Miss Knight, the teacher. I had never seen anyone like her before. She had a very red face, a tight black satin dress, a lot of jangly beads and a frizzy bird's nest of hair.

'Come along, Olive Shapley!' she said. 'Didn't you hear me tell you to fold your arms?'

I went very red and, looking round at the other children, copied what they were doing, but it seemed most unnatural.

'And sit up ... sit up!' said Miss Knight. 'We don't want round-shouldered little girls in this class.'

Then she opened a thin book and began to call out our names. At first I could not understand what was happening. When Gracie's name was called, she said a strange word, unfolded her arms and sat back. I wanted to ask her what the word was, but Gracie would not take any notice of me.

'Olive Shapley,' said Miss Knight. 'Olive Shapley!'

I wanted to say, 'Yes,' but I was swallowing so hard that it would not come out.

'We don't want little girls in this class who can't answer to their names properly,' said Miss Knight, but luckily she went on to the next one and I cautiously unfolded my arms and sat back.

Then came Scripture. No one bothered me. For the first time I breathed more easily and even ventured to look about me at the unfamiliar surroundings. My eye took in the wooden floor and the sharp little desks; the tall locked cupboards and the dark red hot-water pipes; the picture, high up on the wall, of a boy, a cat and a dead fish. Always my eyes came back to the alarming Miss Knight; somehow more alarming because I, too young then for the intricacies of English spelling, did not know about the 'K' at the beginning of her name. 'Miss Night-Night-Night,' I thought, and the world seemed dark indeed.

Then it was time for writing.

'Come here, Olive Shapley,' said Miss Knight, busily cleaning the blackboard, 'and sit at my desk. I want to see how advanced you are.'

I picked up my new pencilbox with the draughtboard lid and slowly went out to the front of the class. I climbed on to Miss Knight's chair, slid back the lid of the box a little and peeped inside; I saw rows of shining pencils – all colours – and all sharpened to meticulously fine points by my father. He had done them last night while my mother was laying out my clean white socks and small black buttoned boots, the new handkerchief with the 'O' embroidered in the corner, and the green and white gingham frock with the French knots in which it had been decided that I should make my first appearance at school. I was horrified to feel a lump coming in my throat. I began to wonder what my mother was doing on this long, long morning. As I thought of the familiar routine of the housework, I knew for the first time the pains of separation.

'Now, Olive,' said Miss Knight briskly, 'no day dreaming. I want you to write your full name on this label, and then we'll stick it on your pencilbox.' She put a sheet of pink blotting paper on the desk and a shiny label with a gummed back.

'Get out a pencil, Olive,' she said, 'and don't waste any more time.'

She turned back to the class who were beginning to become restive and I selected my red pencil with a soft lead. I grasped it firmly and bent over the desk.

'Oh no-no-no-no-no,' said a voice at my elbow, and I was so frightened that I almost fell off the chair. 'Oh no-no-no; we don't hold pencils in our *left* hand. We hold pencils in our *right* hand, don't we, children?'

'Yes, Miss Knight,' chorused the class, glad of any diversion.

'Here's a little girl who thinks we hold pencils in our *left* hand,' said Miss Knight, pleased with her success.

The class giggled and I blushed, but managed to say, 'I always hold things in my left hand for everything. I can't write at all with my other hand.'

'Now, Olive,' said Miss Knight, 'we never say "can't" in this class, do we, children?'

'No, Miss Knight,' chanted the class.

'Say that after me, Olive,' said Miss Knight. 'We never say "can't" in this class.'

'We never say "can't" in this class,' I said, filled with rage and shame.

'Because it's your first day,' said Miss Knight, 'you may use your left hand, but you must tell your father and mother that they will have to break you of the habit immediately.'

She turned away to the blackboard, and I, my hopes of doing something to please this terrifying teacher now sadly dampened, bent again over the desk. Breathing hard, my tongue out, legs twisted round the chair-rail, slowly and with infinite pains, I traced it out ... OLIVE MARY SHAPLEY ... I remembered everything my father had told me and I did it beautifully.

'Hurry up, Olive,' said Miss Knight. 'Have you finished yet?'

'Yes,' I said.

'Well, bring it over here then,' said Miss Knight.

I went across the room with my label, but as Miss Knight took it from me, a frown came on her face and my knees began to shake.

'I don't think you're a very truthful little girl,' said Miss Knight.

I went very red and then pale.

'When your mother brought you in here this morning,' went on Miss Knight, 'you told me you could write.'

'Yes,' I said, lost and bewildered.

'This,' said Miss Knight, 'is not writing. This is ... what is it, Gracie Munns?'

'Printing,' said Gracie, with a self-satisfied smirk.

'Printing,' said Miss Knight. 'Now go and *write* your name and be quick about it.' She crumpled up the label and threw it into the waste paper basket. 'The LCC,' she said, 'does not provide us with labels for us to waste them.'

I stood rooted to the spot. I knew instinctively that this wasn't only my shame. I realised that I had disgraced my mother and father as well. With despair I thought of last night's excitement and of my mother getting my clothes ready. I thought of my father carefully making points to my pencils, and I remembered how, only that morning, he had cleared the breakfast things out of the way and once more, slowly and patiently and lovingly, had helped me trace the OLIVE MARY SHAPLEY on the back of one of his letters, so that I should surprise them all at school with my lovely printing. I felt as though *he* had been crumpled up along with the sticky label and flung into the waste paper basket.

'Come along,' said Miss Knight. 'I can't have little girls who *sulk* in my class ...'

At last my brother was fetched from the Big Boys' Department and told to take me home.

'And tell your mother I don't want her back until she's learnt not to be a cry-baby,' said Miss Knight. 'I can't have cry-babies in my class.'

'Old cat,' said Bill when we were in the playground. Then he found the clean new handkerchief with the 'O' in the corner, in the pocket of the green and white gingham frock, and tried to wipe away his little sister's tears. The knife had gone too deep, and not even the security of home and mother and the special dinner in honour of my first day at school could console me, though it wasn't until late that evening that the whole story came out and they had to promise me that I shouldn't ever go back to Miss Knight.

Next morning my mother took me over to the school and left me in the playground while she talked to the headmistress; I prayed that Miss Knight would not look out of the window and see me. The headmistress soon came out and, taking me into her warm room with the coal fire, kissed me and gave me a peppermint humbug. Then she took me and my mother along to the babies' class where they were playing 'Nuts 'n May'. I saw that the room was bright and sunny and had nice pictures, low down so that you could see them, and no desks at all, only little chairs and tables. There was a teacher in a green smock and she was young and pretty. She took my hand and showed me the vases of flowers on the window ledges, the bowls that would be planted with bulbs, the jam-jars with tiddlers in them, the green wire cages with stick insects inside, and the bootboxes full of silkworms.

Then she sat down and took me on her knee and said, 'A little bird told me you do lovely printing. Do you think, if I gave you a big sheet of paper, you could print OLIVE MARY SHAPLEY for me right across the top?'

2 1920–29 – Childhood

It seems to me now that I spent a great part of my childhood wishing that I were someone else. Not the daughter of a belted earl, but the child of a poor clergyman or an overworked doctor.

I would have chosen to be poor professional class and beautiful. In fact, I was lower middle class and plain. When I was old enough to read *Little Women*, I knew exactly where I fitted in, and a fantasy life with the March family sustained me for years. During World War Two, when I was working in New York, I had a chance to spend a weekend in Concord, Massachusetts, birthplace of Louisa M. Alcott, the author of *Little Women*. I sent out for a copy of the book from Brentano's and when the boy from the drug store brought up my lunch, I was soaked in tears. Whole chapters of the book sprang complete into my mind; I hardly needed to turn the pages. There is a great deal to be said for a romantic attitude towards life.

I was born on 10 April 1910 at 10 Tresco Road, Peckham, southeast London. My mother had named me after Olive Schreiner, the author of *Story of an African Farm*. I grew up with a mystic feeling about the letter 'O'. It still seems to me to have a most satisfying calm about it.

10 Tresco Road was one of a row of small, semi-detached villas, bay-windowed, a tiny garden in front with a dusty privet hedge shutting us off from the road. We were separated from the next house by a very narrow passage, which I still walk up and down almost nightly in my dreams. The back garden was small and shady, full of Solomon's Seal and London Pride, colourless flowers. I once sat on the rockery and thought the word 'stone' to myself over and over again with such intensity that earth and sky reeled about me. It was a very interesting experiment, but I never dared try it again.

One of my clearest memories is of my mother standing on an upturned tea-chest, talking to her friends on the other side of the

9

garden wall, no doubt standing on *their* upturned tea-chests. All my mother's family were tremendous talkers. There was something very comforting to a child about this flow of half-understood, highly inflected, grown-up talk; voices for amazement, for shocked surprise, for disbelief; voices promising startling revelations. My mother could make a drama out of buying four Chelsea buns for tea, and I came to expect this from her.

Once, when I was very small, sitting under the kitchen table playing with a doll, a dashing maiden aunt (most families had them in those days) told my mother a gruesome story of a woman who had been buried alive. Only as the clods began to fall on the lowered coffin did she come out of her coma and hammer on the lid, begging to be let out. The pattern of the bobble-fringe of the chenille tablecloth is burnt into my brain, but my mother and aunt, I remember, sipped their tea and turned lightly to some other topic. My mother never knew that I had been there. If she had, I suppose, she would have been sorry and perturbed, but she could not have guessed the agonies I was to go through. Years later I asked my father if it were possible for a person to be buried alive. 'Nonsense,' he said. 'How could one be sure?' I asked. 'Sever a vein under the arm,' he said. I longed to ask my parents to leave a note, to be discovered on their death, asking that this should be done, but the moment never came.

The one thing that dominated my childhood was fear of death. Angels with flaming swords, seen in illustrations and later in dreams, ranked over the lilac trees in the back garden; all so far from the teachings of my rational, antiseptic, Unitarian upbringing. The little chapel in Peckham, with pews that I always think of as pitch pine, with strips of red carpet on the seats. No hassocks; Unitarians tended not to kneel. No altar, but a table with a starched white cloth and a cutglass vase of flowers. Lessons as often read from the Talmud, the works of Rabindranath Tagore or a play by George Bernard Shaw as from the Bible; and back to our home for Sunday lunch with the preacher, who might have been a Buddhist monk or a Hungarian bishop, or a coalminer from Rotherham who had had a late call to the religious life. My parents were very active in our church; my father ran the Sunday school and, because the minister was unmarried, my mother acted as unofficial hostess for visitors.

Our minister was a gaunt, fiery Shetland Islander with the magnificent name of Magnus Cluness Ratter. He had a passionate belief in the power of knowledge, and the streets of that part of south London have always reminded me of his after-service disquisitions as we ran along beside his enormous strides, listening to talk on Feuerbach and the magnificence of Rembrandt. As we young people grew up Magnus Ratter taught us to examine history and ideas, think for ourselves and express our thoughts. He was a very impressive man and, due in no small way to his influence, within two years three of us from his tiny flock got places at Oxford. The Unitarian Church already had women ministers then and right up until my time at Oxford I thought that I myself would become a minister.

Our church was the source of most things in our life when I was a child. There was the Friday dancing class, when the older ones taught the younger ones ballroom dancing. We all learnt to waltz in a slightly outdated but elegant manner, and do the Lancers, the Veleta and the Boston Two-Step. The only music was the piano and in the interval we had tea or weak lemonade and biscuits. As we grew older, we became rather critical of these occasions, but we learnt our steps.

There were also the Saturday rambles. In those days Croydon was almost country and Coulsdon a long way out. Most expeditions started from Rye Lane Station, Peckham, after an early Saturday lunch. Tea was taken at a small café or farmhouse. We took our rambles seriously and learnt the names of trees and birds. It was all extremely unsophisticated. Many friendships and love affairs bloomed and faded in the course of our rambles.

I remember vividly one summer scene in a country bedroom with sloping roof, with cabbage roses on the washstand china and soap smelling of lemons. The ladies were washing their hands while the gentlemen waited for us outside in the garden among the wasps. Suddenly two middle-aged ladies began to quarrel in restrained but deadly voices.

'Nothing,' said the first one, 'nothing could be cleaner than these towels. Three of them, huckaback towels, and all *spotlessly* clean!' I can see her now, sensible tweeds, flat shoes, pork-pie hat, her solid curves making her look like a tailor's dummy against the light.

The second one, frail and rather elegant with thin wrists and a turned-down mouth, agreed but continued to wipe her hands on a pocket handkerchief. Then she took a packet of Papiers Poudres and a mirror out of her bag and, turning away to the window, began to rub one of the delicious-smelling little sheets over her face. The first lady's hands shook as she poured out the water into the bowl, and her voice shook even more as she said it was a good thing we were not all so particular. The other said in a frozen voice, 'It is an idiosyncrasy of mine never to use towels in strange houses.'

On the way home, over the rattling of the train wheels, I said to my father, 'What does "huckaback" mean, and "idiosyncrasy"?' And I still cannot think of one word without the other leaping into my mind. My mother later explained to my father that jealousy had arisen because one of the ladies had taken a thread of cotton off the minister's coat. That day I had a fascinating glimpse of the world of grown-ups, and the tensions that lay between them and could flare up over an idiotically small thing like a towel.

People talk constantly of the difficulties of being young today. I cannot believe that anything could be more difficult, more constrained, more defeating, than the youth of those of us born in the early years of this century. On the other hand, I cannot believe that children today can ever possibly have the sharpness of our memories.

I was obsessed by physical beauty as a child. Everything in my good Unitarian upbringing told me that this was wrong, but it remained my yardstick. I could never come to terms with the basic unfairness of life; the pigmentation of a skin or the bone structure of an eye socket seemed to me to be one of those irreversible things that made or marred one's life. Children see through the kindly adult comment, 'But looks don't matter. It is you that matters.' It is not, at least not until you are old enough to make yourself matter, and by then you will have suffered infinite misery. I often think that it was my mother who gave me this feeling about beauty. She was not beautiful, or even pretty, though she was handsome and had a great charm of manner. In every family photograph (and those were the days when most families had their cumbersome plate cameras) her own face was poked out with a pin. It was many years before I realised how disturbing I had found this.

Looking back on my childhood, I think I was always impatient to get on to the adult life that lay ahead, and always terrified that I would fail to measure up to it; that I alone, of the several million people in this country, had been singled out to grow into some kind of monster.

It was at school, of course, the upper reaches of the infants' school, that our lives became dominated by 'babies'. Just 'babies'.

The word was enough to make us all dissolve into hopeless giggles, but we felt the mystery and it seemed impenetrable. One day I sensed that I was near to enlightenment. I had been kept in at playtime to paint a relief map of Scotland, made out of plasticine, and two other girls had been kept in too. One of them was 'foreign' and was known not to wear knickers; the other was 'rude' and the night before her mother had had her fifth baby. Heady company indeed. My ears nearly fell off trying to catch the details of the birth. All I could hear was blood – buckets of it, and cottonwool – rolls of it. I could have cried from frustration; this was no help at all.

A few nights later, coming back from the fancy dress dance at the local baths, all was revealed to me by a girl called Mabel Eckers. 'Babies come out of your belly-button in balloons,' she said, 'and the doctor is there to burst the balloon before they suffocate.' This sounded reasonable and she exuded authority. After my mother and I had left her, I cried all the way home. I was dressed as a daffodil in two shades of yellow butter-muslin, my calyx hat had given me endless trouble, and my new shoes were half a size too small. My mother said things like, 'overtired' and 'plenty of early nights', and I did not know whether I was crying for my undignified fancy-dress, my big feet, or for the difficulties that I could see ahead with that damned balloon.

I think that the first real moment of terror I had, the first feeling that the adult world of beauty and sensuality (though I had no word for it) might not be for me, came one Christmas when I was, perhaps, nine years old. It had been a family Christmas and three of us, me, a cousin of my own age and an older girl who was pretty and engaged to one of the family, had been sharing my parents' big brass bed. I remember waking up and watching the engaged girl dress to go to her work as a typist in something called 'The City'. As the morning light filtered through the green venetian blinds, she stood in front of the mirror, powdering her shoulders, the satin straps of her petticoat gleaming. I still cannot describe what it did to me. This is it, I thought, this is being a woman. I hated, more than ever, the sight of my liberty bodice hanging limply over the chair. It seemed to me impossible that I would ever attain to gleaming shoulder-straps. The picture is still as clear in my mind as a Bonnard painting; a woman dressing in a subaqueous light.

As I remember it, an uneventful, tomboyish childhood was pierced from time to time by these disturbing pictures. When I was taken by my father, improbably, to eat my first meal in Soho, sipping my first glass of wine, the whole experience was ruined for me by the sight of a couple on the other side of the little restaurant smiling at each other across a lamp-lit table and unfurling starched white napkins. I was possessed by envy of them, and rage that I was still imprisoned in a young girl's body and the humiliating young girl's clothes of that time. I can recall the exact feeling of rage, impatience and fear that gripped me. It must have made me very often an impossible daughter, but it put me on my guard as a mother.

Along with my desire to grow up and be a femme fatale and sit for ever at lamp-lit tables, unfurling white napkins, drinking wine and looking into the eyes of a young man, I wanted to be free. Children, especially girl-children, were in chains, and my own children's apparent unconcern about their freedom has always surprised me.

When I was young little girls were sharply differentiated from little boys. We were considered more delicate (though I was always as strong as a horse), we went to bed earlier, we 'rested' on holidays after lunch, we did not paddle or bathe on the first day by the seaside. To a little girl feeling herself as strong as her brothers and at least as adventurous, and furthermore not in the least interested at that age in her feminine vocation, and feeling sure that she was going to muff it anyhow, it was a kind of torture.

Our clothes were the great dividing feature. How could one feel free, or even have self-respect, clothed in garments that were designed to *take away* self-respect? Combinations, drawers, liberty vests, starched petticoats with scratchy lace, all apparently purposeless and hideous. Sensible knickers had elastic that was always too tight or too slack, sometimes one of each, so that one leg felt as if it had a tourniquet while on the other material dangled down below the level of your dress. Black woollen stockings itched and, even clean from the washtub, smelt dirty in a flat, sweaty way. The brims of rough straw hats scratched and left a serrated red mark round your forehead for an hour afterwards. Hat elastic bit under your tender chin. We had to wear dresses we hated, that were wrong for coltish, unformed young bodies. But what did it matter that you knew they were wrong and made a mock of you? No wonder some of us vented our anger on other things quite unconnected. Looking at children, girls, today in their simple, comfortable, soft, boyish clothes, I wonder how they cannot help being angelic in temperament!

It took me years to learn that the whole of happiness was not to be found across a restaurant table or even in comfortable clothes. However, the fact that freedom was a double-edged blessing was something I learnt very soon.

Very often on Saturdays we visited relations on the outskirts of London. The last part of our journey home was by the 78 bus from Liverpool Street. The stiff, uncomfortable clothes one had to wear, the long hot midday dinners, the grown-up talk; all this I hated. I always looked forward to the 78 bus. Its route took in Tower Bridge. With luck, the bridge might be up and, sitting in the front seat of the open upper deck, one would have the feeling of the ordered pattern of the world coming to an exciting end, as the grey roadway rose in front of one's eyes, pieces of dung sticking to the asphalt. There was the hooting of the tugs, the lights in the water and, further on, the wicked mystery of the public houses. If we were early, the streets would be quiet, light streaming from the windows, noise and singing bellying out, the 'poor' children shivering on the doorsteps, waiting for their parents. If we were late, we could see, from our safe seats on the top of the bus, the fights beginning on the street corners outside the pubs. Delicious glimpses, never long enough, of another, more powerful life. We would pass the ends of the side streets where the market people were beginning to pack up under their naphtha flares, the women looking like gypsies with wrinkled brown faces, gold rings in their ears, huge aprons and men's caps.

One night, because it looked like rain, my parents insisted that I went inside the bus with them. My brother Bill whipped upstairs. It is the first time I am conscious of ever having made a scene deliberately. I was lost to all feelings of shame; I howled and stamped and begged. My parents let me go and I scrambled on top and slid into the back seat, but it was a totally empty triumph.

It began to rain in earnest. I remembered how kind and good my parents were, and how I had shamed them. My brother, in the front seat, turned round and put his tongue out at me. I slid down in the seat and pulled the heavy leather apron over me that in those days was attached to the seat to afford the passenger protection from the rain. I can remember now the corrugated texture, the weight and smell of those aprons. It was a dark, damp little house, with rain thudding over my head, and I longed to go and sit with my parents in the warm, beery interior of the bus full of Saturday night Cockney good humour.

From all our weekend family gatherings I have some very clear memories. Two of my mother's brothers were socialists and the talk was often of politics. 'Campbell Bannerman', 'Lloyd George', 'Bonar Law' are some of the splendid names I remember from these times. My uncle Ernest was a compositor, 'the aristocrats of the printing trade', as he often said, and the mysterious word 'NATSOPA' rang out very often in their furious conversations. I loved this word NATSOPA, but for years had no idea what it could possibly mean.

My father's incantations were different, quieter somehow. I could say 'South Place Ethical Society' and 'Spurgeon's Tabernacle' before I knew nursery rhymes. The best of all, now happily spoken again, is *The Ragged Trousered Philanthropists*. For a long time, when I was older, I bore a grudge against my father. Once, in a family argument with the socialist brothers-in-law, he delivered himself of the statement, 'I think Labour and vote Conservative.' This seemed to me unforgivable at the time, but I came to realise that it was completely in tune with his gentle, unassertive nature and his overpowering wish to be fair. Many years after his death I came to know Tibetans and I know that my father would have felt happy with Tibetan Buddhism, with its infinite compassion and middle way.

I realise now that I rather unfairly upbraided my parents about their gentleness, in which they were quite different from many other grown-ups I met. A formidable example was a schoolfriend's 'Auntie Annie'. When my friend and I were about nine we went to stay with her in her country cottage in Sussex. Auntie Annie was a headmistress, a tall, gaunt lady, and had an absolute conviction that she knew best, a quality I never found in my parents. She was a suffragette, which I was told but without explanation, and that word has always seemed to me one of the most frightening words in the English language. It was years before I understood the significance of Auntie Annie's egg-cosies crocheted in purple and green.

While bitterly resenting my lower middle-class prison, I think I always realised that I had been lucky in my parents. My father was passionately interested in many things. On the rare occasions when he was left to read me to sleep, the book he chose was always *The Egyptian Book of the Dead*, which was his idea of an enthralling bedside companion. He also took me to my first music hall, the Camberwell Palace, to see Ernie Lotinga one Saturday night. I remember my mother's horror when we got back, but she need not have worried; the jokes were certainly above my head and many, I suspect, above my father's.

However small the house we lived in, my father had a study, and I can see the book titles now: Bradlaugh's *Tracts*, Annie Besant's *Karma*, Edward Carpenter's *Light of the World*. Strangely enough it was through my father that I got my first glimpse of the great world of human emotions. Delivered to our house every week was a horrible journal called the *Family Herald Supplement*, two columns of small print on each page containing the sloppiest love stories. The hero's name was invariably Garth and in the end the governess always married him. The stories were unmitigated tripe. My father read them every week with unashamed pleasure. 'I like them because I know the stories will always have a happy ending,' he used to say. Everybody laughed at him and he laughed too. No one laughed louder than I did, but I devoured the stories when alone, and hid them under the cushions of the basket chair if I heard anyone coming.

My father loved London and on many a Saturday afternoon we took the tram to Westminster. He was careless of the obvious sights and left them to others, but we would walk miles to see a beautifully carved lintel or a few Roman bricks left in a wall. His taste in architecture was always Romanesque: St Bartholomew the Great in Smithfield and, on holiday every summer in Kent, we made a pilgrimage to Barfreston Church. All his life he wanted to see Kilpeck Church in Herefordshire; and when I finally made a detour to see it myself, there, indeed, were the small figures in Phrygian caps, just as my father had said. The Dordogne would have seemed an impossible dream to my father, but when my children and I have been driving in France from one church to another, I have often thought of him and this seems to me to be the way immortality lies.

When I was twelve we moved from Peckham to Dulwich. I never grew as attached to Dulwich Park as I was to Peckham Park, but all my family loved Dulwich Village. On our walks my father made sure we admired the wrought iron gates of the little burying-ground and the wide street with its little greens and enormous chestnut trees and elaborate fountain at the top. Sometimes we would take the left fork down College Road and sometimes the right fork to Dulwich Picture Gallery.

I developed a very special relationship with the gallery over those years. We sometimes took our church visitors there after lunch and I also went often on my own. Dulwich Picture Gallery had an interesting history. A Mr Desenfans had collected all the pictures together to become the nucleus of a national gallery for Poland. However, when Poland was partitioned, the idea was abandoned and the pictures stayed behind in England to be the glory of Dulwich.

I often seemed to be the gallery's only visitor, tiptoeing very circumspectly up and down the glacier-like floor between its elegant dark red walls. I had my favourite pictures, all portraits, which became like trusted and unchanging old friends. I always went first to have a look at Rembrandt's *The Girl at the Window*, which I heard was supposed to have been the little servant in Rembrandt's household. She had a plump and pleasant face, a little tail of hair and kind brown eyes. Then there were two tall, narrow pictures of Spanish peasant boys by Murillo. I remember too the Velasquez portrait of Philip IV with his melancholy Habsburg face. The landscapes, mostly by the unpronounceable Cuyps, did not appeal to me and after a time I did not even see them.

None of my family was much interested in pictures, so I discovered them for myself and had no preconceived ideas about them. I developed into a perfect example of someone who 'knows what they like', and my attitude to the pictures was very constant, static really. I never came to know anything more about them than I learnt by leaning on the shining brass rail and staring fixedly at them as they hung on the walls.

The gallery's chief attendant was an old man in a blue and gold frock coat and a top hat. He was impressive but distant and seemed to spend more time sorting the postcards than tending to the pictures. But his assistant and I became good friends. He was a youngish, extraordinarily pale man who had been wounded in the war, so I understood, and could only do a very light job. He seemed to find nothing strange in my constant visits and, though not talkative, was kind and welcoming. 'The Murillos are looking nice this morning,' he would say quietly as he strolled past. I was very thrilled when he once got permission to show me some of the valuable books that were not on general display.

Before my family moved to Dulwich I was already a pupil at the Mary Datchelor Girls' School in Camberwell Green, which I attended from the age of ten, in 1920, to nineteen. Although respectable and, by today's standards, probably reasonably strict, this school was forward thinking and I think that it marked my formative years. The headmistress was Dr Dorothy Brock, a beautiful woman who had the charisma of a Miss Jean Brodie and the warmth of a Mr Chips. Girls from other schools, when they came to play hockey at Datchelor, would gasp in disbelief when Dr Brock appeared and say, 'That's surely not your *headmistress*, is it?'

The school placed great importance on helping others. I wonder whether any other school in those days supported so many charities and gave so much service. It was itself supported by the Clothworkers' Company in Mincing Lane, a patron the establishment was always very proud to own. We were a Camberwell school and Camberwell was a major concern but, if we had a bed in King's College Hospital, we also supported one in West Africa. We gave financial support to an Indian girl and Boris, our Polish war orphan. There were regular collections for the Ragged School Mission. We were often told, 'Try to give your own money and not your parents'.' The oldest, and perhaps the most memorable, of all these activities was the Dorcas Society; not just the great ritual of the annual Dorcas Social, but those informal groups on Friday afternoons after school, when we talked and argued and some of us unravelled our baby's vest yet again.

Dr Brock set a very high value on this part of the school's tradition. In one of her reports she wrote: 'The chief form of social service which a school can give to the community is to send out people who have something worth giving to the world and the desire to give it.'

It was during these years, in between the wars, that the Mary Datchelor's reputation as one of the great music schools of the country was built up. Even the most unmusical pupils were affected by the high place that it was given in the curriculum. The constant preoccupation of other people, if not oneself, with music was bound to have an effect. There were the interhouse competitions, the concerts, the recitals and, the most original idea of all, half-hours of musical appreciation during lunch time. Even those who felt they only went to sit on the warm radiators at the side of the hall learnt that the making of music was something to be treated with respect. Those years also saw the emergence of those lofty-browed, unapproachable people, the 'music students'. We held them in awe, not knowing that we were going to meet them again in later years, caring for musical standards in schools all over England.

It seems to me now that another great privilege of being a Datchelor girl, and this certainly came directly from Dr Brock herself, was the chance to meet and often to talk to people of distinction. Schoolgirl life was lived at a fairly prosaic level, and for most of us in those pre-television days it was the school that gave us fascinating glimpses of people who had made their mark in the larger world. Professor Gilbert Murray, Dr Mackail and Dr Maude Royden are some that I remember. I have the most vivid memory of a talk, a wickedly humorous talk, given by the theatre critic St John Ervine. In it he explored the romantic novels of Miss Ethel M. Dell, a curious choice for a schoolgirl audience. I remember now the relief I felt when I realised that Life, with a capital 'L', was not entirely an earnest affair, but would have its hilarious moments too. I was very impressed by that light-hearted talk, but I realise that not many headmistresses of that period would have let Mr St John Ervine loose upon their flock.

I remember another visitor, the handsome violinist Jean Pougnet, and the electric shock that passed through the hall as 200 or so girls fell in love simultaneously. After his recital some of the worst affected of us went to the noisy Lyons café at Camberwell Green to eat maple nut sundaes; those maple nut sundaes sustained Datchelor girls through many crises, and with our school hats and our hated gloves tucked into the elastic of our knickers we could imagine we were indistinguishable from the other customers.

For Dr Brock herself these years were ones of recognition in many fields. Nevertheless, in my memory the quality that stands out was her great physical beauty. She would have been quick to tell me that beauty of character is more important, but we were immensely proud of her elegance and charm. I can remember the exact shade of grey of the velvet hair band she wore on my first morning prayers, her graceful walk, the habit she had of holding her head slightly to one side, and her beautiful clothes. I think she gave us a feeling of security. We knew she was valued in the world outside the school, and we knew very well that, however dazzling the platform party on prize day, she would, by her charm and wit, be the star in her scarlet and blue robes.

I am certain also that we were grateful to her because she liked our mothers. Schoolgirls are always uneasy when school and home meet, but Dr Brock took great trouble with our mothers and I think she was unusual in this.

It was not a school that was turned inward and our budding personalities were treated with a respect that I think must have been rare in those days. As one who embraced Hinduism,

Buddhism, Spiritualism and Marxism in quick succession, I never found Dr Brock anything but attentive and helpful. She agreed so wholeheartedly to my defiant request to read *The Bhagavadgita* when it was my turn for reading the lesson at prayers that I went back to the New Testament after all.

I would not have liked to face her anger very often. In spite of her tolerance and wonderful sense of humour, she could be very sharp. When Remove A fought a noisy battle with Remove B on the upper corridor over the merits of Shelley and Keats, smashing the glass of Keats's portrait with a poker, she was very angry indeed. I am sure, however, that after watching us slink out of her study, she made a most amusing story of it for the school secretary Miss Morse.

It was during my time at the Mary Datchelor that, at the age of thirteen, I was invited to a party by a schoolfriend, Kathleen Perry. We were all sitting round having tea when Kathleen's mother came into the room and announced that the family had recently acquired a 'crystal set'. We were lined up in the corridor and, one by one, taken into the sitting-room where Kathleen's father clamped heavy earphones on to our heads and fiddled with something he called 'the cat's whisker'. I had never heard of 'the wireless' and the first time round I had no idea that I was even *meant* to hear anything. But I got a second turn and this time I knew what to expect. After a while I heard an extremely crackly, faraway voice singing '*Omaha, I'm a-coming home to you ...*'. I was impressed by this, but not overly so.

At the end of my schooldays I was ready to look around me and discover my path in life, but I was not optimistic about any wide variety of choice. A lot of girls at that time, if they were bright in any way, unless they were going to be doctors or musicians, thought they were going to teach. It was really the only thing held out for most of us. We all felt we wanted to marry at some point, but we wanted a job first. I wanted to go to university and thought that I would then either become a Unitarian minister or teach history and Latin.

My love of history came from both my father's influence and the inspired teaching of Frances Kennedy at the Mary Datchelor School, who taught me in my final years. I knew about Oxford University from my reading of history and biographies and was especially attracted by its beautiful setting. The school encouraged me to apply there. My parents were also very supportive but in no way put pressure on me. They were not ambitious for my brother and me in career terms. They gave us our freedom and just wanted us to be happy and fulfilled.

I got a place at Oxford to read history and decided to pursue particularly my love of the medieval period. The special period I chose was from about 900 to about 1200 and then I did the Italian Renaissance for my special subject. Since the major relevant books were not in English, I had to learn Italian well enough to read them. I can still read Italian, without ever really having spoken it.

I had three years in the sixth form at school, so I was nineteen when I went up to Oxford. My last year was almost like a year at university, and there were only two or three of us being taught together. I felt very lucky in this, since it was a great introduction to life beyond school and going on to higher education.

3 1929–34 – Oxford

Oxford was the beginning of a new life altogether. I went to St Hugh's College, which was a Church of England women's college. It had very high standards of politeness, morality and everything else. There was not much to distinguish the social life of women undergraduates at that time from that of the pupils of the genteel boarding schools which a lot of them had just left.

We had 'chaperone rules'. The only way you could meet a man alone was to have tea very publicly in a tea shop. A walk in a park, a punting expedition, a ride in a car or a meal in a restaurant were all regarded as highly suspect activities, and heavily penalised. You could go to a men's college for afternoon tea, but only in pairs. You could entertain a gentleman yourself for tea in your room, but also of course with a college friend there. For this you also had to drag your bed out into the corridor, a task which often required the help of your male guest and was guaranteed to cause hilarity if not acute embarrassment!

I continued to enjoy history while at Oxford, but not, I must admit, with quite the same fervour as in my final years at school. Students are very lucky, but higher education in late adolescence has always seemed to me to come at precisely the wrong time to concentrate on it productively. Life just presents too many other glorious options at that time. So, looking back, my studies are not the main thing I remember of my student days. It was here that, like so many, I became an adult. My tutor in the ways of the world was a young woman of my own age who made a great impression on me from the beginning.

On the very first night there, in the Junior Common Room sitting around after supper, I was on a window seat with a sturdy, red-headed girl in a brown velvet dress with a lace collar, clearly made by her mother. We started to talk. She was a Yorkshire girl, now living in Hyde, Cheshire, on the outskirts of Manchester. She spent most of the evening telling me how infinitely superior the north was to the south and what poor characters we southerners were. Her name was then Barbara Betts, later Barbara Castle, MP, and now Baroness Castle of Blackburn. She came to my eightieth birthday party and, to me, she has not changed at all.

Barbara and I became firm friends. She was very advanced for her time. Her family were staunch socialists and she was, even then, committed to her beliefs. Although this was admired by her contemporaries, including me, it also generated a certain nervousness in them. The *Liverpool Echo* has quoted one of Barbara's early acquaintances as saying, 'She used to lecture a bit', and another, 'One always felt inadequate with Barbara' (13 December 1967). The outstanding thing about her was her dedication to her aims. We all thought it would be nice to get a First and nice to be beautiful, but she was the only one who did anything about it. I remember her creaming her face and hands at night and wearing gloves, drinking fruit juice, eating rusks and reading some obscure economics handbook all at the same time. She was determined to be balanced. I was quite scared of her at times.

One summer, during the vacation, I went to stay with Barbara and her family in Hyde. Barbara's brother, Jimmie, was there. He was a forester and Barbara was very fond of him. Jimmie surprised me by trying to persuade me to go to bed with him and of course I was horrified. I certainly could not do it. On our last night, he took me to a pub and pursued this again, and I turned him down again. When I returned to the house, I climbed with Barbara into her parents' big double bed that we were sharing. As I lay there, I thought about Jimmie's offer and how nice he was and finally my own sexual curiosity, not to mention that of all our little group at St Hugh's, got the better of me. I got out of bed, picked my way across the cold linoleum of the landing and woke Jimmie up. He dutifully obliged. The memory of that experience is hazy now, but I do remember getting on the train to London with Barbara the next day. Somewhere just before Stockport I suddenly thought, 'I am no longer a virgin!' Barbara leaned across the railway carriage, tapped my knee and said, 'And you can take that silly smile off your face.'

My holiday with Barbara also gave me one of the big love affairs of my life, and one to which I have remained faithful all my life. It was then that I fell for the north of England. For the first twenty years of my life I had looked around anxiously for that place which I could somehow hold in my hand. I never came within miles of finding it until I went to the north for the first time.

No one, I imagine, could look at Hyde dispassionately and say it was beautiful, but then, I still cannot look at it dispassionately any more than I could all those years ago. Being a southerner, I did see it as romantic. It had rows of small grey houses, steep cobbled streets, sad little shops, clanging trams and a grim park on a hillside. That first time I went there it was Wakes Week; all the mills were shut and the whole town was on holiday. It was all of a piece, it had a shape, it had a focus in a way that a suburb revolving around tennis parties and the eight-thirty to town could never have. For the first time in my life I felt that I had come home. The countryside of the Peak comes down almost to the edge of the town and later I walked over that country, tore my feet to ribbons (being used to the turf of the South Downs), but came back enslaved to that wild landscape, tussocky grass and heather, and peat streams where you bathed in icy dark brown water and came out clothed in an invisible garment of silk.

At that time Barbara longed with an even fiercer intensity to get away from Hyde. I remember our talk on that holiday, two separate monologues hardly even impinging on each other, in which we laid our plans for life. On the day before we left for London together I went out for a last solitary prowl around the town and vowed that I would one day return. Arriving back at the Betts' house, I found Barbara splashing around in a highly scented bath and singing while Mrs Betts hastily stitched a spray of gardenias on the hat with which her daughter was going to take London by storm.

For Barbara London was at that time the gateway to the kind of life she wanted, a life in politics. There was never anything slipshod about Barbara and there is not now. She was always very clear headed and very hard working. She is a decorative creature, I think, but you have to be more than decorative to get as far as she has.

There was another girl who joined us in our particular university friendship who, although less famous than Barbara Castle, was as unique in her own way. She was called Freda Houlston and she came from Derbyshire. She was strikingly beautiful and was sometimes referred to by other undergraduates as 'the Mona Lisa'. She was a romantic and an Anglo-Catholic and very interested in religion; I can remember her reading the lives of the saints and the mystics. By contrast Barbara was unmoved by religion and my own interest in it rapidly became replaced by politics. During the first walk that the three of us took together in the University

Parks, we were passing some poplars and Freda said, 'How lovely they are without their leaves. The boughs look like the hair of some Botticelli angel.' Barbara stopped dead in her tracks, looked at her and said, 'My God, what a damnably silly thing to say. I hope you're not going to go on like this all the time!'

Freda fell in love with an Indian student at Hertford during our last year and decided to marry him. The reaction to this was violent. Her mother, her friends and her college were all opposed to the match. She became ill and had a nervous breakdown, and was later admitted to a mental hospital. Barbara and I, still flouting the bigotries of the period, stuck by Freda and did all we could to see her through her illness. She did marry her Indian lover and went to live in India with him. It was many years later, in the Himalayas, that Freda and I were to meet again. She had become a Tibetan Buddhist nun.

I also became involved with an Indian while at university. However, I did not experience the emotional pain that Freda suffered. There were very few of them, mostly rich Indians, and I loved them and their company. I also loved their food. I remember that some colleges had banned cooking by their Indian students in their rooms, because the exotic smells drifting round the staircases contrasted so unfairly with what was being served up in college dining halls! My first real lover was a Muslim. His father was a high court judge or something similar. He was about seven years older than me and had already taken a degree somewhere in India. He was a lovely gentle man and he knew a great deal about life and love and politics. Later on he spent some years in prison for his beliefs. The eastern people put a great value on love making. I thought I was very lucky to be initiated by somebody like that. His politics again pointed the way for me, but I did not think of marrying him.

I did not think of marrying anybody then, but it was nonetheless pretty unusual to have an affair outside marriage. Barbara was the one I looked to. She had grown up, was emancipated and also she knew quite a lot about sex. We others did not. When we came up to university at the age of nineteen we were ignorant to a degree you cannot imagine now. There was one girl in our college who was known not to be a virgin and we all looked upon her with enormous respect. Barbara so disliked the muddle we were all in that she collected a shilling each from six of us and sent off for the book *Planned Parenthood* by Michael Fielding. It was a very clear little book with lots of diagrams. We all read it and then

Barbara tested us on it, which was delightfully typical of her. She wanted to make sure we got it straight. There was another very helpful writer at that time, Joan Malleson, who went under the name 'Medica'. She was a doctor who wrote books, very careful books, with simple diagrams of vaginas and penises. I was to interview her later on *Woman's Hour* and I remembered how very important she had been in our lives.

It interests me how we had no instruction on how to avoid getting pregnant. We had heard of French letters, as they were then called, and I supposed that the careful men would have one, but I cannot remember anyone knowing any useful details. We did not discuss our sexual lives with our parents, because we did not want to distress them in any way. When my mother was in her eighties, I did ask her why she had never taught me the facts of life and she replied, 'Olive, I hadn't the words!' I think this was true; they would not have known how to begin speaking about these things and you did not read much about them in those days, certainly not in newspapers or magazines. We all just muddled through and trusted to instinct. Many years later when I read Mary McCarthy's book, *The Group*, I realised that the young women graduated in exactly the same year as my group at Oxford, and had the same interests and the same problems as us. The sexual experience of myself and others I knew at Oxford hardly amounted to a revolution, but looking back I suppose it was part of a kind of loosening up after the first two decades of the century.

Another important part of my consciousness was music, in particular jazz. We used to break bounds and go out to a pub somewhere in Henley-on-Thames. The music seemed very daring but the dancing was still fairly formal then. We also used to go to Reading and London. One of my great trips to London was to hear Duke Ellington. He had come to England for the first time and gave his first concert at the Elephant and Castle. I went with my boyfriend, Peter Floud. So that we could be sure of getting tickets, we spent the night on the pavement alongside dance-band musicians from all over Europe, who had turned out to hear the Duke.

Peter and I also went to various political conferences. One I remember particularly was in Paris, in the Salle de la Mutualité. On the last day some of the Paris taxi drivers went on strike and took us to Compiègne where the Armistice was signed. We all stood there, clenched our fists and made some sort of oath. I can remember young miners from Salzburg singing beautifully. Then we came back to Paris over the hills and were arrested; the police had become nervous by then! We spent the night in jail, which of course pleased us no end; we really felt we had arrived. Peter's father was rather high up in the Civil Service and he had us let out, which was a bit of a disappointment.

My previous political experience was limited. I had been a Labour candidate in a school election, but that was about all. At Oxford political alignment was becoming apparent, and if you were interested in politics, you were likely either to be a fascist or a communist. Oswald Mosley was becoming a force on the extreme right. Communism attracted some students at both Oxford and Cambridge and they would go to meetings and on demonstrations together. In Cambridge there was a communist don, who enlisted Philby, Burgess and Maclean as members of the Communist Party, and they began the activities which would result in a major spy scandal in later years.

A lot of us at Oxford were also members of the party for a time, but if our membership had been discovered, we would have been sent down from our various colleges. So, because the party felt that we were valuable where we were, we were not permitted to become fully paid-up members. We started a thing called the October Club, which was really a communist organisation. We had meetings and other events, read a lot of Marx and Engels and discussed them endlessly. However, I do not remember any member of the senior staff being involved with our political activities. It was probably because of this that, unlike the Cambridge spies, we drifted away from extreme politics when we graduated. I went back to the Labour Party afterwards.

My political group at Oxford was so muddle-headed. We were not extreme about some issues, but passionately so about others. For example, we were anti-empire, which was a radical stance at that time. I remember the weekend when the Hunger Marchers came through Oxford, and we all devoted ourselves to looking after them, washing their feet and feeding them. It was an incredible sight. They had walked all the way from Jarrow and some of their shoes were in tatters. Things like that brought tears to our eyes and we were very romantic about it, but in a rather vague way. Nonetheless, when the Spanish Civil War came, a number of the students I had known went to fight and some died.

My brief flirtation with communism left an enduring blot on the secret files. In my sixties I was visited regularly by a gentleman from MI5 who quizzed me about my activities over a pot of tea.

This did not really worry me and I always looked forward to his visits. It was one of the few occasions that I ever got news of my old friends. Some time after that the Keeper of the Queen's Pictures, Anthony Blunt, was finally exposed as a missing link in the spy chain. I was presumably vindicated at last and was left in peace, my dark past no more than a fond memory of university days.

Barbara never associated herself with the communists at Oxford and Freda was much more interested in spiritual rather than political matters. Nevertheless, we supported each other in our enthusiasms and remained close friends throughout our time there. We would sometimes break bounds at night, climbing through an open window, and go for illicit walks along the towpath. Through these innocent activities we felt in some way liberated from the strictures of college life. We were taking risks, though, as we could have been sent down if we had been caught.

Although my later time at Oxford rapidly came to mean breaking out of what I regarded as the constraints of my background, my life in the first year was closely linked with Manchester College, the main Unitarian college in Britain. I met some very interesting people there who came to give lectures, such as Rabindranath Tagore, the Hindu philosopher. I had a much longer association with another Hindu philosopher, Sarvepalli Radhakrishnan. He was then lecturing at the university, and went on to a most distinguished international career as philosopher and statesman; he was the first Indian to hold a chair at Oxford and became vice-president and then president of India. In those days all undergraduates had to pass divinity moderations, 'Divvers', or you were sent down. Being conscious of my own inadequacies in this area, I used to visit Radhakrishnan in his small north Oxford flat and over cups of tea at his kitchen table he would explain to me the Bible and aspects of Christianity; with his help I passed the exam.

I finished my undergraduate degree at Oxford in 1932 and emerged with only a third. I knew very well that I had not really worked hard, having spent most of my time involving myself in politics, having fun and learning about life, love and men. Nevertheless, despite my undistinguished degree I had much more confidence and more experience of life.

I still had no other plans than to go into teaching. In order to finance my studies at Oxford I had promised to train as a teacher and teach for three years; so I stayed in Oxford another year to complete the postgraduate teacher training course. It was a good experience, especially since I was no longer regarded as a student and therefore had more freedom and was able to enjoy Oxford more. The middle term of the course was devoted to teaching practice, and I went to a school in Eltham to teach Latin, where I found that I had to use the direct method. This involved walking up and down in front of the class saying '*ambulo*', meaning 'I walk', and then taking a girl with you and walking up and down saying '*ambulamus*', meaning 'we walk'. It was fairly ridiculous and I never felt that it succeeded in bringing Latin alive for the pupils or taught them anything. That method did not last long, I believe. At the end of the course I also briefly taught Latin at my old school. However, by then teaching jobs were so scarce that the Board of Education eventually tore up the service agreements and positively implored us to find work elsewhere.

Someone suggested that I become a Workers' Education Association lecturer on a new housing estate in Surrey. I did this for a term and a poor job I made of it too. To begin with I was deputed to teach local government, and ever after I knew what it meant to be one jump ahead of the class. I also felt the uselessness of trying to impart knowledge that you yourself do not care about. Up in London in the British Museum I swotted up drains and sanitation and then went back at nights to the farthest flung station on the Underground to the new estate and my first experience of living on my own. My home was the front bedroom of a small semi-detached house on that estate, owned by an elderly couple who ran a fish-and-chip bar. Communication between us was minimal, not least because they came home at night too tired to speak to anybody. I mouldered away in my room, heavily subsidised by my father and feeling that I was living in a kind of limbo. Later I came to know one or two families on the estate, and basked in the warmth and comfort of kitchens and home-cooked food. It was one of the worst times of my life. I was getting nowhere, my classes dwindled before my eyes, there was no one to tell me how to become a better lecturer, and all my Oxford friends seemed to have marvellous jobs or their lives had taken some exciting and unexpected turn. I felt utterly lonely and dreary.

The only people I ever saw who seemed to be alive were an Oxford friend, John Newsom, and his wife, who were running an enormous, empty, echoing beer palace on a windswept corner of the estate. They were about as depressed as I was. The Queen's College, and anchovy toast and sherry, seemed a long way away to John, and the Newsom Report and his many other distinguished activities in education were still a good many years ahead. When it was clear that I was never going to earn more than ten shillings a week as a WEA lecturer, and not even deserve that, I talked it over with my father and decided to go back home, with absolutely no regrets at all.

My father had an idea, and it concerned nursery schools. As a public health inspector, he had always seen the light as far as nursery schools were concerned and, in the early days of her struggle, had been a willing listener and a good friend to Margaret McMillan, the educational pioneer. Margaret McMillan and her sister, Rachel, had become convinced that the early years were the most important ones in a child's life, and Rachel had opened her own nursery and teacher training centre at Deptford during World War One. My father and I went to see Margaret McMillan at the college. As she stood in the churchyard where the first school had been held, her white hair untidy in the wind, large, generous, imperious, all the signs of true greatness on her, she agreed that I should do a one-year postgraduate course there.

In this way one of the happiest times of my life began. The nursery school was like an oasis in what were then the slums of Deptford. I remembered that Peter the Great had lived in this part of London. The Thames flowed wide and sluggish at the end of the street where the school was, and in the streets on summer evenings whole families brought their blankets out and slept on the pavements to escape the bugs. For the first time, I knew what a bug looked like, and how it smelt, and I learnt the smell of dirt and old clothes and hard poverty. I worked in the clinic up the road, saw scabies, and helped to disinfect and learnt the smell of derbac soap and sassafras oil and lysol, all the smells of the poor. I once went to see a mother whose child had stopped coming to school. I found her in a small upstairs room, heavily pregnant and unable to get out of the door unless there was someone there to move one of the two double beds in which the family of six slept. She was caged in that small, stuffy room day after day, unable to squeeze round the end of the bed to get out.

But inside the school there was such goodness and devotion and unselfishness as I have rarely met again. Every moment of the day was crammed and every moment worthwhile. The children began to come at half-past seven; some of them needed a bath, some settled down to breakfast. Our mornings were lively, with walks round the garden, singing, painting, games with water and

sand. We had lunch, and then the little beds were brought out
and the children were rolled up in blankets, thirty or forty settling
down for the nap. Those afternoons felt quietly marvellous;
teachers gone to lunch, students in charge, the small, still bodies,
the peaceful garden outside.

I never liked the course work in the college much. I remember
taking weeks to make a jigsaw puzzle with a fretsaw. I was bad at
all those things, but the work with the children and the families,
when we had contact, still seems to me one of the best things I
ever did. Later, when I had small children of my own, I used to
look back and marvel at how I had managed thirty toddlers!
Individual children blossomed before our eyes. To take a dirty,
verminous, irritable child and make it clean, shining-haired,
active and happy was very satisfying. Today, though the physical
care is no longer so desperately needed, I wonder still how many
small children could use the ordered freedom, stimulus and
community living of a good nursery school.

During my course I got a job over the summer holidays. The
oil magnate, Alexander Duckham, had handed over his home in
Kent as a holiday home for poor London children and a helper
was needed. I applied and was summoned to Sevenoaks station,
where 'transport would be provided'. I was very nervous as I set
off and the transport turned out to be Mr Duckham himself,
driving his Rolls-Royce. He whisked me through the lanes of
Kent, brought me to his cottage on an escarpment above the
Weald, gave me a strong drink, and told me I had the job. It was
a wonderful summer. The weather was marvellous, the children
happy in the huge house and grounds. They came in all ages and
sizes; ragged little children, who screamed at night because they
still felt the rats nibbling their feet in their basement home, some
children with crooked spectacles tied up with string, prim little
girls and naughty defiant boys.

Sometimes in the morning we would go down to the village,
five or six in the old pram, another dozen tagging along. Never
have I felt more wanted, I think it hardly rained that summer,
and we all got brown and fat. Sometimes mothers would come
down for a few days for a holiday. In the evenings there would
often be a summons to the cottage lower down the hill. Mr
Duckham was the only man I have ever known to have his front
hall lined with prone champagne bottles. We would listen to *La
Traviata* on his gramophone, look out over the Weald country,
drink champagne, and then I would go back to the dormitories

and the sleeping children. It was then, I suppose, that I learnt for the first time the inordinate pleasure of doing two opposite things *hard*. The days were hard and full of responsibility, followed by evenings of music and champage. It has always seemed to me a good mixture for life; the champagne tastes better after the smell of derbac soap.

I was by then almost at the end of my year at the Rachel McMillan Training College, but there was little likelihood of a nursery teaching job because, sadly, there were so few nursery schools. Nevertheless I also realised that I was actually more interested in what we now call social work, rather than teaching. However, nobody had the least idea how I might go about pursuing that sort of career. It was then, in late 1934, that my mother saw an advertisement in a newspaper for a *Children's Hour* organiser for the BBC in Manchester. My first reaction to my mother's suggestion that I apply for it was, 'But, mother, I hate the wireless.'

Nevertheless, I did apply and was asked to attend an interview. I remember exactly what I wore (did women of that time always remember events by clothes?). I wore a double-breasted, belted, navy blue gaberdine coat (coats were worn long that year) and a navy blue felt tricorn hat. I must have been an intimidating sight, but I was determined to look responsible. Some time later my new boss said to me, 'You did look awful at the interview. If you'd arrived on a sit-up-and-beg bicycle with a Gladstone bag, we would have *known* you were a midwife!'

There was a slight conflict of interests on my way to the interview. My route to Broadcasting House happened to cross the one by which Princess Marina was going to Westminster Abbey to marry the Duke of Kent. Needless to say, royalty won. I arrived late, very hot and bothered but, much to my surprise, I was offered the job.

4 1934–37 – Recruitment to the BBC

And so it was that my life with the BBC began. There was no nonsense about training you in those days. I had just under one week in London with Derek McCulloch, better known as 'Uncle Mac'. I was told to sit at the side of the studio and watch his *Children's Hour*. I thought it was a very odd scene. Later I found out that Mac had run through his budget and was using his friends in Broadcasting House as an economy measure. One of the friends was Stuart Hibberd, already the BBC's august chief announcer, who in 1936 would utter about King George V some of the most famous words in broadcasting history, 'The King's life is drawing peacefully towards its close.' But on that day in 1934 I sat in the *Children's Hour* studio listening to Stuart Hibberd playing *Cock o' the North* on a tin whistle. I thought, 'They can't be going to pay me £250 a year for doing this.'

On the third day a voice on the telephone from Manchester said, 'Miss Shapley, will you be needing the Northern Orchestra in week two?' I panicked. What could I possibly do with an orchestra? My most responsible job since leaving university had been de-nitting the children in the East End nursery school. However, I said, 'Yes,' and prayed that all would be revealed to me.

On a raw December night in Manchester I got off the London train and walked down the approach of London Road (now Piccadilly) Station. I passed, I remember, a surprising number of advertisements for trusses. The next morning, with my four days of watching Uncle Mac in London behind me, I was to start my job as north regional *Children's Hour* organiser. I would produce five hour-long programmes every week and a sixth on some Saturdays, as the Saturday programme rotated around the regions and was heard nationally. I was twenty-four years old.

The taxi driver took me to the Waverley Hotel in Oldham Street, where I took a room. The very next day a new colleague of mine suggested that I would be better off settling down somewhere straight away and said he knew of a place in south Manchester. He gave me an address to go to in Wilbraham Road, Fallowfield, and I got myself a room in this large, rather crumbling house. It was an odd place, very silent and very dark. The only person I spoke to was a Miss Rowbotham from across the landing, who was kind enough (she gave me a cup of cocoa), but I thought to myself, 'She does have an awful lot of cousins in the Merchant Marine.' No penny dropped until I got back one night to find the front garden full of policemen.

'You can't go in there,' they said.

'But I live there!' I replied.

'Well then, you'd better come along to the station too!'

So it was later that night that I was able to write to my father and say, 'Such fun living in Manchester. Guess what? I'm living in a brothel!' My father's immediate reaction was to send me a ten-pound note to get out.

My next landlady was a Yorkshirewoman called Frances Raby. She had more than her fair share of northern individuality and completed the conquest of this particular southerner at one blow. I have hardly ever met anyone since who has struck me as being so completely alive or with such a gorgeous sense of humour. Miss Raby had had a very tough life, beginning work as a half-timer in a Dewsbury woollen mill when she was only eleven years old. She was a tremendous adult education enthusiast, and much of the pleasure in her life had come to her through friends she had made that way. A year or two before I went to live with her she had handed in her notice at the Halifax factory where she worked, drawn out her savings from the Post Office and gone to Manchester where she knew nobody. She bought a house and set up as a landlady. Never was there a more eccentric and delightful one. All of us who lived there were completely happy under her rather erratic rule. There were nights when we came in late and sat round her blazing kitchen fire with a bowl of onion soup. We listened while she read out the poem or short story she had composed that day while she polished the floors. This more than made up for the occasional mornings when she woke us up with a cup of tea and the words, 'I can't bear the sight of you any more, loves. I'm going to give myself a holiday in Blackpool and you'll have to shift for yourselves.'

I remember coming home late one summer evening and finding no bed at all in my attic room. It took me quite some time to discover that it was in the back garden along with every other bed in the house, all of them neatly turned down for the night. For years our landlady had dreamt of sleeping under the stars and waking up to feel the dawn wind. Now, in her little back garden in Manchester, the dream was coming true. We were going to be part of that dream, whether we liked it or not. Of course we loved it.

Miss Raby's zest for life made her sturdily independent of a lot of things which only money could buy. But she always had good, simple food and a welcoming fire blazing in the grate. I remember the packets of children's plasticine that she could twist into strange and often quite beautiful shapes, the pencils and notebooks in which she wrote the thoughts which came into her head, the glass jar with a few flowers or leaves inside. She welcomed me and my odd BBC friends, all making some kind of living from the arts, and put up with all our untidiness and late hours for the pleasure of our company. Through her I became almost obsessed with the idea of getting people like her on the air. Her jokes seemed to me so much better, so much funnier, than the jokes the scriptwriters wrote, and her point of view on almost anything was worth having. She was certainly one of my inspirations for the experiments I was to make later at putting real live people on radio. In fact, for the first of these programmes in 1938, *£.s.d.*, I largely used her friends, the people she had told me about.

Most of all, I remember, Miss Raby loved the open country and the wild moorland between Lancashire and Yorkshire. When she died her only request was that some friend should take her ashes and sprinkle them on the moors above Halifax.

On my first day in the Manchester studios we had a meeting in the office of the programme director, Archie Harding. His extreme left-wing views had embarrassed the BBC so much that they felt they had no other option than to exile him to the north where he could not 'do so much damage'. He had transformed the BBC North Region with the help of an assortment of talented people, many of whom were to become 'greats' in the field of broadcasting. In the mid 1930s Harding began to experiment with the outrageous idea that 'ordinary' people might have something worth saying on the wireless. He recruited an aspiring poet and writer, D.G. Bridson, and together they began taking the first, tentative steps towards what we now know as the 'documentary'.

The first of these programmes was called *Harry Hopeful* and it began in 1935. Bridson went on to produce a series of innovative industrial features called *Cotton, Steel, Wool* and *Coal*.

When one considers today's technical wizardry the problems of that time seem unbelievable. In 1935 we still had not been given our mobile recording van, which was primitive enough but a boon to us in those early days. Indeed, very little of what was broadcast was recorded at all. This meant that the reality of a situation had to be recreated in the studio, using scripted material, sound effects and trust in good luck. Bridson wanted to get as close to the real thing as possible. To do this he went to people in their homes or workplaces and, after taking notes of the interviews, scripted them. Armed with these scripts, he returned to his subjects with a portable microphone and recorded them reading back their own words. This was by way of a rehearsal. The actual programme was sent out live from the studios in front of an audience which included the relatives and friends of those taking part. Today, as I watch Esther Rantzen or any other television reporter or commentator careering down the Uxbridge Road with microphone in hand, able to record, edit, broadcast, all with the utmost simplicity and sophistication, I cannot help thinking of those early days and the painstaking way we went about achieving our aims.

After that first meeting with Archie Harding I was asked to stay behind. When the room was empty apart from the two of us, he extended his hand and said, 'Welcome, comrade.' I was never a very devout communist, but I could tell that I was among friends. But despite Harding's influence broadcasting at that time was a formal affair. The BBC was a very gentlemanly place. Indeed, there was only one other senior woman on the staff at Manchester. On the first day I said to her, 'I know nothing about broadcasting; you must help me,' and she said, 'The first thing you have to know, dear, is how the gentlemen like their tea.'

In those days every new BBC staff member had to meet Sir John Reith. Reith had been appointed general manager of the British Broadcasting Company in 1922 and was the first director-general of the British Broadcasting Corporation from 1927 to 1938. He therefore directly shaped the way broadcasting developed before the war and indeed the legacy of his high-minded vision of public service broadcasting persists to this day. Staff were summoned by a printed card along the lines of, 'You will wait upon the director-general', with your name and the date and time filled in. I went to London at the appointed time and, very nervous, was ushered into the great man's office, the only room in Broadcasting House, it was said, to have a coal fire. Reith was immensely tall, with a scar right down one side of his face from his severe war injuries. He seemed to uncoil from behind his desk as he stood up to shake my hand. 'Good afternoon, Miss Shape-ly,' he said, in his precise Scottish voice. He was the first, but by no means the last, person to mispronounce my name; 'Miss Shapely' has plagued me throughout my life. The meeting was brief and could hardly be described as a relaxed conversation. Reith's opening remark did not help. Referring to a senior staff member in Manchester, he said, 'Tell me, is … still drinking?'

Back at the BBC in Manchester I found the atmosphere more congenial. I worked hard, but occasionally found time in the lunch hour to go with some colleagues to dance at the Ritz Ballroom. I had started ballroom dancing at Oxford, where I broke the rules to go dancing with my boyfriend, Peter. I absolutely loved it and became rather good. Immediately before being accepted by the BBC I had actually started a job teaching at a dancing school in London. Who knows what might have happened with that career if I had not applied for the BBC job!

I took to my new job and its location with alacrity. I was in the north of England at last and enjoyed finding out about its people and customs. I found an honesty and a courage in the people of the towns I visited, which I found attractive and rather touching qualities. In a hat shop shortly after my arrival I watched a customer trying on several hats, while the assistant stood by politely. The customer finally turned round in one hat to the assistant, who said, 'Eh, love, you look *terrible.*'

London was still a very far-away place and in the 1930s the north was made up of many tightly knit communities, many people never venturing much further than Blackpool or Southport, and then only once a year during Wakes Week. Everybody knew everybody else's business and amid the stereotypical 'net curtain twitchers' there was support and help to be got from one's neighbours. My first friend in Manchester was Thomas Matthews, who was a violinist with the Hallé Orchestra. Through him I met his sister, Mamie Rogerson, and her husband, Haydn, a cellist. One evening I rang the Rogersons and was told by the telephonist at the local exchange, 'Oh no, I can't put you through. Mrs Rogerson is spending the evening with Mrs Wadsworth and her Haydn is practising his cello and she doesn't want him disturbing.'

This was a warm and courageous place, but it was also a restricted one. For those who did not conform, life in those towns could be cruel. I felt that I was lucky to be part of a group that stood outside some of the ethics of the society we lived in. I had never totally conformed and there were many like me at the BBC.

Looking back, I think it was in the area of relationships and sex that some of us were rather ahead of our time. Nevertheless, there were definitely different standards for men and women. It was a new idea for a woman to explore her sexuality and one that it was not really wise to advocate publicly, especially if you were one of the women doing it. There was pressure both from society and from family to get married at some point. The raising of a family was the female's raison d'être and sexual activity was the man's pleasure and a woman's duty. Contraception was left to the discretion of the man and, when unwanted pregnancies did occur, it was reasonably easy for a man to avoid any responsibility in the matter. Unmarried mothers were outcasts from society and very often the only help at hand were the horrific back-street abortionists.

A few weeks after joining the BBC I found that I was pregnant, and knew this meant that I would certainly be fired. The father had a senior position and, unusually, was put in a situation whereby he might lose his own job because of the incident. It was because of this, and not out of sympathy for me, that he eventually gave me the financial help I needed to avoid a scandal.

There was no question of my letting the pregnancy continue. I simply did not feel ready to bear a child, and the stigma of having an illegitimate baby was very great then and did not change until years afterwards. I had also just started a job that I could see I was going to love. So, I decided to seek an abortion. In the end I had to go to three different people. The whole thing was extremely dangerous and very painful. The first man I went to literally told me to sit down on a stool and drop my drawers, and he stuck something up. This did not work at all and in fact I could have died from the injuries. Then I went to a woman, again locally, but still the abortion did not happen. Eventually I went to another, ghastly, woman in Kent who charged the earth. By this time I was pretty far on in the pregnancy and the father had had to give me the money I needed to finish the job. The woman I went to had to flee the country very soon after my visit. Her boyfriend came in and watched the proceedings without so much as a by your leave and afterwards I was shaking so much that she tied me down to the bed with ropes. I had been delivered of two perfectly formed baby boys, twins.

I was still very ill. In the end a nursing home in Manchester said that they would try to clear up all the terrible mistakes that had been made. However, they insisted that my family was told. I summoned the courage to tell my mother and she came up. She was wonderful, absolutely wonderful. She supported me entirely, though it must have been a terrific shock for her.

My new life in Manchester and the BBC resumed and I immersed myself in what looked like being a fascinating career ahead of me. One of the things I enjoyed most was being able to get out and see so much of the north. It was soon clear that I had to have a car, so that I could not only get around easily for work but also enjoy the countryside in my spare time. I bought an old Ford convertible and set about learning to drive, as it turned out just managing to avoid the driving test, which was introduced in June 1935. My instructor was a young colleague, David Porter, who had joined the BBC at the same time as me and was an announcer and variety assistant. David's father was a racing driver in Ireland and David himself drove with some panache. I remember him taking me out on to the Chester Road and making me accelerate up to quite a speed for those days, saying, 'From the very beginning you must drive fast or you'll never learn.' I took his advice and within a week drove alone across the country to Middlesbrough!

The job was pure joy, because in those days regional broadcasting really meant something. We did not take a great deal from London, certainly not in *Children's Hour*. The scripts would be sent from London and we would broadcast our own version from Manchester. We, in the north, did our own version of the *Toytown* series, so loved by the children, with Doris Gambell as Larry the Lamb. The region stretched from the Scottish border down to about Ashbourne in Derbyshire and from Wales to the North Sea. Anything in that vast, varied region was material for programmes and in 1934 very little of it had been used.

At that time *Children's Hour* tackled everything, including at least two full-length live plays a week. Some of the programmes are still remembered. A few years ago a Manchester headmaster told me that he had never forgotten Shorty and Conky, the two Cockney characters from Franklyn Kelsey's serials, *The Children of the Sun* and *The Island in the Mist*. It was always said that the miners of Wigan used to bet on the outcome of the various episodes at the pit bottom. There was not always time to rehearse the speaking parts. Once a character was set, I left it to the actors. Mr Kelsey's lavish effects – earthquakes, hurricanes, explosions – took up all our rehearsal time. The two effects boys used to emerge dripping from the small room with the water tank, the wind machine, the coconut shells and the record of the BBC seagulls.

Wilfred Pickles, later to become a household name, would often take time off from his official job in those early days to act in our plays. That meant six parts and help with the effects for the standard fee of three guineas. Wilfred was versatile. He could change from the leader of the howling French mob to the aristocrat on the guillotine without apparently drawing breath. He was the kind of actor we needed. 'That chap of thine's talking whenever I switch on the wireless,' said one of his father's Halifax neighbours about this time. 'One day he's Julius Caesar and the next he's a blinkin' rabbit.'

I met Wilfred and his wife, Mabel, at the very beginning of my life with the BBC. We had been rehearsing a play and all the cast had come out together into one of those mean, wet Manchester evenings. The puddles between the stone setts in Piccadilly were like black ink and the trams clanked dismally by. I was standing there bracing myself to face a solitary egg in my lodgings when Wilfred, whom I hardly knew, said, 'Look here, why don't you come home with me and meet my wife?' When I said the conventional things about unexpected guests being a nuisance, he said, 'That's all right, we'll get some fish and chips on the way back.' It *was* all right and as we sat round the fire I felt a hard lump of loneliness inside me beginning to melt away. It was a very friendly, welcoming house and Wilfred was a wonderful teller of tales. I remember that Mabel did not let me turn out again that night, but put me in her and Wilfred's own bed. I do not know to this day where they slept.

On one of those early evenings I had been taken by Wilfred and some other colleagues to the Haunch of Venison, a pub in Lever Street much patronised by the BBC. A couple of men at the table next to ours were talking rather bluntly about some ladies of their acquaintance and assessing their attributes. One of them said that though a particular 'lass' was a nice person, she was not much to look at. The other replied reflectively, 'Ay, but we don't fuck faces in Lancashire.' Wilfred glanced at me nervously, but I carried on sipping my drink and did not flinch, thereby presumably passing the BBC shockability test!

Wilfred was always ready for the odd jobs that turned up in those hair-raising plays. 'Wilfred, get the coconut shells, will you, and be a horse cantering down the road ... sorry, that horse has only got three legs ... fine, it's got four now.' In one play I remember, when we had shot back to the Middle Ages, I had to have the effect of knights in armour clanking up the echoing passage of an old castle. This was not very easy, but Wilfred and the effects boy were sure that they could fix something. When we got to that scene, I turned up the microphone of the effects studio slowly and ... there we were, back 600 years and my knights were slowly coming towards me up that stone passage. I slipped across to see what they were doing. There were Wilfred and the effects boy, roller-skates on their feet, precariously marking time on a large stone slab.

The story I most like to remember about him was when some years later I was producing an evening play called *Never Come Monday* by the late Eric Knight. It was a curious piece, a fantasy and not at all easy to do. Wilfred was playing the lead. However, although we all worked hard, the play very obstinately refused to come right. On the evening it was due to go on the air Wilfred, Mabel and I were driving across to the Leeds studio, none of us happy about the play, going over it, trying to put a finger on its weakness. Then Wilfred suddenly stopped the car and said, 'You know what's wrong, don't you? I shouldn't be playing the lead; it's Dick Gregson's part.' It took a minute for this to sink in and then he said, 'Well, we'd better hurry up if you're going to make that switch.' Whenever I am asked what was the worst moment of my career, I usually say the one when I called the cast together and said, 'Look here, chaps, it's only an hour before we go on the air, but I've made a mistake and this is what I'm going to do ...'

We made the switch and Dick Gregson stepped straight into the lead. Wilfred, with some of his better wisecracks, took over various small parts and 'voices' that Dick had been playing. The cast really put their backs into it and it was a very cheerful party that motored home over the moors that night. Of course one could not have risked it with less experienced actors, but then only someone as good a trouper and as sure of his own worth as Wilfred would have made the suggestion.

Wilfred Pickles' broadcasting career steadily developed and during the war he moved to London and achieved fame as the newsreader with the northern accent, with his famous 'Good neet' getting a mixed reception. I met up with him again in Manchester after the war, where my husband, John, was programme director. We had returned from America, where John had picked up the idea of an audience participation game show. He thought that this unscripted format would work in Britain, but with the added interest of visiting a different place each week rather than staying in the studio. John asked Wilfred to visit him at our home in Didsbury and there he described his idea and asked Wilfred to host the programme. This was the beginning of *Have a Go, Joe*, which became *Have a Go* when it became a national feature. The programme lasted twenty-one years, till 1967, and was enormously successful. It shot Wilfred to fame, with Violet Carson at the piano and the producer, Barney Colehan, handing out the prize money ('Give 'im the money, Barney'). Later it was produced by Stephen Williams, with Mabel Pickles dispensing the prizes ('Mabel at the table') and Harry Hudson at the piano. Barney Colehan went on to produce the long-running television show *The Good Old Days*.

While Wilfred was working out with John the details of *Have a Go* he gave our children a very appealing floppy doll, a pig, which one of them still has; they called him 'Wilfred Pickles'. We went by train on holiday to Wales one year and my daughter spent the journey dressing and undressing the doll with a lovely frilly set of clothes she had persuaded me to buy. We got out at a small station and as the train was pulling out, Christina let out a loud wail, 'Wilfred Pickles has lost his knickers.' Wilfred's name was one of the best known in the country and I can hear now the concerned but puzzled Welsh voices along the platform repeating this news to each other.

The *Children's Hour* cast included Doris Gambell and also Muriel Levy, and they were even more versatile than Wilfred. They could act, sing and play the piano. Muriel, a Liverpudlian, wrote two or three sketches a week for us, in green ink on the backs of envelopes in the train between Liverpool and Manchester. Violet Carson, later to become the redoubtable Ena Sharples on *Coronation Street*, I first remember coming in to play a baby frog in one of Henry Reed's brilliant 'cartoons'. Henry Reed worked a lot for the BBC and was the wonderfully talented composer and pianist with Henry Hall's band.

Once a month we held children's auditions for the feature *Young Artists*, when mothers had to be forcibly held back in the waiting room while little boys fought their way through *The Lost Chord* on the trumpet. Being the north of England, many tap-dancers and performers on the spoons applied for auditions and, rather surprisingly it seems to me now, were often used in programmes. Five hours every week was a lot of time to fill, and I extended the contributions by young artists to include programmes from Newcastle and Leeds as well as Manchester.

One of my scoops was when a very pretty and composed schoolgirl in a gym tunic came in for an audition and sang *Peter's Pop Keeps a Lollipop Shop*. The next week when she was on the air and halfway through her second song, the manager from the Argyle Theatre, Birkenhead, rang up to offer her her first professional date. Her name was Pat Kirkwood. Soon after that she left school and went on in the 1940s and 1950s to a dazzling career in musical comedies, pantomime and films, including Hollywood.

A new item which I introduced was *Your Own Ideas*, which continued right up until *Children's Hour* ended in 1964. It featured poems, stories and music written by young listeners. We also had monthly competitions; three certificates and you got a silver pencil. A bank manager once told me what an emotional moment it had been for him when he came to the studios to receive his pencil. In one of these competitions the children were asked to draw their impressions of us, and the prize went to a little girl who drew us all sleeping peacefully together in an outsize bed. It seemed that they thought of us as a friendly lot. I am still referred to as 'Auntie Olive', although where the title came from remains a mystery to me. I disapproved of the 'Auntie' and 'Uncle' notion and insisted for some reason on being called plain 'Anna'. It did not work. I may have been Anna on the airwaves, but from then on I became known as Auntie Olive in the BBC canteen, the pub and just about anywhere else where *Children's Hour* was mentioned.

Because *Children's Hour* was an afternoon programme, we were able to use the Rusholme Repertory Company. Mary Hayley Bell, later to marry John Mills, would sometimes oblige. T. Leslie Jackson, 'Jacko', was assistant stage manager to the company. He later became producer of *What's My Line?*, *This Is Your Life* and *Call My Bluff*. Some of our Rusholme actors would 'lunch' rather too well and there would be difficulties. One of our regulars was so rarely sober that we would invariably place a bucket outside the studio in case he should become ill and have need of it during the broadcast. He sometimes did.

As I had hoped in that first week in the job, the mysteries of what to do with an orchestra were soon revealed to me. Before long I would think nothing of engaging the BBC Northern

Orchestra to play especially for us. We made great use of Jack Hardy's Little Orchestra and we also had, I remember, a genuine Hawaiian trio, exotic even in cosmopolitan Manchester.

The most loved programme was certainly *Out with Romany*, which had begun in the North Region the year before I joined the BBC and was heard nationally from 1938. Romany was in real life a Methodist minister, the Reverend G. Bramwell Evens. He was a naturalist with a great gift for conveying to children his knowledge and love of the countryside. Every week he pretended to go on a nature ramble with his dog Raq and two children, in fact Muriel Levy and Doris Gambell. It was no use telling the audience that they were not in the open air, climbing real stiles and finding real birds' nests. There were long silences when the three performers were looking at a bird in the branches of a tree, and little shrieks of dismay when somebody walked into a stream. The illusion was complete, with the help of those early effects records. Raq always came to the studio and I can see now the look of surprise on his face when his master whistled to him and another, ghostly Raq answered on a record. The BBC did not want to deceive; we always said that these programmes came from a studio, but from the letters we got it was quite clear that many listeners just did not believe us.

We were never much bothered about timing in those days. 'Goodness,' I would say, looking at the clock, 'more than fifteen minutes to go and we've finished already. Well, Auntie Doris can sing a song and Noel [Morris] can read a poem and I'll go and ring up Uncle Harold.' Harold Dehn would leave his warehouse and the piles of cloth waiting to be shipped to Africa, take his bowler hat and banjo off the peg and dash over and oblige with one of his comic songs. Other *Children's Hour* team members were Harry Hopewell and the pianist Charles Kelly. We all enjoyed ourselves enormously and we felt very close to our audience.

It was expected at that time that the BBC regional staff would play many parts. In addition to producing *Children's Hour*, I sometimes read the northern news and the potato prices, introduced brass bands and acted as liaison between the BBC and the Free Trade Hall on Hallé nights. Once I even read the rugby league results, but because I read 'Keighley' the way it looked to me (it is pronounced 'Keethley'), I was never asked to do it again.

Our versatility was sometimes called upon during crises. One day I arrived at Broadcasting House to be greeted eagerly by the commissionaire, saying, 'Oh, Miss Shapley, I'm so glad you're here.

Mr Porter hasn't come in yet and the orchestra is just about to start their concert.' I went straight to the studio, grabbed the announcer's script and while the orchestra was tuning up, struggled with the fearsome names of foreign composers. All broadcasts were live then and you had to get it right the first time round. Minutes before we went on the air, the door was flung open and a figure appeared at the top of the stairs leading down into the studio. It was David Porter in pyjamas and dressing-gown, hair standing on end. He had overslept, but a wild drive in a taxi from his lodgings had saved the day.

One of my early studio appearances was silent but memorable. D.G. Bridson was preparing his feature, *Coal*, and in his continued determination to break away from the tyranny of the scripted programme put a group of Durham miners into the Newcastle studio and told them to talk. After a few minutes I was sent in with a large piece of cardboard on which Bridson had hastily chalked, 'Do not say BLOODY or BUGGER.' These are not really swear words in the north-east, but for many people are woven into the fabric of everyday speech. The sight of these poor men trying vainly to form some sort of a sentence without resort to them was enough to have me sent back into the studio to say, 'As you were.' There was a terrible row about it. It seemed likely that Bridson would be sacked. Luckily for the BBC, as well as for Bridson himself, he was not.

We did a great many dialect plays in those days. The first one that I was asked to produce was unintelligible to me. Robin Whitworth, senior drama producer, told me to check with the cast: 'If there's no advertising or dirt, just let them get on with it.' I later produced plays by T. Thompson, one of the best known dialect writers, and by then was understanding a good deal more. I recalled all this later on, during the war, when I had to produce some programmes in Portuguese. They were quite easy compared with an early feature on the Holmfirth flood in the Holmfirth dialect.

When I came to the north I heard for the first time the story about the plague at Eyam. It is a story of great poignancy and I felt strongly that it should be brought to a wide audience through radio. Eyam is a quiet village in Derbyshire, set among the wild moors of the Peak District. In the autumn of 1665 the plague of London was at its height and many thousands were dying. A box of clothes was sent from London to a tailor at Eyam. The clothes were damp and the servant who dried them at a fire became ill and died of the plague. When others died in that house, the village knew that the plague had taken root in Eyam and people waited in horror for it to spread. Many thought of getting out of the village to try to escape the disease, which was a death warrant. But then an extraordinary thing happened. The rector, William Mompesson, realised that if people left the village they could spread the plague to other areas in the north of England. He got the villagers together and begged them to stay in Eyam so that the plague would go no further. He promised that he would not leave them. A line was drawn around the village a mile from its centre, beyond which no one would go. People from other villages came to arranged spots on the boundary to leave supplies. In all 350 people stayed in Eyam with Mompesson, and a year later, when the plague was over, only eighty-three people were left to tell the story of their horror.

I produced a historical radio play called *Plague at Eyam*, which I considered a great privilege to do. Actors can often be quite distanced from the material they are handling, and indeed it is often better for their professional job if they are. But this was different. The cast got so absorbed in the story that I suggested they might like to go together to Eyam to feel the place for themselves. I contacted the present rector and we all went out in a coach which the BBC organised. It was the most emotional experience walking round the churchyard looking at the tombstones of all those brave people of almost 300 years ago. The year of the Eyam plague felt so near to us, and to the people of the village it clearly seemed like yesterday. I have never forgotten that experience and I never cease to be moved when I think of Eyam.

5 1937-39 - Radio Documentaries

The first stage of my early career at the BBC lasted from December 1934 to the end of 1939. For almost three years I stayed in my position as *Children's Hour* organiser, North Region. Then, after a brief spell in the staff training school, I was promoted to assistant producer, North Region.

Despite my self-confessed romantic attitude to my new home, I was certainly not oblivious to the economic and social conditions around me. In the early 1930 the depression was at its height and for many Britons, but particularly those in industrial areas, it was a time of extreme deprivation and suffering. Once I was taken to see a family living in indescribable poverty in a derelict mill, illegally I suppose, the five children sleeping head to foot like sardines in a broken down bed. Nobody could stay politically neutral after seeing things like that. It affected all of us.

Slowly this was being reflected in the programmes that were being made. Our programme ideas, however, could not have advanced much further without some crucial technical developments. In 1937 the Manchester studios were refitted with the latest equipment, including the new and improved dramatic control panel already in use in London. We also acquired our new mobile recording unit. I was fascinated by the possibility of combining these facilities, and began to concentrate my work on making programmes in which recorded actuality was mixed, through the panel, with studio presentation and commentary. Paddy Scannell and David Cardiff have described very clearly the recording innovations:

> The recording van was twenty-seven feet long and weighed, when fully loaded, more than seven tons. Its maximum speed was twenty miles an hour. Inside were two turntables, each

operated by a technician. The recording time of each disc was a maximum of four minutes. As one disc came to an end, recording was continued on the other turntable, thus securing uninterrupted continuity of a sort. The new equipment could accommodate up to six discs at a time, with remote control to lower the pick-up head onto the precise groove at which to begin the required recorded insert.

Two recording vans had originally been commissioned by London to collect topical items for inclusion in the news bulletins. But they were unsuited for this and were passed over to the regions. Wales, Scotland and West Region, however, had many hilly and narrow roads which the vans could not negotiate. So by the time one of them arrived in Manchester there was some uncertainty as to whether they had any useful purpose at all. Bridson had used it for *Steel* but only for background effects. (Scannell and Cardiff, 1991, p. 345)

When I had the chance of using this equipment I tried to structure my programmes in a straightforward way, with a narrative commentary introducing and linking the recorded material which formed the substance of the programme. This is how Wilfred Pickles introduced my first 'actuality', as we called it then. It was *£.s.d.: A Study in Shopping*.

Good evening everybody. Before we get going in this shopping programme there are one or two things I want to tell you about it. Now it's what I call a 'homely' programme. No flourish of trumpets about it, you know, but the sort of programme you'll recognise yourselves in maybe. The records you're going to hear were made at a little town called Sowerby Bridge. Sowerby Brigg I call it, coming from that part of the country myself.

I remember very clearly venturing out for the first time with the enormous recording van to prepare this programme. We caused a sensation when we parked the thing in Sowerby Bridge. I, feeling an utter fool and holding a microphone at the end of a long lead, disappeared into the side door of the Co-operative Stores and recorded a conversation between a shop assistant and a millworker called Joe Lum from down the valley, who wanted to buy what he called 'a pair of booits'. People were not used then to having a microphone thrust in front of them with the instruction to 'be natural – just be natural!' The three of us who were there that day sweated over our little recording but, in a humble way, I think we were making broadcasting history. The programme was, of course, received very calmly at the time, except by the head of programmes. Nevertheless, he eventually said, 'All right, go ahead, do some more.' And so for a year or two I lived a strange life, in the cabs of long-distance lorries, down coalmines, in dosshouses, on longboats on the canals. Every so often someone said wistfully, 'You know we gave you this job so you could produce a women's magazine programme,' but nothing could stop me.

By the time I made my last 'documentary' programme during this phase of my career, a year and a half later, I had developed more fully and established my own programme style. For *Canal Journey* I recorded men and women working on the Leeds–Liverpool canal, with the help of a fourteen-year-old, Archie Thompson, whose genuine curiosity inspired very direct questioning. I kept my own linking commentary to a minimum and let the canal people speak for themselves. In my introduction I said:

> On this occasion I went after the human story – as the newspapers say – and tried to get the canal people I met to tell in their own words something of what their life is like. In spite of all the jokes to the contrary they are not a very voluble race and some of them found it hard to believe that anyone could find the details of their ordinary life interesting and, when they had been reassured on this point, it wasn't very easy for them to put their ideas into words. All the records you'll hear were made without script or rehearsal.

There were some strong dialects. I am not certain whether this should have been a cause for celebration or despair, given our country's confusions and contradictions (still) about dialect and accents. The *Listener* radio critic, though generally complimentary about the programme, was in no doubt; there was too much 'obscure dialect', some participants being 'downright unintelligible', and he was 'prepared to swear that very few Londoners understood more than one word in six' (31 August 1939, p. 446). So much for bringing the voice of the people to the nation!

Despite the apparent problems posed by some 'ordinary' English people in communicating with their fellow countrymen, I believed passionately that broadcasting was at last on the right track. It was very exciting to be part of that change, though at the time, of course, I did not see it in any historical perspective. But Scannell and Cardiff have since commented that I was the first to take the van all over the region to record people talking in their homes, at work and on the streets. They went on to assess my contribution to broadcasting in very flattering terms, suggesting that, single-handed, I 'brought to maturity the use of recorded actuality as the basis of the radio feature in those last few years before the war' and that my programmes 'broke new grounds for radio both in technique and in their subject matter'. They further commented that 'such reportage, combined with her sympathetic skill as an interviewer (a quite new technique which she had to discover for herself), led one contemporary critic to describe Shapley's programmes as "little masterpieces of understanding and authenticity"' (Scannell and Cardiff, 1991, pp. 345, 347).

Unlike *Canal Journey* there had been no problems of intelligibility in *Broadcasting with the Lid Off*, since the voices we heard were mostly of BBC staff going about their work and they therefore represented a suitably Reithian range of humanity. Not everybody at the BBC relished the exposure at the time, though I think in the end it was generally agreed that our professional integrity had not collapsed around us. I had no doubt that it could only enhance the listeners' legitimate interest in the BBC, and I must admit that I immensely enjoyed conveying the interest and excitement of broadcasting.

Manchester itself played a great part in all our lives at the BBC. Many programmes were hatched in one or another of those dark little basement restaurants where elderly Turks rattled their dominoes and smoked foul-smelling tobacco. The Oyster Bar in Lever Street was where we celebrated; their champagne was incredibly cheap. But Archie Harding also encouraged us to travel. We crossed to Leeds by Nont Sarah's pub in all weathers and struggled over the Buttertubs in snow and ice. We would record a brass band in Barrow-in-Furness in the morning and audition a choir in Newcastle a few hours later, having travelled by way of High Force and Haltwhistle. The whole magnificent north of England was open to us and we took our programmes from every corner of it.

For us, though, the travel was only part of our work, the means to an end. In *Night Journey* I looked at the world of the professionals, the long-distance lorry drivers. It was a fascinating one, which aroused in me great admiration for this section of the workforce, largely unseen and unsung. It was quite an arduous job even reporting on it. One night I rode for ten hours on an eight-ton lorry carrying fourteen tons of chemicals and textiles, while a fine rain fell and I wondered how one would even tackle a car journey on that road. I left no stone unturned in my quest for a full picture. That meant a night in a damp ditch on Shap, with microphone ready to catch the first rumble of the fish lorries as they thundered down from Scotland. The engineer, who was crouched down beside me, asked, 'When's your next programme, Olive?'

'Well,' I said, 'next month we're going down a mine so we can get a microphone to the coal face.'

'Thank God,' he said. 'With any luck, I shall be on holiday.'

In another documentary, *Homeless People*, I tried to convey something of the lives of people who were even more invisible than the lorry drivers. I cast my net very wide: casual wards, night shelters, Salvation Army lodging-houses, hostels, training centres and orphanages. It was a rude awakening for me and, I think, for the listeners, even towards the end of that decade which had seen such poverty and despair. The programme was, of course, mostly very sad, but it by no means painted a depressing picture about human nature; I witnessed great dignity and humanity among both the givers and receivers of help to the homeless. Looking back now on my programme, I see that it both tackled a revolutionary subject for that time and did it in a revolutionary style. Maybe some observers thought that it was not a suitable subject for broadcasting. Documentary producers have always trod a delicate line and it is hard to refute accusations of exploitation and voyeurism. Forty-five years later the television channel, Channel 4, devoted two whole weeks to a season of programmes on homelessness. This interested me, not so much because documentaries are now a major part of broadcasting, but because this topic is still there to be covered and so extensively.

Homeless People was very nearly finished when a newspaper editor in Newcastle told me of a community of French monks settled at Scorton in Yorkshire. Apparently these good people ran a hospital for homeless incurables. He rang them up for me then and there, and it was suggested that I call in that evening on my way back to Manchester. I had a very limited acquaintance with monks and the only thing I could think of was to rub off my lipstick and put on a rather withdrawn look. I need not have worried. When I drove up to the gatehouse, there was an eager young monk hanging out of the window. 'Hello,' he said. 'Wonderful to see you. Now, the first thing you must see is my bedroom!' In his bedroom there was a complete small radio transmitting station; this monk, Brother Clement, was obsessed by radio. Within a few minutes he and I were broadcasting Strauss waltzes to the patients.

It was my programme *Miners' Wives* which created almost the most publicity at the time, and this was no doubt partly because I managed to persuade the BBC to let me take one of the participants abroad, more or less the equivalent of going on Concorde today! First I went and lived for about a week with the Emmerson family in Craghead, a mining village in County Durham. Mr Emmerson was a checkweighman at the local pit. Through the family I got an insight into the life of the whole community, but particularly the problems of the women, who spoke very eloquently for my recordings.

The programme was prepared only six months before war broke out and I thought a European twist would make it more interesting. Our contact in France was an Englishman, in fact the batman in World War One of my BBC colleague Donald Boyd, who had married a Frenchwoman. They lived in Marles-les-Mines, near Béthune, and Mrs Emmerson and I travelled there by train, boat and taxi, and stayed for a week with a family which had three men working in the pits. Mrs Emmerson was naturally apprehensive during our long winter journey, and hated London on the way through. However, as the ancient taxi bumped along the road from Béthune past the familiar-looking pit-head shafts and huge conical slag heaps, her spirits began to rise. When we overtook a group of miners walking along the road in their dark Sunday suits and light caps and mufflers, she turned to me and said, 'You know, lass, they couldn't be anything but miners. I think it's the way they walk.' She settled in to that family, with the help of my rather poor interpreting, as if she had just gone down the road from Craghead. Back in England she spoke in the programme about her impressions of the way of life in the two mining villages.

As is probably clear, I was fascinated by the nuts and bolts of other people's jobs and lives, and one of my programmes looked at twenty-four hours in the life of a big hotel from the staff point of view. *Hotel Splendide* remained discreetly anonymous at the time, but I do remember a very interesting weekend in Scarborough, gathering material for the programme, at the luxurious hotel run by Tom Laughton, the brother of film actor Charles Laughton. Here again, as with my other programmes, the interest of such a setting seemed all too obvious to me, but few broadcasters were yet interested in exploiting all these possibilities. There was certainly more scope for innovation then than now, when we have over seventy years of radio and about forty-five years of television behind us.

The presenters that I used regularly for my documentary programmes were Wilfred Pickles, whom I knew well from the *Children's Hour* days, Joan Littlewood and Jimmie Miller (who later changed his name to Ewan MacColl). Joan and Jimmie had been recruited separately to work as writers and actors in the team around Archie Harding at that time. Joan had walked all the way from London to Manchester, reputedly eating potatoes from the fields along the way. Jimmie had originally been spotted outside a city-centre theatre, playing his music for coppers. They got married and were both heavily involved in radical theatre, creating after the war the famous Theatre Workshop.

Joan Littlewood and I produced what was probably the most unfair and biased programme ever put out by the BBC. We called it, with a nod to Engels, *The Classic Soil*. Engels had described Manchester as 'the classic soil ... where capitalism flourished'. By recording much of the programme in Salford flea market among an odd little group of families who lived in a condemned warehouse in Pollard Street, we proved to our satisfaction and everyone else's intense annoyance that basically Manchester was unchanged since Engels wrote his famous denunciation of the city in 1844. I remember feeling that we needed a statement from a pregnant woman to describe what it was like bringing a new life into this phantasmagoric Manchester that we were creating. Joan was sent out to find someone and, being a perfectionist, came back to Broadcasting House with not one but eight ladies all in advanced stages of pregnancy. They were very sad bundles of humanity, some with small children attached. An awed commissionnaire ushered them into the studio and they came up to the microphone one by one to give an account of themselves. I do not know what they made of it, but we then all had lunch in the BBC canteen and chatted over cups of tea. Since this programme is one of the few pre-war ones of which a recording still exists, it has tended to get a regular airing over the years, sounding ever more crackled and archaic every time I hear it!

Working with Joan was quite an experience, but she, Jimmie and I also had a holiday in France together, which was equally memorable. We set off in my battered little open car and crossed the Channel. Somewhere down the coast we broke down and ended up in a café, where a kindly taxi driver took pity on us. He arranged for the car to be repaired and said he would take us to a place where we could camp. He took us to a causeway down the road and we carried our tent over to a little island. By the time we got the tent up, it was getting dark and there was quite a wind up. Jimmie went and raided a few blocks of stone from a mound inside some railings nearby, and these held the tent flaps down nicely. We crawled out of the tent in the morning and our first sight was our taxi driver swimming over from the mainland with food strapped on his head! We all had breakfast together and were just thinking of getting dressed when a little party of people looking remarkably like pilgrims appeared at the railings and all stood round reverently. We discovered that we had pitched our tent next to the tomb of the famous French writer, Chateaubriand. The French pilgrims were not overly impressed with the English campers.

A few days later we were in Paris and I remember driving down the Champs Élysées with Jimmie sitting in the front. Suddenly we realised that people were laughing and pointing at the car. We turned round and there was Joan, sitting in the back on top of all our luggage, doing a ridiculous pantomime! By that stage we were running out of money and I took us to a restaurant where I knew the owner. He let Joan and me wash up for a few days, while Jimmie played his guitar and sang beautifully in the restaurant, and we made enough money to get us back to Manchester.

There is a particular programme from this era that I remember with the same sort of thrill as my programme about the plague at Eyam. It was *The Quiet House at Haworth*. I wanted to do a programme about the Brontë sisters, but instead of a straight literary programme which was fairly standard fare, I decided to make the Brontë Parsonage Museum at Haworth the focus, and to reconstruct the life the Brontës must have lived there. It was an eerie affair, broadcast one evening in spring. The light was beginning to fade over the moors and throw the crowded tombstones into relief, and the dusk was starting to fill the corners of the old house. We had microphones in several of the rooms, and brought some of the Brontës' possessions to them and talked

about them with the museum custodian and the secretary of the
Brontë Society. There was Anne's workbox with the rusting needle
still stuck through the reel of thread; the comb Emily used the
day she died; poems of Charlotte's, unpublished, in spidery yellow
writing.

The first participant was Miss Ann Tempest, who was ninety-
three years old. She sat in one of the high-backed chairs in 'the
parlour', which Mr Brontë had used as a study, and I introduced
her as the only living person old enough to remember the Brontë
family:

> I think you will be interested to know that she has very definite
> views indeed on the story she has to tell, and her family say
> that her story never changes and that not a whole army of
> newspaper reporters and BBC officials can induce her to
> remember anything new! She has lived in Haworth all her life
> and to her, as to a great many of her neighbours, the most
> famous woman in England, the most talked of novelist, was
> 'nowt but Parson's dowter'.

Miss Tempest could recollect some of Mr Brontë's sermons and
quoted the texts he had used. She remembered 'Miss Charlotte'
taking the Sunday school class, but had forgotten the name of
'the other one', 'a wild young thing' with long black hair and a
dog. She would have been very small when Emily died, but she
probably heard talk of her as she grew up. I shall never forget her
quavering old voice spinning that tenuous thread between us and
those fascinating ghosts we thought had gone for ever.

I produced two other major programmes just before the outbreak
of war that are interesting in retrospect because they involved
collaboration with other, very distinguished, people in pioneering
fields. *They Speak for Themselves* was a radio inquiry into the Mass
Observation movement begun in 1937, and was presented by Tom
Harrisson and Charles Madge, two of the movement's founders.
The programme allowed the researchers to explain their purpose
and also looked critically at the methods of sociological research
used by Mass Observation. Some subjects already explored were
illustrated, including the reactions of the 'man in the street' to
international crises. According to Scannell and Cardiff:

> it is worth noting that the only serious comment on radio, as
> far as we know, about the critical implications of the Munich

crisis, between the event itself and the outbreak of war, comes in this North Region feature programme. The introduction to the programme and a later section, which uses actors to reconstruct the swings in public opinion at the time of the crisis, both point to the information gap between rulers and ruled, and the ignorance of the British public about what was happening in Europe and the aims of British policy. (Scannell and Cardiff, 1991, p. 348)

Some months earlier I had been invited by Alberto Cavalcanti to an evening of documentary film showing at the Academy Cinema in London. Cavalcanti was a Brazilian film maker, who had worked a great deal in Paris and London and was now with the GPO Film Unit. At the end of the film evening, Cavalcanti announced that they would play a radio documentary which, though lacking the visual aspect appropriate to that evening's selection, was 'an important and valuable piece'. This, to my surprise, turned out to be my *Homeless People*. Soon after this, the BBC and the GPO Film Unit decided at the same time to make documentaries about the health services, which led to a unique collaborative effort and sharing of material for film and radio. Cavalcanti asked that I produce the radio programme *Health for the Nation*, and in early 1939 I was sent down from Manchester for a week to prepare it. The narrator was Ralph Richardson and he used to pick me up at the Whitestone Pond in Hampstead in his little open red car to go out for our day's work.

It was exciting to go to London to do that particular job, but I still knew that I wanted to stay with the BBC in the north. As it turned out, I was not to be there much longer and I would not return to live till after the war, when I settled there again with my husband John and our family. Nevertheless, when I later lived in London I always fancied that the north began at Euston. Within five minutes of leaving the terminus I would find myself in friendly chat with four or five people in the carriage, all of whom were either related to my best friends in Manchester, or had lived in the same road that I had once lived in, or went to the same shop in St Ann's Square for their children's winter pyjamas. Euston left behind, Manchester seemed to take on the proportions of a fair-sized village, and by this I mean no possible criticism of it. To a Londoner particularly it seemed quite miraculous that a place so big could still retain the friendliness of a small backwater. You could stretch out your hand and touch all your friends. You could walk out of your house on a cold winter's night and be at almost any of their firesides in a few minutes. I found that when I arrived back in London its sprawling anonymity would depress and frighten me.

I can remember the distinct flavour of all the seasons and celebrations of Manchester during my early years there: spring in the sooty parks with their magnificent array of flowers, which seemed so much longer and somehow more impressive than those in the south; winter, when the cars coming in from the Pennines clanked their chains through the streets; the sounds of horses' feet on cobbles and the feel of those same cobbles through thin shoes; the bolts of white cotton goods dropping through the air from the windows of warehouses in the narrow streets on to the carts below.

A particular personality I associate with Manchester at this time is Sir Thomas Beecham, and with him certain Hallé concerts which were a nightmare as well as a pleasure. Sometimes, if a concert was to be broadcast, I was sent along as the BBC official in charge, with the job of seeing that the concert in the hall started at the right moment for the people listening at home on their radio sets. This was usually fairly simple, except for those concerts which Sir Thomas was conducting. One could never be sure whether he would stride on to the platform five minutes before the appointed time, and then the plaintive tones of my voice over the telephone to BBC headquarters would be backed up by a fine performance of Beethoven's third *Leonora Overture* in full swing, or whether he would remain firmly closeted in his dressing-room long after the announced time, while the minutes ticked past and the announcer in the studio did his gallant best to fill them.

But I remember meeting Sir Thomas on another occasion, which was entirely delightful. He had been conducting the BBC Northern Orchestra in Newcastle. The concert was held in the magnificent City Hall and it was something of an event. After it was over we took Sir Thomas out to the George Inn at Chollerford for supper. The George, I suppose, must have one of the most delightful situations of all English inns – on the banks of the Tyne, a low grey stone building, with gardens full of rock plants dropping down to the river. We had a very good supper, cold roast beef and salad, and Sir Thomas was in wonderful form, telling stories which kept the whole table laughing. The dining-room was full of families from Newcastle, who had come out on that fine summer evening to stroll by the river and have supper there. The whole place seemed pleasantly aware of the great man in their midst and there was an undercurrent of excitement. Just as the meal was finishing, a young man, very shy but grimly determined, came over and said, 'Thank you so much, sir. The Sibelius was wonderful.' A kind of murmur went round the room and I can see now Sir Thomas sitting at the head of the table and acknowledging the tribute with a very slow inclination of the head, which he alone could have made arrogant and modest at the same time. But it was a remarkable feeling in that low-ceilinged dining-room, looking out on the lovely Tyne, and exciting to be on the fringe of it.

As all Mancunians know, the Hallé Orchestra has for a long time been a very important part of that city's history and cultural consciousness. When my family had returned to Manchester after the war I loved the feeling of going to a Sunday afternoon Hallé concert, when the long, ugly streets around Belle Vue were filled with the ordinary people of Manchester going to hear *their* orchestra; the great gaunt King's Hall, redolent of circuses and all-in wrestling; John Barbirolli pacing up and down the ringmaster's room before making his dramatic entry; Clifford Curzon, perhaps, in the passage, flexing his fingers, waiting to go on and play a concerto for that magnificent and attentive audience. In the Free Trade Hall the audience would stream up the stairs, and ladies crowd into the antiquated cloakroom. There would be familiar faces both around you in the hall and on the platform and later, going home on the bus, you would still be surrounded by concert goers. Perhaps one of the second fiddles would be sitting two seats ahead with his wife and his mother, and the leader of the woodwind would be leaning over the back of the seat in front to chat.

Manchester was a great place for parties, and here again music often played a part. One of the nicest we ever had in our house was when Dr Malcolm Sargent came to conduct the BBC Northern Orchestra in a concert of modern English music. Some of us realised then that, if he had not been a great conductor, he would probably have been a well-known pianist.

Unfortunately the supply of music in our house was very limited. I had stopped short at Chaminade's *Autumn* at an early age and the only music I had bought since then was of the variety of *Simple Songs for Little People*. So we sent out an SOS and the biggest find was a copy of the César Franck Sonata for violin and piano, which Sargent and Thomas Matthews, the young

Manchester violinist, played beautifully. It was a fine warm summer evening in July, all the windows were thrown up and the heads of some of the family of eight children who lived next door could be seen bobbing about from time to time in the front garden. I remember I had long given up any attempt to keep my elder son, Dan, in bed, and he sat on the stairs in his pyjamas listening to the music and the talk, and scraping out the trifle dishes with a large spoon.

Another memorable occasion was the night before Gracie Fields made her comeback after the war years. Bowker Andrews, BBC North Region's variety director, was in charge of the programmes in which she was to appear. He had flown out to Capri a month or two before to discuss every detail of every broadcast with her, and the night before the first one some of us gathered in his house for supper and to meet Gracie. I had to take along my new baby, Christina, then a few weeks old and looking rather fetching all in white with pink ribbons. I remember how Gracie pounced on her and picked her up out of her carrycot and talked to her before she was put firmly to sleep in the Andrews' bedroom. Gracie was delightful that night, rather quiet, thinking no doubt of tomorrow's concert in Rochdale, and I realised then how very handsome she was. Mostly, I remember, I was struck by her beautiful bones. The bone structure of her face was something very satisfying to look at, and the strength and grace of her arms and hands.

As she came out of the Andrews' front door to go back to her hotel, two or three grubby little boys with home-made fishing rods and jam-jars came past and Gracie, dropping into the broadest Lancashire, told them exactly what their mothers would have to say to them when they got home. And they, of course, gave back as good as they got. I do not think they knew who she was, but they went off grinning from ear to ear.

The broadcast was exciting enough on the night, but the high spot was when Gracie came out on the balcony of the town hall afterwards and sang to the enormous crowd in the square below. There was a storm brewing, I remember, and the sky was livid. It was a wonderful night and, for her, must have been a wonderful homecoming.

One of the things that most intrigued a southerner about the north in those days was the lack of commercialism in everyday things. When I came back to Manchester from New York at the end of the war, with one small child and another on the way, I tried very hard to buy a clothes horse, a 'maiden' as it is called in the north. In the suburb where we lived, Didsbury, this turned out to be an impossibility. Like so many household articles, a maiden was a rare and expensive bird then and, although I was desperate and quite ready to pay the price asked of me, none of the local shopkeepers would consider selling to me. 'Oh no, love,' they all said, 'you can't pay 18s. 11d. for a clothes horse. It's robbery. You just wait a month or two and we'll have something cheaper in by then.' After New York, I could not believe my ears. This could have happened to you anywhere in Manchester.

I once stayed with some friends who were in the throes of having their hall and stairs painted. I had forgotten about this and when I came out of my room in the morning on the way to the bathroom, I practically measured my length on the bare boards on the landing over the squatting figure of a painter who was just, very neatly, putting some finishing touches to the skirting board by my door. 'Eh, love,' he said, as I recovered myself, 'that gave you a fair fright, didn't it?' In a moment we were involved in a long chat about the weather and the price of eggs and a good many other things. The workmen would do anything for you, from looking after your dinner in the oven to sitting a baby on the pot in an emergency. Once, when the bit of road in front of our house was being resurfaced, Christina was put out in her pram and propped up with cushions all through a very cold week in winter to watch this fascinating operation. I shall never forget the kind driver of the steamroller who put on his brake every so often as he passed the pram, climbed down from his seat, wiped the baby's nose with the handkerchief pinned on to her coat and then got back to his steamrollering. This sort of incident was typical of Manchester. I remember also my children often singing a very fine collection of old music hall songs taught to them through long mornings by Leslie, our beloved electrician, who happened to be rewiring at the time when they had measles.

If, as a southerner, you fell for the north, you fell very hard indeed. I believe there was no middle way. Either you kept your eyes turned to the south and thought of yourself as an exile, or you came to love your new home passionately and felt lost when you had to leave it.

However, I knew one ex-Mancunian at that time who was quite clear that he did not want to go back and live there: Eric Newton, the well-known art critic and chairman on many occasions of the BBC's Sunday morning programme *The Critics*.

He was born in Manchester and went to school there, but refused to admit any nostalgic memories of it. He remembered with some pleasure when he was a schoolboy cycling every Sunday afternoon in Delamere Forest, but he said that after so many years in the north he still was most aware of feeling starved of the sun. His idea of heaven, formed by Manchester, was Provence. I asked him if he did not think that Stockport could look pretty wonderful too, with a fine sunset over the town, but he refused to be drawn. (Incidentally, I considered Stockport to be one of the grandest and most dramatic urban landscapes in the world.) Eric Newton, however, commented on the other side of the coin on this issue. He felt that it was the people coming from the provinces who made the best use of London; young people who have suffered all their lives from a slight feeling of starvation, longing for more pictures, more music, more plays than the ordinary provincial town could provide. I think he was probably right but then, on the other hand, things had a scarcity value in the provinces. In Manchester, for instance, a week of ballet was something to be looked forward to, planned for, saved up for. In London, where perhaps five ballet companies were giving nightly performances, the chances were that you did not go to any of them.

Perhaps I was hopelessly sentimental. Certainly I often infuriated the indigenous northerner. However, I never lost the thrill of the London train rattling into Stockport. On the last lap of the journey, whenever I could, I would lean out of the window and see that grand bit of urban landscape; mill chimneys, the huge viaduct astride the grey town, the tumbling Mersey and the sombre green hills beyond.

I look back on those first years in the north with enormous pleasure and a certain nostalgia. The towns were beautiful in their way, the countryside breathtaking, the people vital; and of course my job at the BBC varied and interesting. However, although it was good to meet people and fascinating to have such close glimpses of their lives and work, I think I was sickened by it at times. Perhaps all journalists feel the same. Sometimes I had the feeling that the whole world was doing an honest job of work apart from me. There was nothing very honest, it seemed to me, in walking into a hospital, say, picking the brains of a man who had been working on a piece of research for years, tidying up what he had to say, recording the surface of it, getting into my car and driving off, then going to a remand home or a mental hospital and doing the same thing. My subjects were always left behind doing the work. A BBC colleague used to call it 'dabbling in other people's realities'. I loved it, of course, but just occasionally I would get the feeling that real life was going on without me.

I have to admit that these feelings never lasted for very long at that time, and there was always ample human contact and intimacy. In Burnley I interviewed a woman called Miranda Roberts, a housewife. I had had a feeling for some time that she was good material, but unfortunately she had never really come across in the studio. With our new technical expertise, I was able to sit opposite her at her fireside and, miraculously, a wealth of stories and observations came out. As we settled down to talk, Miranda summed up the advantages of our cumbersome new equipment and also, possibly, my attitude towards the radio broadcasting of that time, saying, 'It's just thee and me, love.'

6 1939–41 – Outbreak of War

'Cupid takes a bow – at BBC' announced the *Daily Mail* on 16 June 1939. The *Daily Dispatch* of the same day carried the 'news which burst like a bombshell on Broadcasting House, Manchester, yesterday' and went on: 'owing to what the BBC would describe as a technical hitch, news of the romance leaked out about a week before the contracting parties intended that the announcement should have been made'. Yes, indeed. The 'girl whose voice is known to millions of northern radio listeners' and John Salt, the BBC's north regional programme director, had decided to marry and our plans for a quiet start to our life together had failed dismally!

John and I had met three years before through our work in the BBC and had been involved with each other for some time. We did not, though, have any particular plans to marry. However, as with so many other couples at that time, the increasing likelihood of Britain going to war forced us to think about the future and take steps to ward off what we felt would be inevitable separation. John was thirty-four and I was twenty-nine. John's father had died the previous year and his mother and two sisters lived in a lovely house in Yorkshire, the Old Rectory in Thorp Arch, the little village opposite Boston Spa on the River Wharfe.

John Scarlett Alexander Salt had come to the BBC via an unlikely route. He was a Yorkshireman and a great-grandson of Sir Titus Salt, the famous Bradford wool merchant and mill owner. Titus built Saltaire, the model industrial village centred on a huge mill, completed in 1853, in the then open country to the north of the city on the banks of the River Aire. John's roots were also embedded in another part of Yorkshire manufacturing history, since his paternal grandmother was Catherine Crossley of the extensive Crossley family, carpet makers of Halifax. Among his mother's ancestors was General Scarlett, who in 1854 had led the charge of the Heavy Brigade at Balaclava. It always amused John that over time this highly successful military operation had become well and truly overshadowed by the disastrous efforts of the Light Brigade.

Though interested in his family history and proud of past achievements, John also had a fundamental belief in the worth of all individuals and their potential to develop in unexpected ways. His background was privileged and he himself abundantly blessed, but in everything he always set himself very high standards. To be lucky in life's lottery was for him a starting point, not a complacent end in itself.

The path his family had chosen for him was conventional. He was sent to a preparatory school in Yorkshire, followed by the naval colleges at Osborne and Dartmouth. He later transferred to the army and went to the Royal Military Academy at Woolwich before being commissioned in the Royal Engineers. Here he got the chance to go to Cambridge. He was in the first group of army officers to do this and they all had to work extremely hard to get their degrees in two years instead of three. John achieved first class honours in mechanical sciences, and also managed to pursue the sports he loved, particularly athletics and hockey. His career as an army officer led him to specialise in aerial survey work, in which he was a pioneer. After some years' survey work in the Middle East, particularly Sinai, he wrote a book on the technical aspects of air survey. He then became the youngest officer appointed to the War Office.

By all the obvious yardsticks John was pursuing a successful military career. Nevertheless, he grew increasingly dissatisfied with many aspects of service life and anxious also to explore other capabilities he felt within him of a more intellectual and creative kind. In 1933, on a cruise with his mother off the Dalmatian coast, he met Jardine Brown, a senior BBC official, who suggested to him then and during their ensuing friendship that there was interesting and challenging work to be done in the still rather novel field of broadcasting.

In the following year an opportunity arose and John resigned from the War Office, to apparently universal amazement, and joined the BBC as an assistant in the Talks Department. This department has been described as being at that time 'probably the most exciting area of broadcasting to work in' (Scannell and Cardiff, 1991, p. 153). To quote from John's letters, he did indeed find 'the whole foundation of the job ... very absorbing, and absolutely worth while'. He revelled in the variety of people at the BBC and found most of them 'intensely alive'. For him one of his most exciting projects during this period in Talks was the production of a series of programmes called *The Dangers of Being Human*, in which the topic of psychoanalysis was tackled in broadcasting for the first time. Through this initiative John met people in a field which fascinated him, and one of them wrote a book based on the series. Because of his technical background John was an unusual and useful person for the BBC to have on the programme staff, most of whom came from the arts.

Two years later John took the chance that he wanted of moving to the North Region and soon after became director of programmes, replacing Archie Harding who had become co-director of the new staff training school. In Manchester his professional interests broadened into features and documentaries and this coincided with my own wishes, as a member of his staff, to experiment in these areas. John proved to be a supportive and imaginative boss, who let the programme makers have their way in their efforts to develop broadcasting techniques and broaden both subject matter and, it was hoped, radio's appeal to listeners. He was an impressive administrator and an equally impressive human being, as I discovered.

I was very sad that my father had not had the opportunity to meet John, as I knew they would have liked each other. My father had taken early retirement from London County Council in 1935 because of ill health and had then developed Parkinson's disease. He died early in 1939 at the age of sixty-eight.

Even after the publicity surrounding our impending marriage had died down John and I hardly had a tranquil lead up to our marriage on Bastille Day, 14 July 1939. His demanding job remained busy and I was in the final stages of preparing with Joan Littlewood *The Classic Soil*, which was due to be broadcast a week before the wedding. I got fairly exhausted trudging up and down tenement stairs and round cobbled slum areas gathering material for the programme, but of course the interest and necessity of finishing the job kept me going. John and I also faced the uncertainty of the BBC's attitude to employing staff married to each other and, because the situation was not common, it took some time to resolve. There was generally considerable opposition then to the idea of married women working at all. The outcome was that I would have to resign from the permanent staff but would be able to continue with BBC work on a contract basis.

I did not question the justice of this policy at the time. It was many years before employment conditions in any area of work changed for women generally and married women in particular. Furthermore, although I had no intention of giving up my career altogether, I did welcome the chance to have a break and take stock of my new circumstances. My instinct then was that for a woman the combination of running a home and pursuing a career would inevitably present difficulties. Furthermore, through all the later changes in my own life and despite very great shifts in societal and family attitudes and practices, I never saw any reason to change my mind. I gave a lot of thought over the years to the question of 'leading a double life', especially when I was asked to speak at girls' school speech days.

John and I decided to try to rent a cottage out in the hills beyond Manchester, as a complete change from our lives in the pleasant and leafy suburbs to the south of the city. After our honeymoon in France we did find a charming little house, Ghyll Royd, in Hollingworth, right on the edge of the Peak District, and prepared to move in. We arrived with most of our possessions on the first day of September, anxious to get settled before the winter, but of course well aware that war was imminent. As we sat among furniture and packing cases, John went out to telephone the office and was told to take the night train down to London and start a new job. So, we drove straight back into Manchester and went to Didsbury to pick up our colleague, Donald Boyd, who was also going on the train. Poor Donald met us white-faced and said, 'How do you kill rabbits?' His family had gone off into the country and left the rabbits. He had to strangle them. We all then drove sadly to London Road Station, which was an amazing sight. It was how I had always imagined World War One: people with their families, young soldiers being kissed and embraced, women weeping. For me personally this was probably the most emotional night of the war. I could not face spending it on my own in John's flat in Rusholme, so I went back to Didsbury to the Rogersons' house. Mamie and the children had left because everyone thought there would be bombs dropping at any time. It seemed as though half the Hallé Orchestra had also turned up to join Haydn, and we all slept on the floor. So, John and I never even spent one night at Ghyll Royd. Strangely, though, for a long time we had a more permanent feeling about it than all the other places we lived in, and looked back on it as a much loved home.

John had been summoned to the post of deputy director of Overseas Intelligence, the department which monitored and analysed foreign broadcasts. When war was declared on 3 September, the significance of the department's role greatly increased and John tackled the demands with enthusiasm. Special reports were produced for the Cabinet, and the governments of allied countries also came to benefit from the department's work.

So, John and I were separated until just before Christmas, while he started his new job in London and I continued with my BBC commitments in Manchester. My final work there included some recordings I made standing in the main street of Bacup, a little Lancashire mill town in one of the evacuee reception areas. The programme, which was broadcast just one week after war broke out, was called *We Have Been Evacuated*, and I introduced it like this:

> When we arrived, the streets were given over to children: the high school girls sauntering arm in arm up the main street in their tidy brown uniforms, children playing football in the steep cobbled side streets, children going shopping for their new mothers, children making friends with policemen and ARP [Air Raid Precautions] wardens.

Throughout the first two years of the war I would continue to produce from London a variety of programmes reflecting the nation's preoccupation with 'the great evacuation question', as it was expressed to me in an early memorandum from a senior staff member. This work obviously meant for me a fair amount of travel away from London. Parents were to be reassured that the evacuation policy was for the best and receiving families needed encouragement in their wartime role and practical advice about coping with their unfamiliar charges. It was not a straightforward matter; when the first evacuation wave was not matched by early attacks on towns and cities, some families started to fetch children back and become less convinced that evacuation was the best thing in any case. So, when Britain was heavily bombed from the later part of 1940, there was nothing like full evacuation in place and many children shared the difficult life of their parents in cellars, air-raid shelters and London underground stations.

This issue was one of many at that time which brought into focus the role of public broadcasting in a national emergency such as war. Programme makers like me inevitably were aware of the delicate line the BBC trod between objective reporting of current events, if there could be such a thing, and outright propaganda on behalf of the government. At my level in the organisation I was not personally involved in the debates on such issues, which have recently been well documented (Scannell and Cardiff, 1991, Chapter 5). Nevertheless, they did circumscribe, however gently, my and everyone else's work, as is clear from another part of the memorandum referred to above:

> I do feel extremely strongly that in the present emergency stress should be laid upon the more courageous, as opposed to the more self-pitying, point of view. Do not mistake me. I am not asking for any distortion of fact, but there is undoubtably a great deal of courage and determination and fortitude latent in this country in every class, and that these should be adequately represented in our feature work seems to me of considerable importance.

I had then just broadcast a major feature in the *Home Front* series, called *Women in Wartime*, which apparently was 'most favourably commented on by the Ministry of Information'. In it I presented nine women talking about their lives and work in wartime, and introduced the programme like this:

> 'Women in Wartime' – to all of us this war means something different, and I am not sure what those of you who are listening are hoping to hear during the next half-hour. I feel I must say immediately that this programme beats no big drums; it gives surprisingly little information, I'm afraid, but to me it represents an attitude of mind – one with which we have all become familiar in the last few weeks. Diverse as these nine talks may seem, they have a strong underlying unity, and in all of them there is considerable courage. But you must accept the choice of these nine as a personal choice. Now, when we think of 'Women in Wartime' we don't perhaps think first of the 'women in uniform' who have now become such a familiar sight in the streets, but of the much larger group, the women who have no uniforms, who are entered in the Register under 'unpaid domestic duties' – I mean, of course, housewives and mothers.

I chose the programme's contributors deliberately for their variety, and all their stories and viewpoints emerged as interesting and often extremely moving in different ways. We heard from a volunteer in uniform and an Auxiliary Territorial Service (ATS) woman. There was Mrs Lum, a Yorkshire housewife, who at the last moment in the recording session put her papers aside and decided to say just what was in her heart; her sincerity was ample compensation for her hesitant, rather stumbling words.

For two women the years 1914–18 were still a very vivid memory. One had been widowed, as had so many others, and now at nearly seventy faced another war and the need to adapt herself again to wartime privations and disturbances. The younger Freda Lingstrom, an artist and writer, spoke for an often overlooked but very large group of women: the 'surplus million', without husbands or children, who had out of the ruins of World War One built for themselves a new kind of life as single working women, but who now did not always fit easily into the pattern of female roles being woven into the present war. One speaker whose profession did fall into the National Service category was Dr Dorothy Brock, still headmistress at my own school, who described the complications of running a large London girls' secondary school split up in four or five village and county schools in Kent: 'In a delightfully human memorandum issued by the Board of Education, we town-dwellers are exhorted to commune with nature and study the cow; and indeed we have.' But she worried about the long-term effect of the disruptions on her pupils' further education and careers, and remarked drily: 'Initiative and the study of the cow are not yet regarded by examiners and employers as satisfactory substitutes for covering the syllabus in mathematics and science and the rest.'

I felt it right that the last word in the programme should go to a Viennese Jewess, for whom the war began earlier than for most listeners, as a reminder that: 'There are women today who have terrible stories to tell. Some of them are living here amongst us, working alongside us, and we must never let our sympathy for them grow cold.' This woman's parents were starving in Vienna, her barrister husband was in Palestine and she was working as a domestic in England, with her only child stranded in Holland.

We are women in flight; we have lost our husbands and our children; our parents and our friends; our homes, our money and our work. Other women everywhere will understand our sorrow at this war and we shall understand theirs.

On my move from Manchester to London John and I finally had the chance to settle down to married life. However, it could hardly be described as normal, since of course no lives were normal at that time. The war worked against planning and looking to the longer term. Though people followed intently the ever changing national and world picture, they could not escape from their own day-to-day lives and so focused on the minutiae of running a home, getting to and from work, doing a job, trying to maintain some of the rhythm and comforting certainties of domestic life and contacts with family and friends.

My initial desire to ease up a bit on my work commitments, so that I could enjoy a period of domesticity, turned out to be difficult to reconcile with the number of jobs I was offered, gratifying though that was. Indeed at times I felt that I had little control over the amount of work I did, or its type. A lot was topical, of course, and so could be regarded as directly linked to the war effort. There was a programme called *Bombed Out*, featuring people who had lost their homes and were living in places such as church halls. I covered Women's Voluntary Service centres and wartime nurseries, and took part in discussions on wartime housekeeping with 'Dominion' housewives. A programme broadcast on Christmas Day 1940 called *From the Children* necessitated for me a very long and cold December week based in Cardiff recording children. These were all worthwhile programmes. Nevertheless, I was conscious that I had inevitably lost some of the freedom and autonomy as a broadcaster that I had been so lucky to enjoy, particularly in the two years immediately before the war.

The personal price we paid for John's responsible and time-consuming job and my unpredictable and scattered contract work was that quite a lot of weeks went by when we hardly saw each other. This was not a situation we relished. However, we did end up in an article called 'Working Partners', in the magazine *Good Housekeeping*, which featured 'three very successful marriages which give the lie to supporters of the old "woman's place is in the home" theory'!

We managed to move quite early to a lovely part of London when we rented a Regency house in Downshire Hill near Hampstead Heath, where with pets and a very capable maid, Rose, we established our new life together. Hampstead was interesting in a continental and bohemian way, with its delicatessens, book shops and the Everyman Cinema, and rather unfashionably dressed residents. It had certainly not yet, though, become the chic and expensive place of later years. Its height above the rest of London and the wonderful heath were big attractions for us. I can remember the almost alpine feel in the air as you emerged from the underground station.

We entertained in a modest and fairly haphazard way, particularly old BBC friends such as Donald Boyd, now a Talks producer in London. We also saw a lot of Freda Lingstrom, a very old family friend of mine, and started seeing Jhoti Ghosh, a Bengali scholar, whom I had met years before when I was at Oxford and who turned out to be living near us in Hampstead. My friend Barbara Betts, who had not yet met Ted Castle, also came to see us. She was at that time doing freelance work for *Picture Post*, was already a borough councillor and had just been appointed to the Metropolitan Water Board. We were certain she would be in Parliament one day. We got to know Ernst and Marianne Kris, who were both psychoanalysts. Ernst had been one of Freud's closest friends and was now his literary executor, and was on John's staff. Not long after, the Krises had to go to America, but we did not lose touch with them. Our first visitor in London was John Rickman. He was a Harley Street psychoanalyst, whom John had got to know several years before through his programmes on psychoanalysis, and who was to remain a very close friend.

Though we enjoyed many aspects of living in London, especially Hampstead with the heath and the cold beauty of the parks in winter, I remember that both John and I missed very keenly the north and our BBC friends in Manchester. In fact I think that I never really felt settled in London during this period. It seems odd that a born and bred Londoner could react that way, but it just went to show how powerfully I had become attached to the north. We used to find it hard sometimes even to imagine that the Yorkshire Dales still existed, so far away did that part of the world seem from our current lives. The summer of 1940 also turned out to be the finest for many years, which added to the frustration of not being able to take any breaks from work and enjoy it to the full.

Very soon we decided to start a family and were delighted when I became pregnant early in 1940. However, I had a miscarriage at three months and then exactly a year later miscarried again at three months. I was particularly unwell this second time and began to worry seriously about whether the dangerous abortion, several years earlier, had jeopardised my chances of bearing a child. During these times my steady schedule of broadcasting commitments was inevitably affected and some work had to be cancelled.

I do remember, though, a rather lighter assignment than my usual war-oriented work, when I interviewed George Formby. To prepare for this I spent a day at Ealing Studios watching him and Pat Kirkwood making a film together. One minute they were relaxed and joking, eating acid drops out of a paper bag, the next they were going intently through a carefully rehearsed scene, on an absurd rustic bridge covered with pink paper studio roses. It was only a few years earlier that I had first seen the very young Pat Kirkwood in her gym tunic in the *Children's Hour* studio in Manchester.

Between our two attempts to have a child John had an important job change, when he became the first director of the BBC's European Service. The staff he recruited were a fascinating mix of people from all over the world, many of them refugees from Europe, and we made some good friends among them. My former connection with the Communist Party provided a brief difficulty for John in his new post; however, the BBC did not act on his offer to resign. The service's hours and languages increased rapidly, with the French service inevitably being particularly strong. By early 1941 there was evidence that the European Service had already assumed a very significant role in world broadcasting. John felt that broadcasting was well and truly coming into its own during the war and would equally contribute to the building up of a new world in its aftermath. He wrote at the time, 'I find the prospect very thrilling, and look forward to playing a very active part in it.'

From September 1940 London and some provincial cities began to suffer the heavy bombing of the blitz. Living near the big expanse of Hampstead Heath was relatively safe and we used to go up on to the heath to watch the air-raids. We went there to watch through binoculars the very first attack on London, on the afternoon of 7 September, when the sky was full of German planes. Later that day the whole sky lit up and we joined hundreds of people on Parliament Hill, sitting about in deck chairs and on the grass, to witness the simply terrifying sight of the fires. There were already three huge ones in the East End and others were starting up.

The week before this I had been doing some work for American programmes in Birmingham, which was getting very regular raids. Many residents were driving out to the countryside every night to sleep in their cars in comparative safety. However, factory workers were carrying on regardless and maintaining remarkable morale. My BBC unit recorded right through a night raid in one of the biggest armament factories. It was very difficult handling the sound equipment in the dark while the planes circled around overhead. I remember well the scene in the air-raid shelter as we made our recordings, and later wrote of:

> Community singing, dancing to a gramophone, and best of all a wonderful little old woman in complete gipsy fancy dress, telling fortunes at 3d a time for the Spitfire Fund. I thought it was so marvellous to have the energy to change your dress completely at midnight when an air-raid warning had gone ... The people were magnificent – furious at being made to stop work during raids – I came back feeling immensely cheered. We recorded an old sailor in a factory one day, who produced more malapropisms in five minutes than anyone I've ever heard. One was (speaking of the morale during raids), 'There wasn't a bit of excitement, there was just a panic.'

Not long after, the area around Broadcasting House in Portland Place was very badly hit and John and I went out the following lunchtime to survey the desolation. It was a dreadful sight. The BBC had not yet had a direct hit, but it seemed inevitable.

A few weeks later I was returning from Cambridge and, as the train pulled in to Liverpool Street Station, I heard the sirens going. I rang John at Broadcasting House and made my way on the crowded underground to join him there. It took a long time and I ended up at Regent's Park Station, where I set off for the BBC on foot. About halfway there the sky suddenly seemed to break overhead and a great noise started up. Bombs screamed and blazing shrapnel danced about in the streets. I realised that this had to be a determined attack on Broadcasting House, but in my panic I continued to try to reach the safety of the building. I was scurrying from doorway to doorway along the deserted street, when suddenly a voice yelled at me, 'Come in here!' and a man pulled me into a wide porch. I was surprised to hear a Mancunian voice say, 'If you're going to the BBC like me, you'd better wait a bit.' We waited and when it seemed that the bombs were within a few yards, we wildly rang the bell of the house to see if we could get in, but there was no answer. Then there was a deafening roar and a cloud of smoke went up, completely enveloping both

Broadcasting House and the BBC's nearby Langham building. We were only about fifty yards away. The stranger said, 'Well, they've got us at last.' I insisted on making a dash for Broadcasting House and found the entrance hall slightly damaged with some minor casualties and John frantically looking for me.

John and I left the building for a while and just missed a bigger hit, which did much more damage to the building and occupants. The place filled up with demolition squads, firemen and first aid people, in addition to the usual contingent of people who had to sleep there that night. It was never safe to leave after dark, so every night Broadcasting House became a huge dormitory with people sleeping on mattresses, in the corridors and stairways and concert hall. There were not only staff members but all kinds of visitors, variety artists, Cabinet ministers and the Home Guard.

Not surprisingly, working conditions became very trying, but it was surprising that there was little actual disruption to scheduled broadcasting output. It was even apparent that many people tended to produce exceptionally good work through their determined cheerfulness!

I remember some other highlights in my own working life during these two years in London, inevitably linked by the wartime theme. On Boxing Day 1940 I had the chance to recall on the air my programme *Miners' Wives*, which had been broadcast a few months before the outbreak of war. The *Postscript* to the original programme, in which Mrs Emmerson became 'Mrs Armstrong', told in full the story of our stay in the French mining village, where:

... the friendship that sprang up between her and these French families was complete. They accepted each other immediately, and the language barrier was no barrier. The pit imposed a certain pattern on their lives, and the French pattern wasn't so very different from the English one. Ties like those cannot be broken. Neither side in the ordinary way has much chance of testing them. Perhaps in a peaceful world we should forget them. But the occasion has come now.

Whatever is happening in Durham, whatever is happening in that little mining town near Béthune, I am sure that Mrs Armstrong does not forget, that Léon and Jules and André, and Rosalie and Bernadette remember, and I am sure that they know that if there is hope for the future it lies in the strength of bonds like these – bonds between the peoples of different

nations which no treachery, no brutality, no tyranny can break.
In such times as these they flower forth in indissoluble
comradeship.

A few months later the *Miners' Wives (Postscript)* programme was
translated and rebroadcast in the BBC's French service.

In 1941 I compiled a programme called *Children in Wartime* for
transmission to America and the Empire, which was later broadcast
in a shortened version in Britain. In it I used material recorded
by parents, teachers and children themselves in various parts of
the country. The Canadian commentator Rooney Pelletier set
the scene:

Here in Britain the children are front-line soldiers. They share
every danger with their parents. With them they are facing death
and destruction, sudden homelessness, hunger and cold and
sleepless nights. And they are behaving magnificently.

We heard an account from a nine-year old London boy of a
daylight air-raid, and a letter to her parents from an evacuated
older schoolgirl. An East End boys' club rehearsed for a concert
in aid of Red Cross funds, a whole school in Harrow spent hours
down in a shelter, and children boarded ships bound for America
and the Dominions. To this kaleidoscope of British children's
experiences in wartime were added importantly some poignant
contributions from young refugees from Europe.

And later that same year I produced a programme called *Women
in Europe* which was in effect an echo of my programme at the
beginning of Britain's war, *Women in Wartime*. In the earlier
programme only one of nine speakers had already had first-hand
experience of this war, the Jewish refugee from Vienna. In the later
programme I also introduced nine speakers in:

... a story of terror and of heroism, of heart-breaking misery and
of sacrifice. It is a story that could be told in millions of different
ways by millions of story-tellers, but it would still be the same
story. It is a story that is being unfolded tonight, at this moment,
in many countries. It is the story of the women of Europe
today.

The first speaker was an Austrian Jewess, whose nightmare had
begun when the Nazis entered Austria on 11 March 1938. The

origins of the other speakers reflected the war's progress: Czechoslovakia, Poland, Denmark and Norway, Holland, Belgium, France, whose plight had become so vivid to us in Britain, and Greece. The final contribution was by Mrs Lum, the British housewife whom we had heard in the earlier programme, who expressed her:

> ... dismay and shame. Dismay that such conditions of horror and suffering could exist in a civilised world, and shame at the grumbling and self-pity in this country ... I thought of my husband and little boy safely at home in Yorkshire listening to this broadcast in front of a good fire, and I knew I'd see them again tomorrow, and the tears came to my eyes.

By the time this programme was broadcast John and I were already preoccupied with a proposal which would change our lives dramatically. The BBC wanted John to join the New York office as deputy to the North American director, Lindsay Wellington. It was also suggested that I should be given every opportunity to do programme work over there. It was not an easy decision; we did not want to leave the country at that time and neither of us wanted to be so far away from our families. However, John's job would be an important one, with a pioneering element which was very appealing. The New York office had two broad roles, which were continually developing: to produce broadcasting material for use in the BBC services from London and to promote British broadcasts in various ways in the United States.

John accepted the job and in his usual thorough way got straight down to reading about American history and the constitution. We were both conscious of our considerable ignorance about American matters and, poring over atlases, began to immerse ourselves in current affairs ranging from labour conditions to the 'race problem'. This was the start of a growing fascination with the life and literature of the country.

So, just after the bombing of Pearl Harbor on 7 December 1941 we wound up our London BBC jobs, packed up our house in Hampstead and waited for news of when we could cross the Atlantic. It looked almost certain that we would sail on Christmas Day.

7 1942–45 – Letters from America

To our surprise we spent that Christmas in Northern Ireland. Amid crowds at Euston Station we had managed to get a sleeper from London to Stranraer and then sailed across to Belfast, witnessing a beautiful sunrise on the way. There we had four restful days before sailing for America. We were well looked after by George Marshall, the BBC's Northern Ireland director, and Ursula Eason, who had joined the BBC there the year before I joined in Manchester, and in the same role as regional *Children's Hour* organiser.

Our passage to America took longer and was rather more exciting than we would have wished. However, in retrospect it seemed to balance our considerable feelings of guilt about leaving Britain in the dark days of the war, feelings which never diminished and indeed intensified as the war progressed. We travelled on a medium-size cargo boat, which was leading a British convoy bound for New York. Not only was the weather at times very bad, including dense fog, bitter frost and a hurricane force gale, but our journey ran parallel with a group of German submarines, which managed to reach Long Island Sound. Our boat lost the other British boats several times, since we were all trying to stay clear of the submarines, and it was eventually ordered to complete the crossing independently. So, we landed at Halifax in Nova Scotia and made our way south to New York by train.

First impressions of places are often very powerful and of course can never be recreated, so John and I felt that it was important to record our reactions to everything around us during the early stages of our new life in America. Within one day of arriving in New York John wrote:

... it is quite definitely one of the most beautiful creations we have ever seen. No one seems to talk very much about the colours, but the changing light on the skyscrapers is exquisite and I had no idea how much use could be made of different colours of brick and stone.

A week later he observed that New York made London look like 'a quiet old country town', with the standard of living in Manhattan 'far beyond anything I had ever imagined'.

One can't really compare it with London because it is an entirely different civilisation; although I have heard many people talk about New York, nothing that anyone has said has ever given me the impression I am now getting. And the extraordinary thing about all this wealth is that in spite of it all the place is essentially friendly.

That January, in 1942, John and I decided that at least one of us should write a letter every Sunday to be sent to both our families in England. We would also keep copies for ourselves as a diary of both our personal and professional lives in America. We were motivated more by a desire not to let these experiences just drift by rather than by any grandiose view to posterity, and managed to keep to this undertaking pretty well. Fifty years later that decision has enabled me to recreate vividly this whole period of my life and I am truly grateful for it.

We both observed with fascination our new surroundings, which for me included women's hats, which I judged hideous: 'I think you could walk down Fifth Avenue with a colander on your head and be unnoticed!' By contrast John's involvement was more serious and bordered as ever on the anthropological:

The great mistake is to assume that because Americans talk the same language they think in the same way; nothing could be more misleading. I am quite sure it is going to take a long time to understand their way of life and point of view; we certainly find the prospect very stimulating and exciting.

Later the *Manchester Guardian* would recall him talking of his experiences among the New Yorkers, 'whom he had studied with the same wonder and detachment as some explorers study the Trobriand Islanders'.

Our initial brief stay in a rather expensive hotel was followed by a few weeks in a small hotel suite in a less fashionable area but conveniently near both the BBC office and Central Park. We had to consider very carefully where and how we should live, since we were to continue to receive British salaries for normal day-to-day expenses and had already realised that the cost of living was about double that of London. The BBC generously covered all the 'extraordinary' medical expenses that we were to incur.

After we had spent some dreary evenings looking at badly furnished apartments, we had a stroke of good fortune. The BBC's special correspondent in America was about to leave New York on a long tour around the country and offered us his beautiful Fifth Avenue apartment at what was, for him, a decidedly uncommercial rent. This generous new colleague was Alistair Cooke and I am glad to say that, even at almost two years older than myself, he is one of the few celebrities appearing in my memoirs whose work is not yet totally consigned to broadcasting archives! His spacious flat was on the fourth floor of a big apartment block, with a side view from the front windows of the trees and the lake in Central Park. It had a grand piano for me to play and, to our especial delight, an excellent small library of books about America which Alistair had built up since his arrival a few years earlier. Our luck was complete by our taking on Mabel, a highly intelligent and efficient part-time maid from Harlem. She was charming to look at, very dark and plump with a broad smile, and wore bright blue print dresses and snowy aprons. Her services were to extend way beyond the domestic when she proved to be both a marvellous broadcaster and a contact for my BBC work. I used to visit Mabel and her husband at home and through them learnt a great deal about black people. She introduced me to other people in her community and I found I could move around safely gathering material for programmes. This was an unusual situation for a newly arrived foreigner and I felt very privileged.

The BBC's New York office had expanded rapidly since its opening with just two staff in 1935. As we were arriving it was on the move, from the British Empire Building to the International Building at 630 Fifth Avenue, which was part of the Rockefeller Centre. The BBC took up residence at the eastern end of the thirty-third floor. While our American colleagues could concentrate wholly on settling in to their new offices, John and I were understandably distracted by the breathtaking views from the windows. To the north we looked down on Central Park towards the George Washington Bridge and the Hudson River; to the south we peered through a forest of skyscrapers to the Statue of Liberty and Ellis Island; and to the east lay the wharf on Fifty-third Street which the 'Dead End Kids' films had made famous. Over to the west were the docks and we later witnessed the extraordinary sunset caused by smoke rising from the French liner, the *Normandie*, as it floated engulfed by fire across the city before coming to rest in the mud like a great whale. We were always entranced by the particular bit of New York around our office and its seasonal changes. The little winter ice rink in Rockefeller Plaza became a pool again in the summer, surrounded by pots of shrubs, and tables and chairs under brightly coloured umbrellas.

The BBC's own new studio was not going to be ready for some months, so in the meantime we used the facilities of the NBC and CBS. The arrangement was very efficient, but inevitably rather less relaxed than the early days in Broadcasting House in Manchester, where one could break off in the middle of rehearsal to have a cup of tea with the engineers.

The office's role, as I have mentioned, was two-fold: to produce broadcasting material in America for use in any BBC service from London, known as 'eastbound' traffic; and to promote British broadcasts in various ways in the United States, known as 'westbound' traffic. John, as deputy director, and his boss, Lindsay Wellington, were responsible for developing all aspects of this work and, very importantly, liaising with their American counterparts in broadcasting and gauging reactions from British and American audiences.

Eastbound topical material, called News and Special Events, was transmitted on every day of the week except Sunday via a special radio beam-telephone circuit to Broadcasting House, London, where it was recorded and sorted out for use. The more general feature programmes were recorded in New York and then flown across to London in a bomber by co-operation with the Atlantic Ferry Command. We also sent to the BBC in London popular American programmes, such as the Bob Hope and Jack Benny shows from Hollywood, and individual items such as a talk by Greta Garbo for the Swedish service or a joint religious service between Westminster Abbey and Washington Cathedral. Finally, material was also gathered with our own portable recording gear, for example the reports of the special correspondent, Alistair Cooke, as he travelled round the country.

The BBC was equally anxious to promote its westbound North American Service, operating from London. The service ran from early evening (New York time) to just after midnight with a full schedule of news, talks, features and entertainment. Because short-wave listening was not widespread in America, the New York office publicised the service and tried to get stations in all states to rebroadcast locally. Audience research was obviously a very important aspect of this work, and the BBC had its own staff as well as co-operating with other established organisations such as Gallup Polls.

John tackled his new job with great enthusiasm and continued his efforts to brief himself on the American political, economic and social environment. He remarked that 'here the mental landscape is new and vast, with very few points on it that are sufficiently familiar to be taken for granted'. For a usually well-informed, observant and cautious person, this was challenging but also frustrating.

Quite soon after we had both started our regular daily jobs the BBC agreed to my suggestion that I work in a more flexible manner. Though the office was a most congenial place with interesting and committed staff, I was overwhelmed by the amount of fascinating material that lay out in the streets of New York and beyond. There were sights and sounds and impressions to convey back to people in Britain, and confident and articulate Americans of all types and ages to record for people back home to hear. I was certain that I could use all the skills that I had built up in my BBC career so far to produce innovative and worthwhile programmes. The prospect was very exciting.

We also found that generally American broadcasting styles and techniques were not as creative as those which had been long pioneered and developed within the BBC. This was possibly because American radio had largely been developed commercially. At that time it tended to be the public broadcasting organisations around the world which were allowed to be innovative and experimental, unconstrained by commercial considerations. These impresssions were confirmed by American colleagues and others we met in broadcasting and it was partly what attracted Americans to the BBC office.

After taking some weeks to find my bearings in the new environment and develop some broadcasting ideas I proposed to Derek McCulloch (Mac), *Children's Hour* director in London, that I should do a regular newsletter from America. The idea was well received, and the target age range, timing and programme regularity agreed. A crucial issue to be decided was to what extent the war should be brought into the talks. My own feeling was that it was best to present the American scene emphasising the permanent elements in it, with only incidental references to the war. This coincided with the *Children's Hour* policy adopted since war began. As Mac wrote: 'We have been very careful about the war over here in *Children's Hour* because children get it so much in school and, lamentably, [have] had so much of it in actual fact.' I first introduced the new series in the *Radio Times*:

> When I was a child, America was for me, quite simply, the country of the March family, the immortal March family of *Little Women*. Since then my knowledge has widened a little, but when I first stepped inside a New England home, I recognised immediately that long-familiar atmosphere of cookies, pickled limes and Thanksgiving turkeys, and the prospect of living in America took on a new significance.
>
> I'm sure that children today are much better informed than I was about America, but I'm also sure that there's still a place for stories about it. If I can do anything in these talks to put this country of unmanageable size and complexity into some sort of perspective for the children, I think it's by telling them stories about it, real-life stories with a full measure of the rather pedestrian detail that all the best stories have.
>
> … And while I think that there'll be plenty to tell about the countryside itself, and while I'd like to build up for them a series of pictures that they can remember, I'm sure it's the stories about the people that are really important. Of course, it will be a fine day for me if I can ever begin a talk with, 'Last night, children, I watched the sun set over the Painted Desert …,' but I think they are more likely to prick up their ears if the talk begins, 'This is the true story of Topsy, a little negro girl who lives at 821 East 19th Street. She has eyes like bootbuttons and hair like a woolly mat. She has five brothers and six sisters and their names are …'

My first *Fortnightly Newsletter* for *Children's Hour* was broadcast in Britain on 8 May 1942. It was a scene-setter called *Letter from America*. Four years later its grown-up namesake would begin its career quietly in the capable hands of Alistair Cooke and the rest, as they say, is history. This is how I introduced my first children's newsletter:

Hello, children! Isn't it strange that just saying those two words, 'Hello, children', seems to bring England and home nearer to me than anything has brought them for the last three months. I suppose it's because I've said 'Hello, children' so often in the old days that I half expect to look up and find that this smart New York broadcasting studio has changed into the old familiar one in Manchester. Well, whatever it is, it's a very good feeling to be in touch with you all again; it makes the 5,000 miles of ocean between us shrink to just a little trickle of water.

I expect Mac will have told you that I'm over here in America to work for the BBC, but what I'm sure he didn't tell you was that one of the jobs I'd most like to do while I'm here is to act as a sort of special correspondent for you – for the *Children's Hour*. Ever since I stepped off the boat that brought me from England, I've been thinking how many things there are in America that you might like to hear about; things that you wouldn't be likely to find in newspapers or in books or learn about in school. I'd like to build up for you a picture of America and Americans, so that when people talk about Lend-Lease or Arms Production or Anglo-American Friendship, you can immediately think of some American family, some American house, and some picture will come to your mind that will make these rather dull things come alive.

Supposing you decided that you would like me to be your special correspondent over here; what are the kind of things you'd like to hear about? If I know, you see, I can go round with one eye open and one ear cocked for you all the time. But in the meantime, shall I suggest some of the things that I want to do and see in this country?

I went on to tell them about New York, the views from our BBC office, and Central Park and the Bronx Zoo, then full of children playing in their school holiday. I suggested things they might be interested in: a school near the East River with children of all races together, the industrial cities and vast farming areas, famous natural sights – Niagara Falls, the Grand Canyon, the Painted Desert and the Mississippi, and the huge powerful American trains:

... but most of all I want to get to know some people here, because I'm certain that no country ever really comes alive for you until you know people in it, until you know them well enough to walk into their houses at any time and know they'll welcome you. Are these the kind of things you'd like to hear about?

Well, let's have a last look at New York. The sun has gone down, the sky has turned to the bright electric blue of the New York twilight and the lights are coming out in the buildings. In our office, it's very quiet. We can hear a dull hum of traffic, and an occasional motor-horn, sometimes a siren from a boat on the river. Below us, thirty-three storeys, is a little open-air skating rink. If we open our windows and poke our heads out we can look down on the little insect-like figures on the ice, and if we strain our ears we can hear, very, very faintly, the sounds of *The Skaters' Waltz*. I almost believe that you can hear it too. Well, anyhow, I think you'd like New York alright. Goodnight.

Well, we got a wonderful reponse from children in Britain, who had very clear ideas about what they wanted to know about America. Their interests and preconceptions were based on what was available to them: books, radio, limited and often rather stereotyped films, maybe relatives or friends in America and, of course, American troops in Britain. It is difficult today to imagine that at that time for most British children and indeed adults America could have been a different planet. The ignorance, of course, worked both ways. Even today, despite a constant cultural and information exchange (perhaps rather too one-way for some British sensitivities), I am not convinced that the barriers of real understanding are necessarily much lower than they were then. Americans and Britons are still surprised to discover, despite a common language, their differences in personality and outlook, just as John and I did all those years ago.

I did thirty-eight children's newsletters in all, regularly till mid 1943 and then intermittently till my last talk in April 1945, which was on the death of President Roosevelt. Two talks were about American public schools, PS 150 and PS 43, the second in response to all the questions we got from British children, who were endlessly fascinated by the very different American education system and school culture. I told them about Independence Day, Thanksgiving Day and Christmas, and about summer and autumn in New York. I described a New York drugstore, the Third Avenue 'el' or elevated railway, and the New York Rodeo. I talked of

famous places, like Washington, DC and the White House, and
not so famous places, like a children's library and a typical New
England country house. I did not miss the chance to enthuse about
my visit to the home in Concord, Massachusetts of Louisa M.
Alcott, author of *Little Women*. I once allowed myself the luxury
of reminiscing about England, feeling able in my exile to see the
'wood for the trees' and suggesting that if my thoughts encouraged
the children 'to just open your eyes a shade wider for even a few
seconds to see what lies about you, to see what you have inherited,
then that's good enough'.

I thought the children would be interested to hear about
American radio, mostly commercial and employing hundreds of
thousands of people, with its advertisements and quizzes and soap
operas, so very different from the high-minded and stately BBC.
I did not ignore the war totally and compared rationing in America
with what the children were experiencing in Britain. Peter Weiss,
a thirteen-year-old New Yorker, talked about his family and
friends and school. Predictably, there was much clamour for
information about 'an American cop', and Patrolman Bryant, a
black policeman from Harlem, obliged with descriptions of
everything from his gun to the local children's clubs helping
with the war effort. Unpredictably he ended our interview with
a magnificent rendering of *Ol' Man River* in the deepest bass voice.
The children loved to hear about differences in clothes, behaviour
and language between young Americans and Britons and I reported
several times on these – objectively, I hope, and often admiringly:

> And then the American language is so clever and provides for
> so many emergencies. Where we have to painfully go round a
> situation, an American shrugs his shoulders and says, 'So what?',
> and that just about says all there is to say; or when we're
> struggling to express our complicated feelings on something,
> he will say, with an air of finality, 'Well, I guess it's just kinda
> one of those things,' and really there doesn't seem anything
> more to add.

One of the highlights, for me at least, was the participation of
Mrs Eleanor Roosevelt, who was not only the president's wife but
a widely admired person in her own right. The North American
director wrote to her proposing that she broadcast to the children
of Britain, and she immediately invited me to the White House
to discuss the programme. So, there I was one hot afternoon

sitting on the famous great back porch, looking out over the beautiful gardens and drinking tea out of tall glasses with clinking cubes of ice in it. I was immensely impressed by Mrs Roosevelt; she was modest, gentle and serious and had great charm. She later came to the BBC studio in New York to do the broadcast, accompanied by one security guard. Despite her efforts to remain unobtrusive, the whole BBC office was thrilled by her visit and it attracted a good deal of press interest.

I asked Mrs Roosevelt how British children could help American soldiers enjoy being in Britain and she said:

I imagine that whenever British children stop to speak to American soldiers they are doing a real kindness, for nearly all young Americans love children. Many of our soldiers now overseas either have children of their own or small brothers and sisters and they probably miss them. Therefore, to see children or to go into a home where there are children, would be a real pleasure.

Through an early talk, *Statue of Liberty*, where I described my visit with four New York children, I tried to give some context and meaning to this great copper engineering masterpiece, in addition to the amazing statistics which children love: mouth – three feet wide; nose – four feet six inches long; waist – thirty-five feet; weight – 225 tons; height of torch above sea level – 300 feet:

And it came to my mind then, and I expect it has come to yours, 'This is all very well, but just what does this liberty really mean?' And I looked round at our party, yours and mine, and I thought: 'There's Phyllis and Gordon, typical American schoolchildren, I suppose, friendly and not a bit shy, used to saying what they think and having their point of view respected – it's easy to see that they have been brought up as you have been, in a free and democratic country.'

Then I looked at Louise, with her dark skin and white teeth, her scarlet sandals and bright green gloves, Louise who loves ballet dancing more than anything in the world, but who plans to be a hospital nurse when she grows up; Louise, who was born in the Deep South and whose great-grandparents were almost certainly slaves. And then I looked at Albert who had come to America two years ago when he was only five years old; Albert who was too small, when they brought him out on deck to see the Statue of Liberty, to realise what he was escaping from in Germany, but who will know well enough one day.

And as the ferry bumped against the New York landing stage, I asked the children if they had any messages for you in England. 'Tell them,' said Gordon, 'we're not afraid either.' 'Let them know about our air-raid drill in school,' said Phyllis. And Louise, in her Southern drawl, said, 'Tell them we'll always be pleased to see them whether they come laughing or crying.' But Albert, who was getting a little tired of it all, hadn't any message for you, and Gordon looked at him rather coldly and said, 'I guess Albert just came for the trip.' Goodnight, children.

John and I found Americans outgoing, friendly and very hospitable, and from our first days in New York we were invited to a stream of cocktail and dinner parties by BBC colleagues and other people we met. I suppose we were objects of interest and we also brought first-hand accounts of life in wartime Britain for those who wanted to hear them. Nevertheless, we found that nuggets of real friendship did not appear readily in these settings, partly because American and English conversation styles and social expectations were so different. It was clear to us why some Americans confessed to finding Britons at best shy and gauche and at worst snobbish and condescending, and indeed I am sure they did meet enough Britons who conformed to the stereotype. We worried about our own image and tried hard to bridge the gap we perceived. But, as John observed about conversation in America compared with that in Britain:

> ... it serves quite a different purpose. In America no one ever listens to anyone else – except, of course, when it concerns practical things like projects, schedules and dollars. If Mr A makes a statement X, and Mr B makes a statement Y, then X and Y don't blend to form a conversational pattern – they cannon off each other like a couple of billiard balls. The result is that you never actually get anywhere by conversation; it seems clear that from a sociological point of view, their means of communicating with each other is something quite different, but I haven't yet discovered what it is. This peculiarity seems to be universal, though it only achieves its complete form at a women's party.

That last remark was based on my field reports back from lunch parties, where everyone talked at the top of their voices all the time. It was quite a shock and made me realise how low-key and circumspect (Americans would say cold and devious!) British people are. Nonetheless, despite the forcefulness of Americans, we often found them strangely conformist; at times I longed for the originality of a Miss Raby, a Mrs Emmerson or a Mrs Lum.

Of course, as radio broadcasters we had a professional interest in verbal communication and its possible bearing on Anglo-American relations. John later conducted an experiment in which two groups of students at Columbia University listened to an identical script read in English and American voices and then described their impressions of the speaker. The 'English' group thought the speaker was 'a typical English character' with the following traits: 'sense of domination, aloof, snobbish, commanding, little imagination, very dry, staid, conservative, phlegmatic, colourless, ineffectual'. The 'American' group heard a speaker who was: 'vigorous, enthusiastic, good natured, conscientious, diplomatic, alert, alive, energetic, analytically keen, polished, worldly, tolerant'. The BBC was clearly right to take the medium of its messages seriously.

Despite anxieties over what were clearly going to be our social inadequacies in America, we did make some good new friends, renewed old friendships and thoroughly enjoyed visitors from England. Donald Boyd came out from Britain to do an extensive tour for the BBC all over the States in a car with recording equipment. He found Americans intrigued that Britons wanted to find out more about them through BBC reports, but he also discovered much interest in Britain, which was encouraging for the 'westbound' side of John's work. Geoffrey (D.G.) Bridson, our colleague from Manchester, spent six months in America doing radio features, so we saw him in between his travels. David Porter, also from the Manchester days, visited from an RAF camp in the far north of Saskatchewan, where he was training bomber pilots. And we continued our close friendship with Ernst and Marianne Kris, whom we had known in London.

We also got to know a new family, Paul and Topse Schubert, who lived at Wilton, Connecticut and whose house I described in one of the children's newsletters. Paul worked in the Navy Department, but we knew him through his many broadcasts for the BBC, which he did in addition to a lot of other radio and magazine work. Topse had been a professional photographer in

Hollywood. They were refreshingly unconventional for America and had spent a number of years before the war roaming round Europe, living in villages while Paul did enough writing to keep them alive. They were immensely kind to us and aware of our occasional sense of loss and disorientation in America, and we used to go out by train to stay in their house in the country. It was low and white, on a little hillock with woods on three sides and a clearing in front. It had red shingles on the roof and a blue front door and shutters. In winter we drove through dead brown lanes to sit by pine logs burning in the open hearth of the living room. In summer there was a complete transformation; the grasses were high and the leaves thick and the woods round the house a cool green cave. The house's centre had shifted out to the porch where we sat on rocking-chairs amid boxes of petunias and geraniums. The Schuberts' house was an oasis of old-fashioned American domesticity and calm away from New York, and we loved it.

We had not anticipated when we left Britain after two and a half years of war quite how isolating that experience would be in America and how cut off from Europe we would feel. We were almost hurt by a general lack of inquisitiveness to find out more about the war, both the background and even events as they unfolded. John remarked that to many Americans 'the war in Europe appears as a civil war between tiresome old muddlers who are always bobbing up asking for help'. To be sure, this was now America's war too; American troops were fighting from Britain and going all over the world. Events in Europe were reported in the American press, but we longed to read British accounts and opinions, and share Britain's trials with its population at home. We were very conscious of our safety and found the air-raid precautions and trial blackouts in New York hard to take seriously.

We were especially conscious of the quality and quantity of our food. The American enthusiasm for entertaining frequently and in grand style sat uneasily with us, thinking of what we had left behind. I wrote, 'we feel rather old and weary when gay young things at cocktail parties chatter on about the horrors of only getting two lumps of sugar in their coffee the other day'. When one of John's sisters, an accomplished cook, asked me to describe in detail American eating habits, I just could not give a full account, though I knew she would not begrudge us our good fortune in eating well. I did admit that after our initial excitement over fruit and butter we had begun to accept these things as normal like everyone else. Like many other people in America, we felt that the least we could do was to send some additional food to Britain and so we arranged monthly food parcels for both our families.

We lived for a number of months in Alistair Cooke's particularly stylish and well-appointed apartment on Fifth Avenue. However, we were struck everywhere by the miraculous everyday standards of American comfort and efficiency compared with those in Britain. Indeed Americans in Britain would probably have hesitated to associate these notions with British homes at all. New York kitchens looked magnificent to us, with neat and efficient storage, large refrigerators ('ice boxes') and electric appliances like toasters, which we had never seen before. Bedrooms had huge walk-in closets instead of cramped, clumsy and untidy British wardrobes. Closets were very important; it soon became apparent that status in New York was partly measured by their size and number. Not everything impressed us: I found 'really very dull' a popular American soft drink, which was 'a sort of fizzy lemonade, but brown and rather sweet', and described with some distaste my first encounter with 'a little muslin bag of tea, which you wave hopefully about in hot water'. I have since adapted to both Coca-Cola and tea-bags!

Another aspect of 'mod cons' which intrigued us was the question of New York's climate and what you did, if anything, to modify the temperature. The BBC's office was rather eccentrically not fitted with air conditioning in the hope that the summer's heat would not be too fierce at that height. We noticed that New Yorkers suffered endlessly from colds, sinus trouble and sore throats, which they sensibly pointed out was due to the huge contrasts between outside and indoor temperatures, with very hot heating in winter and very cold air conditioning in summer. John was puzzled; 'however, it's not for me to halt the march of progress and suggest a compromise'.

Dazzled though we were by American domestic luxury, we rarely found much evidence of individuality in decorating and furnishings. Some apartments were almost like stage sets, not places for living, and their styles were changed just as rapidly from, say, French empire to Queen Anne, or whatever that season's fashion dictated. When the time came for us to furnish our first apartment, we rebelled against mock period sofas and love seats, cherubs painted on the walls and gilt mirrors, and caused great consternation by our choice of American country-style furniture in maple. To us these were very attractive simple pieces in a lovely honey-coloured wood, with enduring appeal and inviting any number of different fabrics and individual decorative ideas. We soon found, though, that for New Yorkers maple was only permissible for children's rooms or a couple's first home for a year or so. I remarked at the time that we were going our own way with our 'antiquated European ideas' and indeed we were no doubt considered suitably British and eccentric. One of the attractions for us of the Schuberts' house in the country was that far from reflecting prevailing fashions in interior design, it was simply a confident and comfortable expression of its inhabitants' own tastes.

Our delight and surprise in the New York landscape never diminished during our time there. We found that the geometrical layout of the streets helped us get to know the city fairly quickly and begin to feel at home there. We could not imagine how New Yorkers ever coped with London's chaotic layout. It was not easy, though, to adjust to the dramatic neighbourhood changes, as smart turned to run-down and vice versa, and it was easy to stray as we wandered around between districts. We discovered the elevated railway, with its unexpectedly intimate view of the city as you rode past bedroom windows and the roofs of houses. We took the ferry to Staten Island, with the wonderful view of Lower Manhattan and the Wall Street buildings as the boat drew out. John and I ran about exclaiming, but no one else even seemed to notice it; 'I suppose you can't rhapsodise if you see it every day,' I remarked. We found the buff-pink marble Grand Central Station magnificent, the scale almost too grand for people, with its forty or so 'tracks' and different types of 'car'. John cast his engineer's eye over New York's bridges, all of which we could see from our office windows. His favourite was the Whitestone Bridge, a slender suspension bridge connecting Long Island with the Bronx; it was 'stripped of everything except the bare engineering essentials – just the thin supporting cables, the delicate curve of the roadway, and the graceful towers of white-painted steel', and from a distance appeared as 'two delicately pencilled curves'. For me New York was particularly exciting as a 'melting pot', absorbing people of all colours and nationalities, where you heard many different languages on the streets. In one of my early letters I wrote:

We've both lost our hearts to New York and if we leave it today have seen enough of it to make it always a very nostalgic memory. It is the most extraordinarily beautiful place, and the strange thing to me is that it's so fairylike; that this stone is used so cunningly that it's not oppressive but soaring ... Just now the lake is brilliantly blue and glittering in the sun, and the houses are dazzlingly white. Then at night, when the lights begin to come out, it's even more enchanting.

8 1942–45 – Conversations in America

One of the reasons that I so enjoyed all my BBC career was that my personal and professional interests often merged seamlessly into one other. This was particularly so during our time in New York. I was interested in every aspect of my surroundings and in turn just about anything fitted into the BBC's agenda of informing Britain about America. I am sure this is why both John and I responded so intensely to our experiences there and had such vivid memories when we returned to England. During this period I could never imagine running short of programme ideas.

Despite the BBC's deliberate policy of keeping the war in the background for the *Children's Hour* newsletters, it inevitably remained a strong theme for much of the adult programming. Every Saturday night the BBC used to send out a short-wave broadcast from the American Eagle Club in London. Through the New York office the relatives of the men who were going to speak were notified and told how they could best pick up the broadcast on their sets. Many families wrote to us to tell us how 'their' broadcast was received; I did a talk about this for Britain, called *American Boys Calling Home*, to help build up a picture of the two nations helping each other. I spoke of:

> ... letters of thanks and appreciation, and telling of neighbourly kindness and warm feelings for England. Perhaps this one from South Carolina tells the whole story; 'To know that he was safe and well and so cheerful made our hearts very glad. You are doing a very humane act and one that all parents of sons in the fighting forces appreciate more than words can express. The letter came in time for us to notify our friends. It was quite an exciting evening for our little town. We are so proud to have a son in the RAF.'

The 'New York at War' parade was the most spectacular event John and I attended during our whole time in America, and I did an *Eyewitness* radio report about it. It started at ten o'clock in the morning and went on for eleven hours. All the armed services and the special wartime services were there, with ranks of New York cops, wave after wave of navy blue. There were floats, including one of a fighter plane, Scottish and Irish pipers, and bands playing tunes like *God Bless America* and *Keep the Home Fires Burning*. We had seats near the reviewing stand where President Roosevelt was taking the salute. I remember the contingent of British sailors marching towards us. The Englishman next to me leapt up and shouted at the top of his voice, 'By God! Here's the navy!', just as though the American navy had not been filing past for what seemed like hours!

In my report I concentrated on the non-combatant divisions: war workers (off duty, as the official programme made clear) and the Protective Forces, such as air-raid wardens, nurses, women's voluntary services and the Home Front, where women again played a big part.

I remember that one of the biggest cheers that day went to a dancer, the black entertainer Bill 'Bojangles' Robinson, no longer very young and known as the unofficial mayor of Harlem. In a space cleared in front of a jazz band he appeared, with a wonderful springy walk and in a white suit and straw hat over one eye, twirling his cane. I can see him now as occasionally, to the crowd's delight, he broke into a soft-shoe shuffle, and I can still hear the music, *Sunny Side of the Street*.

One of my programmes which caused quite a stir, at least in the BBC office and among the very superior elevator boys in our staid office block, was *New York Speaks to London*. This was because eighteen people came to take part in it, including a Chinese girl, two black men, the toughest Bronx taxi driver I had ever seen (in his best clothes, making him look even tougher) and, most exotic of all, a pure-blooded Creek Indian princess, Princess Laughing Eyes, and her two children, Spotted Fawn and Little Deer, all in full battle regalia and carrying tom-toms. The participants got on marvellously together as they waited to broadcast live to the forces. They then revealed in turn to the listeners the way in which London was special for them: they had been born or had spent time there; they had a particular image of it or maybe hoped to visit one day; they had a son in the RAF or an evacuated London child in their home. A ten-year-old was the chairman of the

Defense Stamp Committee in her school, and a merchant seaman was helping to keep the sea lanes open between America and Britain. Princess Laughing Eyes, a long-time New York resident, was a Women's Army Auxiliary Corp member and an air-raid warden in Brooklyn, with a brother, Straight Arrow, in the navy. She said her mother wanted to drive a truck because, as she said, 'Indian women have always had to do the hard work and they can do it again ...' My own black maid, Mabel, very composed and relaxed, who was also taking part in the programme, pretty well relieved me of my duties as hostess to the group. I suspected that my programme style had helped to usher in a new age in BBC broadcasting from New York.

Everyone knows nowadays that Thanksgiving, at the end of November, is the American festival which is probably closest to American hearts and celebrates the first harvest gathered in by the Pilgrim Fathers. Many families make major efforts to get together at this time. In the Britain of 1942 this festival was less well known, so that year I produced for the Home Service *A Wartime Thanksgiving Day*. We recorded the programme at the Episcopal church of Saint Matthew in the small New England town of Wilton, Connecticut. Our friends, the Schuberts, had helped set up the connection. It included, interspersed with hymns and prayers, residents explaining how they usually celebrated Thanksgiving and how it was different this year with people away in the forces and doing other war work. The rector and choir had even put on vestments for the occasion 'as a mark of respect for Britain' and the rector, speaking of the community's ties with England, said that 'many of us are deeply moved to be linked to you all so closely for a few minutes by the new and powerful bond of radio'. I had had to work hard in Wilton to overcome people's suspicions about the BBC and this type of broadcast, especially since nothing similar was ever attempted by American radio stations. I achieved, I think, an interesting and sincere programme and it was broadcast by some of the local stations. In England the mayor of Wilton, Wiltshire, and other families in that town had parties of American troops in to dinner and to listen to the programme, so it was one of the ways in which the BBC was trying to help establish some sort of human contact between the nations.

I broadcast an occasional series called *The World Goes By*, where I pursued my vision of conveying to listeners in Britain something of the texture of ordinary life in New York, as a counterpoint to the political and military commentaries which were the stuff of radio bulletins and newspapers. Some of the topics I covered were springtime in New York, the subway and parents' week in the schools. Also keeping low on the ground was *Meet the Ackermans*, a programme about a real family, 'one of America's thirty million families' with their 'very typical' story that 'you could hear with slight variations all over the United States'. I also wrote and produced a fictional serial, *Dear Kay*. This was the story, told in letters written to a friend in England, of an English woman and her husband, sent out to America on a war job, who lived in New York from December 1941 to June 1945. The story, of course, was largely based on the experiences of John and myself, and it allowed me to talk to British people, particularly women at home, in a chatty way about domestic and personal topics, people and travel.

In the same vein, but rather more tricky to produce, was *Conversations in America*, an occasional series of free-ranging talks with ordinary people, though I should add that throughout my broadcasting career I rarely found anybody 'ordinary'! Mabel Dobson, our black maid, was the first subject and I could not have been more fortunate in my choice. She arrived for the recording in a delightful cotton frock and a little concoction on her head which puzzled me by its familiarity until I realised it was a doyley off a cake plate, skewered through with a hatpin. I had got her to write out her life history, which, as I noted, she did 'in a prose style that wouldn't have been more dignified coming from Doctor Johnson'. From that and from our many talks together I had written a conversational script, which we then half read and half spoke before the microphone. She was a wonderful natural broadcaster with a strong voice and rich laugh. Also, totally without intent she represented positively black people to England by coming across as the honest, respectable, hard-working Harlem lady she was. At the end of the programme she made a most moving appeal for the fullest use of black people in the war effort. Even the engineer was red-eyed and told her that it was the finest thing he had ever heard. Mabel caused only one problem. She understood that she should call me 'Miss Shapley', as the other participants would do. However, in her enthusiasm she said, 'I love cooking, you know, and I'm always trying out new dishes for you and Mr ... (shocked silence) ... new dishes for *you*.' It would not have been so bad if she had finished with 'Mr Salt', but it could have been Mr Anybody! I feared for my reputation.

In October 1942 Alistair Cooke was due to return to his apartment, which we had happily occupied for seven months. So, we spent some time during the sweltering summer looking at possible places to rent. We settled on an apartment occupying the whole fifth floor of a brownstone house on East Ninety-third Street. It was small but just right for us and one room looked out on to a tree, worth a few extra dollars in New York real estate. However, it had no elevator, a big minus for most New Yorkers, so the rent was reasonable and we anticipated getting very fit. Our biggest wrench was leaving Mabel. She had not only been a marvellous maid in all the expected ways, but also friendly and supportive during our early months in New York, and a wonderful interpreter of the city to us and informal broadcasting scout. We truly owed her a great deal, and I think in turn she had found us interesting and certainly amusing.

We had barely got established in our new apartment when I became pregnant. So, having decided to try to move to a larger apartment in plenty of time for the birth, we began to look around again. The place we settled on was on the east bank of the Hudson River at One Hundred and Eighty-third Street, just north of the George Washington Bridge. This was definitely not considered a 'good address' by many New Yorkers, but as foreigners we did not feel constrained by such considerations and were thrilled with it. Castle Village was a recent development of five cross-shaped apartment blocks, which had won a design award from the American Institute of Architects. Every apartment had a river view and every room was a 'front room'. It stood high up on a promontory overlooking the Hudson and the cliffs on the other side called the Palisades, which were covered with woods. Even the first-floor apartments had stunning views, but we managed to secure a penthouse, which had the added advantage of a small terrace. John's journey to the office took longer than before – twenty-five minutes on the subway – but this was far outweighed by the pleasure we took in the apartment and its location. We made the move in the spring of 1943.

Back in the autumn of 1942 – before I became pregnant – we had had our first chance to take a holiday in America. For a while we planned to go to Asheville, North Carolina for various reasons, but particularly because it was the home of Thomas Wolfe, the writer whom we both admired greatly and who had died in 1938 aged thirty-eight. However, we had no idea how long we would be in America, so, in the end we decided just to get out of New York and 'do' the country, to get some physical idea of its size and variety – all in two weeks. And we had no regrets.

Accounts of our travels took up many pages of letters to our families, and gave me enough material for no less than seven *Children's Hour* newsletters. The whole journey was a fascinating experience and is still vivid to me now. Of course we had both always been keen amateur observers of people and places, and I was also going for much professional mileage. However, at that time few people's reactions had been blunted by extensive foreign travel, and this was decades before the magnificent travel films that are so familiar to us now.

Much of our itinerary was later plotted by my newsletters: Chicago; Kansas City; El Paso (*City of Conquistadors*); New Mexico (*Indian Country and the Carlsbad Caverns*); Alpine (*A Texas Cowpunching Town*); the Big Bend and Badlands country of Texas (*Cactus Country*); the Rio Grande (*La Cucaracha*); San Antonio (*City of Spanish Missions*) and New Orleans. We ended up with a much better idea of America than we had had before, though John did not 'quite know whether to be more impressed by the diversity or the uniformity'.

Here I think I should just give a flavour of my radio talks to the children. As always, I felt that I should start low on the ground and tell them things that seem to intrigue them, which are often the nuts and bolts of life rather than the highlights and marvels so impressive to adults. So, in *Seeing the States by Railroad* I began:

Although I very much want to tell you *where* I travelled, I think the story really begins with *how* I travelled. Because travelling by train in America bears only the remotest family resemblance to travelling from Clapham Common to Waterloo or even to travelling from London to Inverness.

I covered about 5,000 miles; that's about the distance from London to Constantinople and back; and I've still an awful lot of America to see. I knew, of course, that it was a big country but I suppose, like most people, I had to cover that distance, to sit from dawn to dark some days watching the almost unchanging horizonless landscape slip by ... I had to do that to know in the marrow of my bones and for all time, just how vast it really is. All I can say to you at the moment is what many Americans have said to me when they heard I'd been on this trip: 'Well, it's quite a country, isn't it?,' and well, it is ... it's certainly quite a country!

I then described in detail how our 'tourist sleeper' looked and how it was more like a boat than a train, because people lived on it for days and nights on end. There were no separate compartments, like on British trains (at that time), but long coaches with a centre aisle and seats arranged in little groups of four, with a dressing-room at either end and an ice-water tap for each coach:

As soon as the train starts and begins to gather speed a really surprising thing happens. All these people, who had not set eyes on each other ten minutes before, hastily finish hanging up their coats and putting their best hats away in brown paper bags and start to talk. They move up and down that centre aisle, chatting, asking questions; what state do you come from, where are you going, may I look at your knitting and so on. To a British person this is almost unbelievable. I wonder how many of your parents remember train journeys at home – journeys of five or six hours when the only conversation has been when the gentleman opposite coughed and said, 'Would it inconvenience you if I lowered the window a little?' No, I know it's not like that in wartime, but that's hardly an exaggeration for what it was before. But in America, within half an hour everybody is talking away as though they've been friends for life, bridge parties have been started and the whole train buzzes with friendliness and talk.

I mentioned the porters and dining-car attendants, members of a great black trade union in America, the Brotherhood of Sleeping Car Porters:

And I think one of the pleasantest things about train travel here, to a stranger at least, is the kindness and good humour and very, very good manners of these coloured people who are so important for your comfort during your journey. I remember the first day of my trip we had a very noisy little boy in our coach, and I remember coming back from lunch and finding the coloured porter making up a bed at one end of the coach. When the little boy wanted to know who it was for, I heard the porter say, 'It's for you, 'cause I reckon we're all just about tired of hearing from you.' And although the small boy made a fuss, his mother left him to the porter who just finished making up the bed, popped the small boy inside and buttoned up the curtains. And that was the end of him for an hour or two.

Our time in New York was exciting professionally, but was not without its difficulties in our personal lives. Early in 1942 I had started to suffer quite a severe nervous breakdown. Perhaps my two failed pregnancies, the strain of London during the blitz and the difficulties of adjusting to New York had all begun to take their toll. I got along for some time but soon the physical symptoms became quite overwhelming and we had to take expert advice. My symptoms consisted of a tightening of the throat muscles which made swallowing, eating or even breathing, sometimes, a torment. My throat was examined and there was, of course, no physical cause, but I do not think it is exaggerating to say that for a time I lived in an almost constant dread of dying by strangulation. At its worst I sometimes could not leave home for three or four days at a time and at its best travelling of any kind or shopping was impossible. The only relief I could get in a bad attack was to lie curled up on my side under a blanket (head and all) and in this position make the most determined efforts to relax. I did manage eventually to get my BBC work going in New York, but it was not easy.

Luckily John and I had good friends among the group of refugee psychoanalysts in New York, particularly the Krises, and I was referred to a Viennese woman analyst. Almost from the beginning things began to get better, though there were many relapses. I went to her for fifteen months altogether, mostly five days a week, but very soon began to lead a much more normal life. I know now that I was very lucky; unlike a great many others in a similar situation. I had everything for which to get well, mainly a very happy marriage and the prospect of the children we both wanted. Over the fifty years since that time fashions have come and gone in psychiatric treatment, and the psychoanalytic approach has come under some attack. My only valid contribution to this debate is my belief that my problems then were skilfully addressed by this particular analyst and I am not certain in what other way I would have overcome them.

Six or seven months after the analysis had started I had felt very strongly that I wanted to start another baby, and as soon as I knew I was pregnant early in 1943 I began to feel much more confidence in the success of the analysis. The treatment stopped in June 1943, two months before the baby was born, and I found myself with my feet on comparatively firm ground and in my hands a technique of dealing with other anxiety situations should they arise.

My pregnancy was normal and John and I were delighted with our son, Daniel Alexander, born on 15 August 1943. We took him home from hospital after just seven days (the usual stay was two weeks), and then we could really begin to enjoy him.

The early escape from hospital was to recover from a harrowing experience, even given the fairly barbaric state generally of western childbirth practice at that time. My obstetrician was a kindly Viennese Jewish refugee, but I was not prepared for what giving birth would actually be like; women rarely were in those days and only with hindsight could we see how unnecessarily painful and degrading our experiences were. John and I also discovered later that our doctor had not yet got his citizenship papers and was therefore only allowed to send his patients to one particular hospital, a rapidly declining private one, which closed down soon afterwards. This turned out to be dirty and inefficiently run, with largely undisciplined and irresponsible staff, whom my doctor was clearly rather nervous of and anxious to placate. I could not reproach him in his difficult position.

During an agonising labour I was left alone in a room which led on to the building's fire escape. On that hot summer Saturday night a staff farewell party was going on outside, and while nurses drank, chatted and laughed I could not make myself heard. Someone eventually told me that I was going to be 'a great deal worse' before I was better, and one young nurse said several times, 'You've had your fun, dear, and now you're going to pay for it.' I was then suddenly surrounded by undisguised panic and anaesthetised. I found out later that the foetal heartbeat had disappeared and the baby had the cord round his neck. When I came round, feeling very sick and hearing a baby yelling somewhere in the room, the anaesthetist, a great hulking youth, was slapping my face and saying, 'Come on, you limey, snap out of this.' No one even held the baby up for me to see (I did not see him for ten hours) and I do not recall a kind word from anyone except my own doctor and, of course, John when he was called in. I felt desperately lonely.

This ordeal had actually lasted only six hours, not so long for a first baby, but things did not get better. My wish to breastfeed was met with incredulity and I got no help or encouragement at all from the staff. It was simply not done and seemed to be regarded as positively distasteful. At one point one of the other new mothers was allowed to stand over me, struggling with the baby, and pour scorn on my efforts. I felt like a zoo exhibit.

Many women of my age have similar stories. They were not good experiences and one certainly never forgets them. I am just glad that, at least for many mothers in the world since then, things have got better. My own later births, when I knew about natural childbirth and was better prepared mentally, were much happier. Compared with the tense little person I held in my arms in that New York hospital, when I was so distressed, my third child, who was born quietly and quickly, was placid and looked like a rose petal.

It was in New York also that John's health began to cause worry. He had had various mysterious pains for some years and in America had been treated with injections for low blood pressure. Then very shortly after Dan's birth he was taken ill with appendicitis on a work trip to San Francisco and spent three weeks in hospital where he received excellent care, at vast expense to the BBC. Although those acute pains went and he got by adequately after returning to work, he never regained good health and doctors were puzzled by his symptoms. Of course, diagnosis and treatment were much more primitive affairs in those days.

The following summer he suddenly became seriously ill. On returning from the office one day, he felt faint and vomited a lot of blood. He was rushed to hospital and over the following five days had four transfusions till the bleeding stopped, which got him over the critical period. The problem was diagnosed as a gastric ulcer, which, it was considered, accounted for many of the previous troubles. Treatment was by medicine to heal the stomach and a strict diet of milk, eggs and strained vegetables. The diet was dreary but manageable in America. We wondered how on earth it could be achieved in Britain if we were recalled home. After that John enjoyed some periods of feeling quite well, but mostly struggled. His condition robbed him of a lot of the energy he longed to put into his work and he found this very frustrating.

Just before Dan's birth John and I had the memorable experience of meeting the actor and singer Paul Robeson, who was then at the height of his career and immensely popular in Britain. I found him a very impressive 'famous person'. I am often asked about the famous people I met during my BBC career. Well, I did meet quite a few celebrities, and often they were very pleasant. But as an interviewer it is sometimes hard to connect with such people;

the fame itself overshadows whatever it was that brought them fame in the first place, and you flutter around them painfully aware of your own insignificance. It is an unequal and rather undignified relationship. Also, as is no doubt clear by now, I was usually much more thrilled when I succeeded in bringing unfamous people to the microphone and helped them to tell their story. I found this professionally rewarding and I also made such lovely and enduring friendships along the way.

However, in America both Mrs Roosevelt and Paul Robeson were special. Paul Robeson was born in Princeton in 1898, the son of a pastor in the Presbyterian Church, and grew up with astonishing all-round talent. He won a scholarship to Rutgers University and excelled in academic work, debating and athletics. He then gained a law degree at Columbia University, and was later discovered acting in amateur dramatics while playing football professionally. He went on to a successful acting and singing career on stage and in film. He became an outspoken critic of fascism and performed at hundreds of benefit concerts for oppressed peoples, his wide repertoire including Chinese, Hebrew, Russian and Spanish folk songs. When Robeson was giving a concert in New York John approached him and he agreed to be interviewed by me. He was thoughtful and interesting with a powerful but benign physical presence, and we were delighted with the broadcast. After the recording John came into the studio and suggested that, if he had time, we could take him out to lunch. I can see now that tall handsome black man smiling gently as he said, 'Thank you, Mr Salt, but there isn't a hotel or restaurant in this city that would let me in.' We were stunned and all the BBC office staff were embarrassed and upset. While we in our work were concentrating on Anglo-American relations, there were clearly matters still to be worked out between peoples within America.

Our time in America has a very particular musical association for me. During the 1960s' 'folk boom' in Britain I surprised my guitar-playing children and their friends by my memories of the artists that we first heard in New York and with great excitement broadcast to Britain: Woodie Guthrie, Sonny Terry, Josh White, Burl Ives and a young man, a boy still really, from Kentucky, Pete Seeger. I remember Pete Seeger getting lost in his hotel and ringing us up at the BBC to come and get him out; he found New York terrifying. I think my strongest memory is of Leadbelly, who was so black he was blue. While serving long prison terms for violent crimes he had collected songs of all kinds, slave songs, ballads, prison work songs. He was eventually discovered by John and Alan Lomax, father and son, who were making a collection of folk songs for the Library of Congress in Washington, and he gradually became well known through their concerts. I remember a party we went to given by Burl Ives one hot summer night in an apartment in Greenwich Village. There was all this wonderful music, still fairly raw and unknown. The cops on the beat thundered up the stairs to tell us to stop the noise, and stayed to sing along, loosening their collars and accepting a glass of cold beer.

John became North American director in May 1944 on Lindsay Wellington's return to London. During our time in America the BBC's operations had expanded rapidly. In early 1942 there had been twenty-three staff confined to the New York office. Two years later there were seventy staff, in New York and branch offices in Washington, Chicago, San Francisco and Toronto, of whom sixty-three were American or Canadian. Of the 900 American radio stations about 270 were now regularly carrying BBC programmes, either live or re-broadcast, and output amounted to about 140 station hours a week. Although news, talks and features predominated, there were special 'tie-ups' with stations in the middle west covering large areas, including farming programmes.

Within the New York office John had started weekly lunchtime 'playback' sessions, which made innovative use of the radio medium. Mostly they would involve the entire BBC staff; sometimes though, the BBC would invite in to the office all kinds of people, not just from broadcasting or newspapers, and even people just off the street. They would have a cold lunch and listen to a particular programme: maybe one which we had sent to London, or one from London that we were re-broadcasting in America, or a local Home Service one, or an overseas programme from the American Office of War Information. We found that any programme stimulated thoughts and discussion on relations between Britain and America, which were interesting and valuable. These sessions became quite an event in New York radio circles.

A source of great pride for John, as the BBC's chief representative in America, was the handling by the BBC War Reporting Unit of the D-Day landings on 6 June 1944. The first news the New York office had was at about midnight from a German news agency. Soon after the French programme of the BBC European Service told the French to get thirty-five kilometres from the coast, and then at 3.15 a.m. London gave notice of a statement for universal broadcast at 3.32 a.m. A stream of eye-witness accounts then started to come in, from BBC and American reporters on ships, in the air and, in due course, on the landing beaches. The New York office immediately established its own 'invasion desk' to receive and relay information around the clock in America. The *New York Times* considered that 'the service of the BBC, as D-Day listeners know, was not less than superb. The BBC was not only first with a good deal of the news, but exemplary in its presentation.'

A few months later more than 700 members and guests of the Radio Executives' Club of New York gathered in the Grand Ballroom of the Hotel Roosevelt to pay tribute to the BBC and, as the *Radio Daily* put it, 'its giant effort necessary to the successful prosecution of the war, and the great part it is playing in cementing the relationship of two great Allies, England and the United States'. The director-general, William Haley, spoke from London. John also spoke, as well as Elmer Davis, head of the Office of War Information. The principal speaker was the Earl of Halifax, who was Britain's ambassador in America. Though this sort of occasion was not John's most comfortable milieu, he was very gratified by the recognition accorded to the BBC generally and to the New York office, and graciously received an illuminated scroll with a citation of the BBC's contribution to international radio.

During these years John continued to reflect on America and Americans but came no nearer to wrapping up his thoughts neatly in his mind. On the one hand, he was not swayed by a broadcasting system run by advertisers, whose full force was unleashed at Christmas: 'you can imagine – no, as a matter of fact it is beyond imagination – what it is like turning the knob of your radio set; the Christ child and the Virgin Mary get inextricably mixed up with toothpaste and laxatives from morning till night'. However, there were many refreshing aspects of life in America compared with that in Britain, particularly the classlessness and easy social manners. For example, as a broadcaster he had been astonished by how accessible people were, especially the 'great and the good'; a telephone contact or meeting that would take weeks to set up in Britain would happen instantly in America. John wrote:

> This country has much that is wonderful, and exhilarating, and fascinating, and horrible and extraordinary, and depressing, and

stimulating – in fact it has almost everything a healthy person needs.

I feel I could write two long books – one describing how in spite of all the apparent differences English and Americans are really very much alike, and the other saying that in spite of all the apparent similarities, English and Americans represent two entirely different cultures. And both these theses would be entirely true as far as they went.

It is probably clear from my memories of John and his own writings that he was a very intelligent and thoughtful person. He was fascinated by human psychology and its implications for social action, particularly conflict. Although as prone to instant impressions and prejudices as the next person, he was always conscious that casual, private and apparently harmless views can intensify with alarming speed into implacable and widely held prejudices with dangerous implications. And the world had already had ample opportunity this century to witness what can ensue. His generation had barely known a time when war had not been the major preoccupation and this inevitably coloured an individual's view of their own place in the world:

My own part in it has been so paradoxical. I spent my earlier years actively preparing for it, left the army because it seemed so senseless to spend one's whole life preparing for destruction, and then when the show comes off, I have been very largely out of it.

At that time of such horror for so many people all round the world, many also worried about the long-term effects of the war. This was brought home to us by an apparently short-term domestic incident. When Dan was a small baby, we had had a week away on our own, because I was exhausted; before recovering fully from the birth I had been looking after John following his first major health crisis. Our domestic arrangements, involving a temporary nurse and a newly appointed part-time maid, had not worked out well. While Dan had been adequately cared for physically, he became quite disturbed many months later and the problems seemed to stem from his separation from us that week. A year later John reflected:

It's a sobering thought, that if a small incident like that can affect a child of twelve months so badly, what must be the result of millions of families broken up in Europe. The effect of that is not merely a problem of rehabilitation, but psychological troubles through generations. And there just won't be anything like enough really sane people to cope with it.

From the time of Dan's birth till we returned to England in June 1945 I managed to do some BBC work in New York, including six of the *Children's Hour* newsletters. But the difficulties of unpredictable domestic help and John's health problems, coupled with the demands of a small baby, forced me to admit that my BBC career was likely to be fitful for some time. In many ways it was a relief to accept the situation and I certainly anticipated a full return at some time in the future. Programme ideas still bubbled up, and I was particularly interested in doing something on the differences I was observing between American and British styles of parenting. That, I knew, would wait till I could view it all with the benefit of hindsight.

By the spring of 1945 we knew that we would be returning to England in the summer. John had the chance of a job in London, but chose in the end to take up the position he had had before the war, north regional programme director in Manchester. The decision was positive, because we both felt that the quality of life we wanted lay in the north. But we were also anxious about John's continuing poor health and the wisdom of his taking on a demanding new position in the unfamiliar environment of London. The timing of our journey home caused some anxiety, because our second child was due in December. Luckily, on a preliminary visit back John had managed to organise the purchase of an attractive Victorian family house in West Didsbury, which was just what we wanted. We bought it from Leonard and Bebie Behrens, whom I had known in my earlier days in Manchester. Leonard and Bebie, with their daughters Mary and Ruth, kept a sort of open house at their lovely large house in Didsbury, Netherby. They were deeply involved in the arts in Manchester, particularly music, and were most welcoming to young people.

We had little notice of our departure from New York and flew home from Baltimore Harbor in a clipper along with a lot of very distinguished service personnel. Dan was the only child on board and sat in the saloon completely absorbed in a little model aeroplane from an American 'five and ten cent store.' I can see now the rack above our heads with a row of hats covered in gold braid and Dan's teddy bear tucked among them.

2 Bill and I outside 10 Tresco Road, Peckham, 1914.

1 With my parents and brothers Bill and Frank in 1910.

3 With my cousin Win in our back garden (I am on the left).

4 On a family holiday at Deal, Kent. My father and mother are in the centre deckchairs, with me in front in the striped dress.

5 On vacation from Oxford, with my dog.

6 The very early days of the
Mobile Recording Unit, with my
Ford car, 1937.

7 With Mrs Emmerson
in her kitchen at
Craghead, County
Durham for Miners'
Wives, 1939.
*Photograph courtesy of
the BBC.*

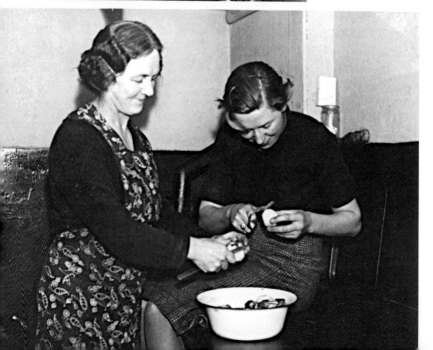

8 John Salt, my first husband.
Photograph Arnold Eagle.

9 Wedding day, 14 July 1939.

10 John and I in
our Hampstead
home, featured
in a magazine
article in 1940.
*Photograph A.W.
Kerr.*

11 John and I with other staff at the weekly lunchtime 'playback' session in the BBC New York office, 1942. *Photograph Jack Manning.*

12 With Mrs Roosevelt during her broadcast to the children of Britain in 1942.

13 Dan's fourth birthday in Yorkshire, August 1947. John was already ill but we did not yet know that he had cancer.

14 During my time as daily presenter of Woman's
Hour, 1949–50.
Photograph courtesy of the BBC.

15 With Dan, Nicholas and Christina in
Hampstead, for my column in *Modern
Woman*, 1949.

16 Christopher Gorton,
my second husband.

17 Rose Hill, Didsbury in the 1950s

Right
18 An early television programme in
the 1950s at Levens Hall, near
Kendal.

19 On the set of *Something to Read* in
1960. I am in the middle, with Brian
Redhead on the left at the front.
Photograph courtesy of the BBC.

20 With Godfrey Winn in the Rose
Hill Trust Nursery in 1970.
Photograph Tom Hanley.

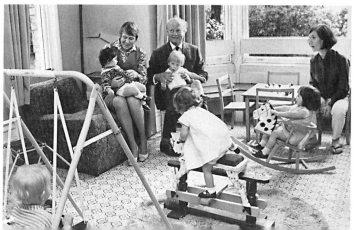

21 Photograph accompanying an
article in *The Guardian* in 1989.
Photograph courtesy of The Guardian.

22 With Barbara Castle on my
eightieth birthday.

9 1945–49 – Return to England

Three and a half years is a fair time to be away from one's own country; long enough to absorb something of the new country, and long enough to get very homesick indeed. As the months went by in New York I found that I was beginning to take an aerial view of England. So much so, that when we came home the actual sight of England from the air seemed only a finishing touch. As our clipper flew in over Cornwall towards Poole Harbour and we looked down and saw the white line of sea breaking against the cliffs, the morning mists curling away from incredibly green meadows, the feudal villages with church and manor-house and fields laid out like the diagrams in history books, it felt like putting in the last piece of a jigsaw puzzle.

We moved into our house at 11 The Beeches, a quiet cul-de-sac in West Didsbury, a Manchester suburb that we both knew very well from our early days in the BBC. The change could not have been more dramatic; from a penthouse in the city of skycrapers to a leafy suburb of a once-great British industrial city. However, as any Didsburian would tell you, Didsbury is not just *any* suburb! But more about Didsbury later.

Just after our arrival John suffered a recurrence of his ulcer trouble. The summer of 1945 was a time of great upheaval for many people amid hopes for a resumed normality, and we were not surprised that John showed some strain over our move back to England and his new job. It was very difficult organising the recommended diet for him, but he got plenty of rest and Dan seemed to benefit by having him around the house for a while.

With the uncertainties of John's health and our next child due in December, we felt we could do with some domestic help. After enquiries we were very lucky to be able to bring to live with us Alice Pye, who had been for many years with our friends the Boyd family, and was extremely gifted with children. She was to stay with my family for almost four years. No one knew then what a roller-coaster time it would be and I cannot imagine how I would have got through it all without her presence.

No sooner had Alice settled in than the new baby threatened to arrive three months early. I had to spend most of this time in bed with my feet propped up on telephone directories in a determined attempt to keep it. John went back to work and Alice looked after Dan. Nicholas John did hang on and was born at the right time, on 7 December 1945 in St Mary's Hospital in Manchester.

I did not then try to resume a full BBC workload, despite the great bonus of having Alice to help look after Dan and Nicholas. I wanted to be able to enjoy my children while they were young. Also, as everyone knows, small children can be exhausting and I was not a young mother. But most of all it was clear that John needed my support both in his job and, as time went on, because of his rapidly deteriorating health. The crises came and went and with each one our feelings of unease grew, though we could barely admit them even to each other. I did not look too far into the future.

In the spring of 1946 I wrote and broadcast, in the north of England Home Service *Fireside Talk* series, a talk called *A Child Comes Home*. In it I put together many of the thoughts I had had over the past four years about children in America and Britain, and particularly my observations since becoming a parent in New York.

> I think the first thing that I noticed on coming home was that we take our children more easily than the Americans do, are less anxious about them, even perhaps enjoy them more, fit them into the pattern of family life with less fuss.

I then apologised for, 'as the Americans say … going out on a limb', but went out on it all the same. Generally speaking, during and just after the war British parents and children were in no position to be as ambitious and materialistic as their American counterparts. Looking back on my remarks now, though, it is clear that some of the acute differences I detected then began to be eroded before long, particularly among older children. In the 1950s the British teenager emerged, with much of the music, films, fashion and language borrowed from America, which began to create a more uniform western youth culture. And listening to parents today it is clear that some of the pressures I witnessed in America, absent in Britain at that time, are now well established here. Nevertheless, I believe that our very distinct national character continues to override a certain amount of this conformity, and that the essence of my observations is still valid. If you disagree, a review of my thoughts of almost fifty years ago is at least of historical interest! Here is the rest of my talk.

Living in New York, I felt it all began with the babies. American babies must be the most highly organised, the most agonised-over babies in the world. Every day, it seemed to me, they were put through a routine of weighing, measuring, temperature-taking, charting, quite unlike anything we are used to here; I found, too, that they had gathered around themselves a jargon which, odd as it sounded to me, was common currency among the mothers I sat with every afternoon in the park. My baby, I discovered, didn't coo, it 'vocalised'. It didn't even dribble, but 'salivated'; it had a 'gross motor drive' and a 'strong manipulatory urge', and a great many other things as well. Now, clearly, if your baby is such a highly technical affair, as were some of those American babies I saw every day, then your stake in its welfare becomes very great indeed; it has just got to be successful. From being the baby which has weighed most, eaten the most spinach, walked earliest, it must go on, if a little girl, to be the prettiest or most poised of all the little girls; if a boy, to be the most aggressive or most masterful of all the little boys. And the American child, boy or girl, feels very early the tremendous value which attaches to this kind of success, and guesses too that to some extent, perhaps, his mother's affection depends upon it. Eat your spinach for mother, go out and make friends, be the most popular little girl, don't be the little boy that all the others push around. All this an American child understands at a very early age, much earlier, I'm sure, than we would want our children to become conscious of such things; he feels that he has to be a success, he has to exploit to the full his personality. Even my own small child was beginning to know that if he wanted to be left to make his own sandpies in his own way in the park, he would probably have to hit two or three other little boys over the head with his spade in the course of the morning! Sometimes we would remember the well-meant compliment of the matron of the New York nursing-home where he was born. 'He's a grand boy,' she said, 'he's going to beat up all the other kids on the block!' This was a new idea to us then, but later we came to understand it; American society, as everybody knows, is highly competitive, and not the least for quite young children.

And then, too, as a result of this you will find that American boys and girls grow up very quickly; there is no prolonged childhood for them, no days of lying fallow; they are living in an adult world and being judged by adult standards much earlier than our own children. If you ever get hold of American illustrated papers, you will remember the many articles on the 'teenagers', their activities and their ideas, their parties and their clothes. You'll know from these articles and from films what these American boys and girls look like, the boys self-possessed and mature-looking, the girls confident and well-groomed. This early flowering has, of course, a very attractive side to it. Most American children and young people have delightfully easy and friendly manners; they're competent and they're poised – you constantly feel there is no social situation too difficult for them to handle. I still think that this aspect of American upbringing is quite excellent, and that we probably have a lot to learn from it. To give a child social ease and fluency of speech at an early age is surely a good thing and, heavens, how fluent those American children are! They love to talk and often they talk surprisingly well. I remember the first New York school I visited. The teacher sat at the back of the class, and I found myself taken under the wing of a small girl of seven, who met me at the door, introduced herself to me, introduced me to the class – all with the greatest composure – put me into a comfortable chair and then, with the help of the others, gave me a most lucid and lively account of the class 'project' for the term – a project on Esquimaux as I remember. It was a school in a water-front district of New York, a very mixed bag of children, but all more than equal to the job of entertaining an unexpected visitor.

How do these American schoolchildren with their 'projects' on every conceivable subject, their typewriters and their filing-cabinets and their quite amazing assurance and fluency compare with our own children – compare with them in school, that is? That obviously can't be settled in a few sentences, but I did sometimes feel that in some American schools the desire to make learning attractive was so strong that some necessary mental discipline was probably being thrown out along with the drudgery. The business of preparing pageants, writing and performing radio scripts, learning to use reference libraries, typewriters and filing-cabinets is arresting and good fun, but it's not education. I found, also, that what might be called the idealisation of the child in American society sometimes had strange results in the schools. The free and friendly relationship between the teacher and the pupils is very pleasant indeed, but I couldn't help feeling that sometimes an almost exaggerated deference was shown to children's quite ordinary remarks. A New York school teacher tells a story about this: she was talking to her class about astronomy and happened to give them the distance from the earth to the moon. One of the boys challenged this, and when she pointed out that these figures were, after all, backed by the country's leading astronomer, he said, alright, but he was sticking to his point. The class turned out to be unanimously on the side of the boy; the astronomer, they said, was welcome to his opinion, and anyone in that class could have theirs!

There is no doubt that in England children bloom more slowly. They are still growing, still expanding, still finding new interests at an age when American boys and girls tend to be completed, finished, polished. It's probably true to say that most English parents don't believe in forcing the pace for their children. We are prepared, I think, in a way that many American parents are not, to let our children go through the uncertainties and awkwardnesses of adolescence in their own way and at their own speed; we are willing to let them pursue their own interests and make their own friendships. We aim perhaps at a later maturity, but a real maturity, founded on many interests and much speculation. I suppose, like American parents, we want above all to make our children happy and well-adjusted members of the society they will have to live in; and in England an individual way of looking at things and intellectual curiosity are still thought valuable.

Not only are American children encouraged to grow up early, but they also grow up into a fairly fixed pattern. Teenage girls everywhere will dress the same, swoon at the same crooner, hold identical parties. It takes a very brave boy or girl to strike out a path for themselves. The pressure of conformity in America is something we can hardly understand in this country. Success lies along well-defined lines, even for children and young people, and if you can't achieve that kind of success, or you don't want it, then you have to take the consequences. As an

American girl, by no means one of the failures, said to me: 'You must understand that it's not enough to be a nice person. You've *got* to be versatile.' Only she pronounced it 'versatle' in the much more forceful American way. It can be a very brutal experience being young in America, if you are plain or shy or backward or haven't as much money as the people you are with. It seemed to me that parents are as much involved in this as their children. A mother's greatest fear is that her daughter will be a wallflower, a father's that his son won't be a good mixer. And as a result of this emphasis on material standards of success, you sometimes have the feeling in America that children don't have the same chance to develop resources within themselves. An English child I knew, coming home after three years in the States, said, 'American children are nice, but they don't know how to play.' When pushed a little, it was discovered that she meant they didn't know how to play imaginatively. But it is harder for them; so early they are swept up into the American passion to 'go places, and see things'. On a wet afternoon, an English mother might possibly persuade her family to amuse themselves in the attic with a box of dressing-up clothes, but an American mother would almost certainly have to find twenty-five cents for the neighbourhood movie.

In a country as enormous and as varied as America, everything is true, and, of course, everything is true about America's children. But I do believe that the things I have spoken about go to make up the kind of childhood and youth that American parents find desirable and worth aiming at for their children. Most of the children I knew were being brought up in New York, but although life is lived a little more slowly in other parts, the general picture is pretty much the same. There's a lot that's most attractive in the way Americans bring up their children, their very real love and devotion for them, the splendid schools they build for them, and the magnificent climate and the grandeur and beauty of the land itself; all combine to give childhood a spaciousness and an enchantment that cannot be denied. But I'm still glad that our American-born child will grow up here in the north of England, and that his younger brother will be a north-countryman from the start; that they'll grow up knowing the hills and lakes of Cumberland, the coastline between Flamborough and Whitby, the towns of Lancashire and the West Riding, the Wall Country and the Yorkshire Dales. And, most of all, of course, I'm glad they'll grow up among north-country people, where I know they will find friends and happiness even if they turn out to be only nice people and not the least bit versatile!

Not very long after Nicholas's birth John and I began to think about having a third child. We had originally talked about having three children, but after my two miscarriages and our various illnesses had been relieved and very grateful to have achieved two healthy boys. We knew that some people might regard as reckless another pregnancy so soon and with an unwell father. But it was just this uncertainty about the future that led us to agree that we should go ahead without delay. We went away for a weekend in the Lake District and there I conceived. Apart from some anxious slipping around on the ice during the fiendish winter of 1946–47, a winter still talked about by those old enough to remember, all went well with the pregnancy. Christina Mary was born on 11 May 1947, a spring baby.

That summer we spent our holiday with John's mother and sisters at their house at Thorp Arch in Yorkshire. Dan had a very happy fourth birthday on a lovely sunny day; Christina slept peacefully while we all sat in the garden and Dan and Nicholas played. John and I felt very fortunate in having completed our family as we wanted. We had overcome quite a few troubles and life looked good.

Then the blow fell. Back in Manchester John suddenly became very ill and was eventually diagnosed as having inoperable stomach cancer. The cancer lay right on the side of his stomach and for this reason, it seemed, had not been detected before in all the X-rays and other tests. The whole pattern of our family's life fell apart and John died on Boxing Day of that year. He was forty-two. Those weeks are still as clear in my memory as if they had happened only a few months ago; that is the nature of bereavement, as many people reading this will know. Below I shall give a fuller account of this time. My words are those I wrote for our children some years after John's death in the belief that I had to leave a proper record for them to understand and hold throughout their lives. Only I could tell the story and it belonged to them.

When John died Dan was not yet four and a half, old enough to be very disturbed by the death, but not old enough fully to comprehend. Our friend John Rickman, kindest and most human of psychoanalysts, impressed on me the need to get the fact of death across: 'It is far more damaging, in the long run, to believe that you have been mysteriously deserted by a loving father, than to have to face up to a horrible blow of fate.' But blows of fate and the irreversibility of death are not easy to explain to a small boy, shaken already by all the mysterious comings and goings in a stricken house, and who could only repeat, 'But *why* hasn't he taken his pyjamas with him?'

If you are an agnostic family there are no immediately comforting pictures to paint; no God in the sky waiting to welcome; no hope of a happy family reunion one day. But we struggled on and, as John Rickman had told me, I never had to relate the fact of death to the other two children; Dan took that job on for me. At different times, much later, all three children came to me separately and wanted to know in great detail how their father had died. I remember the quality of their listening, and that they never needed to ask again; one only had to tell the truth.

People tell you how lucky you are to have children when you are widowed; of course you are, and all the more so as the years go by. But they are also a constant reminder of the loss of the one other person in the world who loved them as you do and with whom you could have shared the little things. There is only you to marvel over the first steps, the first words, the first day at school, the first joke they tell. I found a lot of these events of my children's early years equally joyful and painful.

Children themselves can seem to be largely unaffected by the absence of a parent, and indeed it is right that their day-to-day lives should be as positive and happy as possible. Most mothers, and fathers also in this situation, serve their children very well. But I feel that such a loss can be damaging in the long term unless its significance is acknowledged and young people are actively helped to come to terms with it. When my children became fatherless, single-parent families were almost all created through death and there were far fewer overall than today. At times my children felt conspicuous among their friends by having lost their own father, but he was an acknowledged figure who occupied a positive role in their history. I worry more about families today where the missing parent may be unmentioned or shadowy, or where children can only view them through a curtain of adult bitterness. Particularly in adolescence these issues can matter acutely.

I was grateful to friends who in an easy way brought John alive for my children, and helped me also to remember the good times. Dan, Nicholas, Christina and I often used to talk about the friend of Daddy's who came to see us and told us about a walk that he and Daddy took on the banks of the Hudson River in America one brilliant, cold New Year's Day, with the blue river and ice floes; and how they came back to lunch and Mummy had ready a great bowl of spaghetti and tomato sauce. No one could have made up that kind of story. Children have an ear for circumstantial details; and to be able to see your father for a moment, taking a walk like anybody else's father on a fine morning and coming back and enjoying mountains of spaghetti, is wonderful to a small child, comforting, cosy, a reassurance that you have a father too, and that he was nice and people liked him. My children often talked about their father and always in a very chatty and unmorbid way. Sometimes, as they were growing up a little, we were drawn together in a moment of sadness; we suddenly knew our loss when we saw other children flying kites with their fathers on Sunday afternoons. But it was a real sadness, that we recognised, and it did none of us any harm.

As the children grew up they could not help but become aware of how others remembered John, because old family friends and colleagues would tell them spontaneously about their love and respect for him. We also had a copy of the very personal and moving address given at the memorial service by John Coatman, who was then the BBC's north regional director. Wilfred Pickles wrote about John's death in his first autobiography, *Between You and Me*; on the wreath he sent he had written, 'For John, I shall never forget you' (Pickles, 1949, p. 197). Herbert Smith, a BBC broadcaster and producer in Manchester, later commented about John's openness to new ideas, 'If the item was a success it was your success. If it failed it was his failure. He was a big man physically and mentally' (Hartley, 1987, p. 58).

Over the Whitsun holiday following John's death I left Nicholas and Christina with Alice and took Dan for a weekend to the holiday house in Criccieth of our solicitor and dear family friend, Neil Pearson. Another guest there was Christopher Gorton, a Manchester businessman who, it turned out, had known John before the war. They used to have lunch together at the Reform Club. He had heard of John again when he was dying and told me of the grief he felt and his deep sympathy for me and the

children. He was a lovely man and over the next few years a
friendship developed slowly between us.

Below is what I wrote for my children about ten years after John's
death:

> You all had to face the fact of death at a very early age. The
> circumstances of that death, the fact that you were made
> fatherless so early, still seems to me a thing of enormous sadness
> – a sadness which I think that you, in your teens, are almost
> beginning to feel for the first time. But I cannot believe that
> this has done you any harm. Let's say that it has made you all
> at ease among the great events of life – love, birth, friendship,
> death. You have had to learn early to live with polarities and
> hold them in your minds; to find the good in something which
> seems evil; to know that nothing is wholly black or white,
> good or bad. You know now that things *are*; that they must be
> accepted, not fought against; that contradictions must not be
> eliminated, but held together in the mind. Life, even at its most
> painful, is still life and still wonderful. I hope you have learnt
> all this. I think you have.
>
> It has been difficult to know sometimes how to handle the
> memory of your dead father. One of the few Latin tags I have
> managed to keep in my rather dustbin mind is 'de mortuis nihil
> nisi bonum', but if one only speaks good of the dead, they soon
> become mummified. They become a bore to the living,
> especially, as in your case, to the living who have never known
> them. The only thing is that it is so very hard to find anything
> but good to say about your father, and there are literally
> hundreds of people to bear me out in this.
>
> John Salt appeared to have everything: great good looks, the
> body of an athlete, a first-class brain and birth into a privileged
> class. Of all these gifts, it was only the brain that interested him.
> Never has a handsome man been more indifferent to his looks,
> or a member of the upper class had more hatred of unearned
> income and a feeling for the danger of it and the privileges it
> brings. He resolved to live by the hard rule of Confucius, and
> set up for himself fanatically high standards of honour, work,
> behaviour. Perhaps this was what caused his death. After he died
> much was said about him; 'He never said anything silly,' was
> one comment. One of his greatest friends, the Freudian analyst
> Ernst Kris, wrote from New York when he heard of your father's

death, 'He was the very image of a man.' This was true, but beautifully said. These are the words that comfort.

There had been a long shadow cast on the summer when you, Dan, were four, Nicholas was one and a half and Christina a tiny baby of a few weeks. We came back from our summer holiday with your Salt grandmother at Thorp Arch and, unknown to me, John went to the doctor for a check-up. The doctor arrived at the house, frightened. He had begun to suspect a growth in the stomach. X-rays must be taken at once. 'But it could be a benign growth,' I said. 'There are no benign growths in the stomach,' was his answer. I went back to making the beds in your nursery. I had the cold hand clutching at my heart, so beloved of fiction writers. But like so many things in bad fiction, it was true. Then one event followed another: the X-rays, the exploratory operation, the verdict that this was cancer and inoperable. I remember that I had just brought you all in from a November walk, chill and grey as only Manchester can be, and the doctor came while I was taking off your leggings and coats. The surgeons had seen, there was no hope, I must go now to the nursing home, so that I would be there when John came round from the anaesthetic.

This was the hardest moment of my life. It is terrible to go and sit by the bed of someone you love when a sentence of death has just been passed on them. They become strange to you; you are frightened of them; they lie there so quietly and so harmlessly, but you can hardly approach them from fear. When John came round in that luxurious, warm, dimly-lit hospital room, he was strangely happy. We were so near, and yet separated by a chasm. I was alive; he was dying. The first real secret I had to keep from him was one of such enormity; it had to be well kept. Later I was to question this. It seemed to me that someone so intelligent and so brave must surely want to know that they are going to die. It seemed disloyal to fool him, to tell lies, to live a lie every day and all day, to turn the whole of life into a lie.

The whole of that time is clear and complete to me still. I think I realised dimly that this must be lived through, fully, and that I would have to pass right through and come out, somehow, on the other side. I had had in some ways a sheltered life. Now here was something I could not shrug off, ignore, wait to pass. I had to live it through. The worst time ever, the never-to-be-repeated time of my whole life was the hour before I went to John in hospital, while he was still unconscious. I beat my head against the wall of the fact of his death. I beat my head literally against a wall, and I had about an hour to accept this fact, to make it part of me, to put on the mask I was going to wear for weeks. Nothing was ever so difficult again. I learnt something that has stood me in good stead ever since; that the bad, unwelcome thing must be taken in to the centre of your being and accepted; that it must be looked at and looked at again. There is no other way to live.

Your father came home from the hospital and lived for six weeks. A curious calm settled over the house. He was not well enough to see a great deal of you, but each morning and evening you came in and climbed into bed with him and you all read books together. Dan told him about school, the nursery class, and Nicholas pointed with his fat finger at the book; 'cow' he would say over and over again, 'cow'. Every night at about 11 o'clock I would bring Christina in for her last feed. She was a very pretty baby, dark-haired and very like her father. I remember that she slept in an old Camella sleeping-bag, washed to a soft streaky green. Her father would hold her and we would allow ourselves all the luxury of telling each other how marvellous she was and how lucky we were to have achieved a little girl. This part of the story is quiet, a false peace; huge luxurious coal fire in the bedroom, lamps, and flowers that people sent in. There was no great pain. Sometimes we looked such a normal, happy family, that the whole thing seemed unbelievable.

One of the nearly unbearable days was Nicholas's second birthday, and for this John insisted on getting out of bed and climbing the little flight of stairs to the nursery. I shall never forget how long that journey took. In the nursery were two excited little boys, and the round table in front of the fire with the birthday cake and the candles, and the baby on Alice's lap. There were just the three of you; and Alice, who was a tower of strength; and my mother, kind and calm though her heart was breaking; and me, but I cannot see myself; and your father in a dressing-gown, unbelievably frail; and the three of us knowing that he would not be here for another of your birthdays. Still he did not guess, he did not ask.

As I helped him to shave each morning, it seemed impossible that he should not see, but he did not. Someone said to me at this time that however brave a man is, it is hard to face the fact of your own extinction. But by the end of the third week of December, I realised that John was uneasy. Still nothing was said, but I would catch a look on his face, a look of sadness, of questioning. I knew that we had reached the last phase. This part of the story is about friendship and it should be told. As soon as I saw this look settle on your father's face, I went downstairs to the telephone and put a call through to a man who is also dead now, but I would like you to remember him. His name was John Rickman and he was an analyst and President of the British Institute of Psychoanalysis; a big, quiet man, a Quaker and possessed of great sensitivity and insight. I can never be grateful enough that he was there to be turned to. He came up immediately on the next train from London and I took him into John's bedroom late that night. As I went out of the room, I heard your father say, 'I want the truth. I am going to die, aren't I?' There was silence for a moment and then John Rickman said, 'Yes.'

It is difficult to tell the story of the next week, because we lived it at such a high plane. But some things are worth telling if they are going to help anyone else. Later that same evening John Rickman found me collecting up blankets. 'What are those for?' he said. 'I'm going to make up a bed for myself on the sofa in our bedroom,' I said. 'No, you are not,' he answered. 'You will sleep with your husband as you've always done.' This appalled me. I had adjusted to living with the lie; you will get better; this time next year we'll do this and that. But now I must live with a man who knew he was going to die. 'If you had heard an hour ago that you were on the point of death,' John Rickman said, 'wouldn't you want someone near you through this long, long night?' Of course, he was right, and I held your father in my arms every night until the last. That night I would wake up and see John Rickman's head outlined in the firelight, as he sat in the easy chair, and this was immensely comforting. Nobody ever had a better friend than we had in him.

It had never occurred to me that I would ever tell the story of John Salt's death in this way, for anyone to read. But I think, after all these years, it can be told. It was a noble, courageous death, and was felt to be this by all of us who were near him. John took the fact of death and made it part of him, and I could see that he was determined not to let it spoil the time he had left of life. The door opened again and a lot of people came to see him, and the talk was very good. He was not one for swearing, in fact I hardly ever remember him doing so, but I remember him saying, 'At least now I needn't drink any more of that damned Lucozade. Can you find some wine?' And with one of our friends we drank some Riesling out of our best Heal glasses with little stars on them and we talked about France. We even got out the map of France and argued about the best routes to take and whether Mère Filliou's *volaille* was better than Mère Guy's. We really lived that last week of his life. The weather softened and we had those marvellously mild December days; a blazing coal fire, flowers, books, talk, a lot of laughter.

When John learnt that he was dying, he asked me to bring you children in to our bedroom just once and then no more. He could not bear to see you again and begged me not to talk about you.

Christmas Day was a fine, clear, mild sunny day. John woke early and we talked for a long time before anyone else was about. Only then did he bring himself to mention you. He spoke all your names, slowly and lovingly, and then he said, 'I trust you with them completely. Only promise that you won't let their lives be drab.'

Soon after breakfast he asked me to get the doctor. He told us where to sit; his mother on one side, me on the other, his sister at the foot of the bed. 'I'm very tired now,' he said to the doctor. 'This has gone on long enough. I'd like you to put an end to it.' He said goodbye to us all and I took his hands in mine. He said, 'Olive, don't leave go of my hands until I am asleep.' He never recovered consciousness, though he lived until early on the morning of Boxing Day. It was a strange Christmas Day, going from the bed, where the breaths grew longer and slower and deeper, to the nursery where children had paper hats on and too many sweets, and relatives and friends came and sat and waited with us.

I thought it impossible that I should ever enjoy Christmas again. But of course I have done so. The good family feeling of our Christmases has only been deepened by the memory, now softened, blunted, of that one agonising Christmas Day.

What can I tell you about grief? That it passes, eventually, and that it is a bore to other people. Even the best and most sensitive of friends, and certainly all your acquaintances, long for you to come out of your sadness. There is something unpleasant, it seems to me, about the sight of a suffering human being; something that other human beings do not want to contemplate. As long as you are sorry for yourself, it is quite certain that no one else will be sorry for you. You have to snap out of it, put it behind you, not parade it, not ever bring it out. Ten years later you may talk about it, but not then when you desperately need to. You have to get used to people by-passing your remarks and even physically avoiding you; I remember seeing one or two people crossing the road so they would not have to meet me. You have to take studied cheerfulness and not resent it.

No one could have had better and more concerned friends than we had, but even so there were shocks. I remember that a few days after your father's death, on New Year's Eve, I felt the silent house to be intolerable and the thought of other, happier New Year nights not to be borne. So, I set out to see people. Everywhere I called people were dressing for parties. In my locked-in state I had forgotten that this was what people did on that night of the year. Everywhere slightly irritated husbands were zipping their wives into party dresses and wives were giving last-minute instructions to baby-sitters. Of course they were, and I was grateful to them for seeming embarrassed. Why should they not go out to a party? It was only my world that seemed to have come to an end. This was the first shock I had, that the public mourning was over, that life was going on and that I could not make any more special claims on people's time and attention. It was very salutary. There is so much in Jewish ideas that seems to me right, practical and wise. The year of mourning is a good idea. It is not until one has seen all the seasons come and go, and lived through them alone, that the wounds begin to heal.

10 1949–53 – *Woman's Hour*

In the autumn of 1946 a new radio programme was launched on the Light Programme in London under the control of Norman Collins, the programme head. It was to be a magazine programme for intelligent women and would deal with 'keeping house, health, children, beauty care and home furnishing' and finish with a short serial reading (Donovan, 1992, p. 289). The 2–3 p.m. timeslot was considered just right, after morning chores and lunch and while doing the washing-up before older children came home from school. This was *Woman's Hour*, which was to become one of the BBC's major success stories and is still going strong.

The complete history of *Woman's Hour*, as devotees will agree, is worthy of its own separate history. Some surprising facts stand out. First, contrary to probable expectations when it started, it has often been at the forefront of changing public perceptions of broadcasting taste. This has meant that at times it has been extremely controversial, in both language and content, some would say subversive. Secondly, its listeners are by no means all women. And thirdly, in 1991 its time change to the mornings provoked a major outcry which has not quite died down.

My own active association with the programme, as presenter and producer, lasted on and off for over twenty years. Since then I have several times had a taste of my own medicine by being interviewed myself. Over all these years people's interest in and attachment to *Woman's Hour* has been brought home to me time and time again by its large correspondence and the questions and discussion about it among the community groups I address. When you are in the studio a great deal of broadcasting seems to be launched into the void and it is sometimes hard to visualise the exact audience. But with *Woman's Hour* I always felt that a large section of the audience was fairly constant, and you knew that they listened yesterday and would probably listen again tomorrow, and might even put pen to paper and write you a letter.

At first the programme had a male presenter. He was soon followed by Joan Griffiths, who in early 1949 was due to leave to go to *Housewives' Choice*. I was offered the position of daily presenter (sometimes called 'commère') and started the job in late February, thus becoming the programme's third presenter in its history. The BBC accommodated the juggling act that this move entailed and paid for my weekly commuting from Manchester for some weeks. When I bought a house in London, Alice and the children joined me.

I presented *Woman's Hour* for the next eighteen months and it was an entirely delightful experience. Though I had to be well prepared for the continuity and other live broadcasting, I found this a less frantic job than that of producer, which I had done so much of in the past. It was the programme's team of producers, by and large, who initiated contacts, made arrangements, scripted, recorded and edited material and put together items for transmission.

Woman's Hour was at that time unique among radio shows. Though it certainly tried to lighten the household chores and give listeners a new interest, albeit an appropriately feminine one, it also tried to open a window on the world outside, in a way which listeners themselves may not have had the time or opportunity to do. So, the programme items were always wide ranging, in both subject matter and format: live discussions and interviews, news digests, straight talks, book reviews and, of course, the daily serial. Inevitably the balance has shifted over the years in tune to the radical changes in women's lives, from predominantly housebound topics to more current affairs and employment-related ones. Today's younger listeners would certainly find much to chuckle over in the early programmes.

As the presenter I was obviously one of the few people in the country who heard the whole programme every day without fail, and people often used to say to me, 'What a lot you must know.' What a lot I *ought* to have known! But although I listened each day across the table from the speakers, and certainly found an enormous amount to interest me, I confess that many ideas went in one ear and out the other. When you are partly responsible for the smooth running of a conveyor belt of items, you can never stand back sufficiently to enjoy anything fully. After all, your job is to make sure the listeners do that.

Our speakers were always interesting, whether or not they were used to public speaking or entertainment of some sort. Some 'pros' could be surprisingly nervous and some novices astonishingly assured. People crumpled scripts so that they sounded like bacon sizzling or a storm at sea, muddled their pages and leant comfortably back in their chairs, to the obvious despair of the programme engineer behind the glass screen. Some were very friendly and some put up a barrier, some were just what you expected them to be, some were very baffling; but they were always fun to meet.

Almost all women liked to look nice when they broadcast; a quick dab of lipstick and comb through the hair seemed to boost people's confidence. Quite often people wore hats in the early days, which was fine by us, and some people kicked off their shoes in the studio. I once discreetly encouraged a woman to take off her new corset between rehearsal and transmission, when I had discovered the cause of her pained expression and delivery. The BBC sent out contracts to contributors beforehand and occasionally people arrived clutching two guineas thinking they paid us for taking part in the programme. We liked to be hospitable, but were careful with the lunchtime sherry when it became clear that by two o'clock some women, who hardly ever drank alcohol, were a bit too relaxed even for *Woman's Hour*.

For our Monday guest slot, later renamed 'Guest of the Week', we invited women who had made a name for themselves in some field or other, and of course forty years ago publicly successful women shone even more brightly in the firmament than they do now because there were even fewer of them. I interviewed Margaret Mead, the American anthropologist, and Mrs Roosevelt appeared in a repeat of my previous interview with her for *Children's Hour*. My former headmistress, Dr Brock, now Dame Dorothy Brock, obliged me yet again by appearing in one of my programmes, and I found myself again wondering rather anxiously whether she thought my splendid education had been put to good use or not. Vera Lynn was one of the nicest people I had ever met; no side, no affectations, just a thoroughly nice person, very ready to chat about her house and her little girl. Dame Edith Evans made an appropriately theatrical impact on the *Woman's Hour* studio. She was by no means a beautiful woman, but was very gracious and no one could take their eyes off her. Guests used to choose a piece of music to follow their talk and she chose a rather saccchariny orchestral piece used in *Daphne Laureola*. As her talk ended the music was faded up, Dame Edith rose from her chair and, with the utmost grace and a mixture of sentimental melancholy and burlesque, began to gyrate slowly round the room. My last glimpse of her was wafting majestically through the studio door to that silly music.

Woman's Hour has never been afraid to tackle difficult topics and I am proud of my own role over the years in helping to push back the frontiers of broadcasting acceptability. Many producers working on the programme have known the rather weary nervousness with which their more challenging suggestions have sometimes been received within the BBC. I used to get stern memos along the lines of, 'If Miss Shapley insists on doing an item on the change of life, we insist on seeing the script first.' We were always very careful to warn listeners about such items, giving their exact duration and advising them to turn down their radio sets if they feared offence. This advice was considered necessary also to protect small children who might be listening with mother after *Listen with Mother*. I used to wonder what the average three-year-old would make of a rather technical talk on venereal disease, but such warnings were taken very seriously. Today's audiences are clearly made of sterner stuff and a good thing it is too.

It was not just medical and sexual topics which were considered daring in the early 1950s. Psychology and human relationships were still largely uncharted territory even in ordinary private conversation, and into this area *Woman's Hour* again leapt fearlessly. I chaired a discussion in 1952 called *Women without Men* between five women, including myself: three 'spinsters', as I called them, a divorcee and myself, a widow. Issues which are commonly explored now on radio and television and in magazines, like women's self-image and role in society, loneliness, deprivation of sex or children, and old age, were ranged over with a good deal of frankness for that time. And, as ever, we found that despite male apprehensions these were definitely not taboo topics for our listeners, who welcomed them.

Not that *Woman's Hour* was all dangerous. I think it was balanced, just as life should be ideally, and sometimes it embraced the fanciful. Looking back I am rather surprised at some of the topics I covered with apparent enthusiasm. I must have got carried away in 1953 by the excitement about the coronation robes of peers and peeresses, which were exhibited before the coronation by Norman Hartnell, the royal dressmaker. Mr Hartnell's newly designed alternative robe for a baroness or viscountess was the first major change in peeresses' robes since the reign of Queen Anne. I found that it was 'charming to look at, could be converted into a useful garment afterwards (or is that the wrong thing to say) and only costs something like £30 or £40'. Of the regalia, I liked best the coronet of a marchioness, consisting of four silver balls and four golden strawberry leaves – 'very pretty indeed'. I also noted with approval Mr Hartnell's little caps with floating veils which could be worn by non-titled guests in the abbey: 'beautiful creations in tulle and net, caught up with sequins and jewelled clips'.

> But the robes themselves are somehow unreal. They're pure story book of course, and also, to me, irresistibly reminiscent of the wet afternoons when you were small and 'dressed up' and acted plays ... It was hard to realise that men and women were going to wear them solemnly on a proper occasion. But there they were, crimson and gold, velvet and fur, strawberry leaves and ermine tails, all the traditional colours and patterns of pageantry in this island, and it was impossible not to fall a little bit under their spell.

I am sure that the listeners also were spellbound by the coronation robes, given that the whole country was at that time caught up in coronation fever. But beneath such decorous concerns lurked a different Britain, as I discovered in the late 1960s when a woman wrote in about her husband's apparently incurable warts and we asked listeners to send in their suggestions. This item was the unexpected hit of the northern *Woman's Hour* year, and the office felt rather as if it had been transported back to the Middle Ages! Letters came from respectable sounding suburban addresses begging the poor man to put his hands out of the window and make washing motions in the light of the full moon; to let seventeen black snails crawl all over his warts and leave the slime on for three days; to spit on them when he woke up (with 'fasting spit', as several listeners called it); to rub them with the juice of the greater celandine; to take arsenic tablets (which seemed a little drastic); to apply the woolly insides of broad bean pods; to hide a piece of bacon in the ground and not tell anyone where he had hidden it; to become pregnant (not very practical advice to a man); and, of course, to consult his local wart-charmer (we were doubtful if the Yellow Pages could help here).

Listeners were also stirred into action by my newspaper advertisement when preparing the item, *What Size Did You Say, Madam?* This looked at the problems of women and girls with big feet, a topic in which I had an unashamedly personal interest. The letters flowed in, including agonised ones from fathers saying that their family life was dominated by their daughters' large feet. We had clearly touched another nerve. Other *Woman's Hour* crowd-pleasers I recall were nits and dental phobia. By contrast my meticulously prepared look at Manchester's religious communities for the *Talkabout* programme was no doubt politely received but produced no ripples.

One of the more unusual talks I wrote and broadcast during my time as *Woman's Hour* presenter was *To Travel Hopefully*, which was later repeated. In it I reflected on how you experience travel as it is happening and how your perceptions change in hindsight. I looked back on my train journey across America in 1942:

> As the train raced on, this journey, like so many long-anticipated things, looked like being a failure: I might have been travelling between Rugeley and Stafford for all the excitement I felt ... I was fascinated by what went on *inside* the train ... But the scene *outside* refused to come to life.

I even went on to confess that in Kansas City I bought on impulse a copy of Arnold Bennett's *The Old Wives' Tale* from the station bookstall and saw much of New Mexico and the Rockies through a blur of remembered images of English landscape.

> Does this seem very far-fetched to you and is it the way other people travel? Do you take your pleasures like this? For some of us, I'm sure, nothing is very true or very real while it is happening, but only becomes so, sometimes very long afterwards, in the light of the imagination, when a great deal of the original experience has been pared away and forgotten. It's dangerous, I think, to live like this, but if that's the way life presents itself to you, you won't be able to change it.
>
> ... I don't know about you, but in my memories I know no way of managing the grand and spectacular things. I've never seen the Grand Canyon or Niagara Falls or the Pyramids, but I don't think they'd ever quite come off their postcards for me. So many people have stared at them, exclaimed over them, searched for the right adjective to describe them that I couldn't make them mine in any way.

Even on my way back from a trip to the magnificent Carlsbad Caverns of New Mexico, in the blue and silver luxury coach as it glided through beautiful desolate country:

> In the forefront of this are two women with pince-nez and their endless conversation. Their grandmothers might so easily have come along that same road, in a stage-coach, their ears strained for an Indian yell, their eyes looking for the thin spirals from greasewood fires. It is those two women chattering away in the motor coach about the autumn sales that keep that remote and lovely bit of country alive for me.

El Paso was curious and exotic to an English eye with the streets as full of leathery cowboys in ten-gallon hats and dark little Mexicans as you could possibly want. My sharpest image still, though, is of the Plaza with its magnet of two alligators lying like fallen tree trunks in the middle of the pond.

> I discovered that everybody in El Paso says: 'Meet you at the alligators at six o'clock.' And when you get there you just stand round the railings and listen to the children spelling out DO NOT MOLEST THE ALLIGATORS on a placard in the middle of the pond. It seems curious that anyone should want to molest them, but I remember watching two soldiers spending a painstaking ten minutes trying to spit in an alligator's eye! Anyhow it's all there for me still, crystal-clear and comforting for me to think about.
>
> A few pretty pictures to light up a dark evening? Perhaps, but I'd rather have them than a bag of gold. And I would rather my children had them, in their turn, than almost anything else I can think of. If I could give my children one thing, I think I'd choose to give them a visual memory, give them the power to use their eyes and to make for themselves a store of memories that they could draw upon when the lean years come, when they are tied perhaps to one scene, one routine. This is what *I* mean by travelling hopefully.

I cannot leave my reminiscences of *Woman's Hour* without particular mention of the daily serial. Its popularity was already well established in 1949 and, though modern novels were perhaps most popular of all, I remember that people used to write in to say, for instance, that *Cranford*, which for years had been to them a rather dreary, unread school prize, gathering dust, had, when Molly Rankin read it as a serial, become a living book, full of real people. Through the punishing demands of a daily programme an extraordinarily high standard has been maintained, in choice of books, quality of abridging and aptness of reader. I have always loved the serial, both as a listener and an abridger. It is a great privilege to have the chance to work on a novel dear to you and try to bring it to a new audience. I did a lot of abridging over the years, not all for the *Woman's Hour* serial, and also dramatised adaptations. Among my personal favourites were Charlotte Brontë's *Villette*, Anna Sewell's *Black Beauty* and J.B. Priestley's *Lost Empires*. Kenneth More had agreed to do the *Lost Empires* reading some time in advance and did it beautifully; I remember being very much helped by hearing his voice in my head as I worked.

On a more personal note, I was also grateful to *Woman's Hour* for at times accommodating without fuss my occasional domestic crises, when children had to be brought in to work. Even around 1950, when they were quite young, I was surprised at my children's respectful response to the tense, purposeful atmosphere of the studio. Supplied with a batch of old BBC scripts, typed on one side only, and a pencil apiece they could be relied upon to draw, in dead silence, trains, cats, 'funny people', houses and, for some reason, dustbins – all my children had a passion for drawing dustbins – while the, to them, interminable voice of *Woman's Hour* flowed on above their heads. As they grew older they started to turn the script papers over, leading at times to a rather alarming broadening of their education; I do remember those change of life scripts!

Both during and after my regular *Woman's Hour* stint I continued with other radio work. I always loved any programmes about books, and for some time was an occasional panel member on a programme called *New Books and Old Books*. Three guests used to talk about two books each which they had enjoyed and wanted to recommend; one book was a contemporary work and the other had to be at least twenty years old. This was pure pleasure, at least for the participants; we could indulge our existing passions and explore new works. Some pairs of books that I chose were: Christopher La Farge's *The Sudden Guest* and Thomas Wolfe's *Look Homeward, Angel*; François Mauriac's *The Unknown Sea* and Jean-Jacques Rousseau's *Confessions*; Geoffrey Trease's *Tales out of School* and Louisa M. Alcott's *Little Women* (no surprises with that one); and Katharine Anthony's *The Lambs* and Charles Lamb's *Letters*.

A fellow guest on one of these programmes was John Betjeman. The young producer took us all out to lunch beforehand to a rather grand restaurant and, amid all the ordering of pâté and asparagus spears, Betjeman asked rather apologetically if he could have sausages and mash. When we got back to the studio, he disappeared and turned up with very little time to spare before we went on the air. He was asked to give the engineers some level, sat down at the microphone, smiled disarmingly and said, 'How dreadful, I've lost my script and haven't two consecutive ideas in my head.' The producer went rather green, whereupon Betjeman smiled again and produced from the baggy pockets of his coat a pile of tattered envelopes covered in hieroglyphics. The red light went on while he was still sorting them out in a puzzled sort of way, but he delivered, of course, a wonderful talk, easy and assured, only stopping to give all of us an occasional wicked grin. Apart from being so entertaining John Betjeman had for me a particularly lovely voice and charming personality.

I remember producing a quiet and undramatic programme called *Young Shoreditch*. It was based on the diaries kept by the nine-and ten-year-olds in a junior mixed school in a pretty drab district of London. The writing up of the diaries was done every day after prayers as a matter of course. They were not marked or corrected but the teacher always read them. The children's writing was far from drab and was refreshingly full of incident, variety and colour. The boys predictably concentrated on expeditions on roller-skates and bicycles, with a noticeable absence of girls from their accounts, and the girls filled their diaries with people and personal relationships. I recorded some children reading extracts from their diaries and they were linked with a commentary for the programme. Recording children is quite different from working with adults. They are not, generally speaking, very 'produceable'. You have to take them very much as they are, try to make them feel happy, simplify the mechanics as much as possible, and then tell them to go ahead. Their first performance will probably be their best. The Shoreditch children turned out to be nerveless and rather professional performers, and during every short break of a minute or two plunged themselves into the comics carefully provided by the BBC.

For over two years in London I wrote monthly articles for the now long-defunct magazine *Modern Woman*, many of them focusing on 'the people I meet'. The long list of people featured included Joyce Grenfell, George Cansdale, the superintendent of London Zoo, and his young family, and Richard Dimbleby, the well-known broadcaster, with his young family. This was an enjoyable journalism assignment which also put the jam on my family's bread financially speaking. Readers apparently liked my tales of 'behind the scenes' at *Woman's Hour* and earlier BBC and other reminiscences. I also exploited my own children shamelessly by writing about them, and the magazine went to a lot of trouble to organise photographs and line drawings to illustrate the articles. I remember that the children approved of the photographs, but did not think the drawings looked anything like them. These pieces now seem rather touchingly innocent, as indeed does much of the journalism, radio and television of that time compared with now.

The family photographs for the *Modern Woman* articles were taken at our house at 15 Redington Road, Hampstead. This was a rather shabby late Victorian house in a typical Hampstead street, by no means one of the grander houses in that area but just right for us. It had a sloping back garden with a superb view over London, and there were lots of other families around. The nearest school was a progressive one called Burgess Hill, and I enrolled Dan and Nicholas there. When I dropped them off in the morning, Christina would race in with them and had to be bodily removed with tears and protests. She eventually got to go there herself. The pupils were very uninhibited and seemed to spend a lot of time swinging from trees in the garden, stark naked and turning nut brown in the summer. We all have many happy and funny memories of Burgess Hill and I remember that first names for staff were compulsory. I used to slip up occasionally and say 'Mrs Whatever' and Dan would nudge me, whispering in an agonised way, 'Call her *Kathleen*, Mummy!'

It was in Hampstead that I first took in lodgers, which was the start of my long career as a landlady. I always found the lodgers interesting, but in retrospect our Hampstead ones set a high standard. At one time the dress designer in the attic was being visited for fittings by Diana Dors, just beginning to be known; and Andy Pandy was being conceived, and his signature tune slowly worked out on the piano, in our old dining-room on the ground floor, which was rented by Maria Bird and Freda Lingstrom, the head of Children's Television. This meant that practically everybody in the road, for one reason or another, found us interesting. My children remember being invited into Andy Pandy's flat (as we thought of it) and sitting through the first appearance of two other, quite different, characters, Bill and Ben, the Flowerpot Men. There were a good many noses pressed against the window *then*.

Nowadays most people have little memory of me as a television performer. That is because it was all so long ago! I was asked to work in television before the war in 1938, on a programme on holidays, but had to withdraw due to my father's illness. In that year reception was still confined to the London area and only 5,000 sets had been sold. Television was suspended for seven years on the outbreak of war and then, because of government restrictions on expenditure, was slow to spread beyond London. By 1950 it had reached the Midlands and there were almost 344,000 sets, but that was still less than one home in twenty (Kingsley and Tibballs, 1990, p. 4).

In that year I finally made my start in television, as 'fact finder' for a series of interviews with prominent women called *Women of Today*. I remember particularly Odette Churchill, MBE and holder of the George Cross. She was a Frenchwoman who had married an Englishman and was settled in England with three small daughters when war broke out. She became a secret service agent and worked in France, was captured by the Nazis, imprisoned and tortured for refusing to give information, and was sentenced to death and sent to Ravensbruck concentration camp. She was saved by the arrival of the American forces, married Peter Churchill, with whom she had worked in the French underground, and was now living with her family peacefully in Kensington.

Odette Churchill had endured twenty-six months in prison, of which twenty-three were in solitary confinement, including over three months in total darkness. She had survived her ordeal mentally by 'hearing' familiar music in great detail, mostly Chopin and Tchaikovsky, making journeys, sometimes only to Kew Gardens and sometimes right through France, and reciting poetry, Baudelaire, Lamartine and Victor Hugo. She also had other more prosaic resources to draw on; she redecorated all her friends' houses and refurnished them, and also planned complete wardrobes for her children. She said these imaginary domestic tasks gave her great pleasure. I hardly need to add that she was immensely impressive, but she was not intimidating and I knew that she would really connect with the viewers as a woman.

A popular early television show was *All Your Own*. This was introduced by Huw Wheldon and frequently produced by Cliff Michelmore, and it gave children a chance to display their various talents. I believe that the young guitarist John Williams first appeared on this programme (Kingsley and Tibballs, 1990, p. 20). I introduced it on a few occasions when Huw Wheldon was on holiday.

I had a more regular association with another showcase for young talent, on radio; this was the *First Attempts* series on *Children's Hour*, which I presented for about eighteen months. These sorts of programme seem to have long disappeared from radio and television, and I am not sure whether other outlets have sprung up to replace them. In those unsophisticated days the BBC almost seemed to assume the role of national talent scout, especially *Children's Hour*, which in retrospect played a significant role in many early careers, for example giving opportunities to Vanessa Redgrave, Julie Andrews, Petula Clark, Billie Whitelaw, Beryl Bainbridge, Nigel Davenport, Judith Chalmers, Sandra Chalmers, Peter Wheeler, Robert Powell, Ben Kingsley, Colin Welland, Brian Trueman, Gordon Jackson, Tom Conti and Michael Aspel (Grevatt, 1988, p. 498).

I have very happy memories of the children's television series, *Olive Shapley Tells a Story*, in which I narrated stories for very young children, sometimes in vision and sometimes over the book illustrations. The programmes were done from both the Alexandra Palace and Lime Grove studios and for the narration to camera I had to learn the script; there were no 'idiot cards' or autocues in those days. One of the strange things about performing on television is that for many people it is not as alarming as performing before live audiences. So I was completely unnerved when I went in one day and found the entire band of the Grenadier Guards in the small studio with me; rows and rows of them, with pink faces like geraniums, all looking at me as though I was mad when I started to tell my little story about a mouse. It was one of those stories where everything happens three times and on the live transmission I lost track of which lap I was on. The floor manager, a mind reader like all good floor managers and knowing that I was short sighted, crawled along the floor like a great St Bernard dog, with his scriptboard in his mouth, till he arrived at my knees and mimed the wind-up action, just out of vision. I wound up the story with relief and he crawled back the way he had come and in a moment was ready to start the band off with *Colonel Bogey*. I have to admit that I enjoyed that particular programme more in retrospect than at the time!

My children also liked this series, because, as with the Flowerpot Men, they performed a vital consumer research function, and Dan also tested my lines at home. There were several of the *Epanimondas* stories by Constance Egan, the *Orlando* books by Kathleen Hale, *Buttons* by G. Dewi Roberts, *The Bounceable Ball* by E. Nesbit, *The Theatre Cat* by Noel Streatfield, *The Baby Mouse with a Knot in Its Tail* by Anne Calonne, *The Kitten Who Lost Her Purr* by Marie Oxenford and several stories by Violet Statham about Tilly Posh, an appealing duck in a shawl, which were beautifully illustrated by Harry Rutherford. At one point I remarked rather wistfully in a note to the producer that 'it would be nice to get something that wasn't about baby cats or baby mice', but the tide of writers' and children's tastes flowed on fairly predictable lines.

The huge hits with both my own and the viewing children were Helen Bannerman's *The Story of Little Black Sambo*, originally published in 1899, and its companion, *The Story of Little Black Quibba*. These books are now hard to read without wincing, with parents called Black Mumbo, Black Jumbo and Black Flumbo, and I realise that they are woefully politically incorrect. However, much later my daughter's love of the stories from her childhood eventually overcame her scruples and she read them to her son from our original family copies which have my markings for the television readings. Adam fell for them in turn, insisting on the exact voice inflections and pauses as marked, including my cues such as 'wait for picture'. Thus my television readings of 1953 are likely to live on into the next century, long after these books have probably been banned.

My domestic arrangements underwent a number of changes during the four years we lived in London. Alice, who had been such an important part of our family during the difficult years in Manchester and over the move to London, quite soon decided to return to the north. I then managed to find a woman with a small child who was happy to share my home and help me run it partly in exchange for accommodation. She was unmarried and it was very unusual in those days for a single mother to be bringing up her child. As a mother I never saw any distinction between those of us who were respectably widowed and those who had not been married. We faced exactly the same loneliness and practical problems and I felt that unmarried mothers and their children suffered most unfairly by society's disapproval. Later on in London I employed an older married couple who lived in. This was the first of two couples I employed where the husband turned out to have a shady past and present and the wife was either innocent or accepting. Both arrangements ended abruptly with the involvement of the police and we were left shaking our heads in wonderment. In neither case did the children suffer, but my unerring knack of picking plausible con men became legendary in our family.

Thinking hard about this period I do remember feeling tired, rushed and stressed a fair bit of the time. However, my overall impression is of very happy times with the children and enjoying their growing up; rose-tinted glasses clearly have a useful role to play in reminiscences. Nevertheless, combining a career with a family means walking a tightrope and one is in constant danger of falling off it. I remember one of the worst times was when I was writing a very long radio feature called *Focus on Fashion*. In those days we did not know nearly as much about the odd workings of the fashion industry as we do today, and there was a lot to find out. While I was working on this all my children had chickenpox and the child living with us was also sick, as was the child of my regular help. I have never forgotten the horrors of leaving that rather sordid scene after an early breakfast, in my tight black dress and pearls, sitting all day on little chairs in over-heated salons, watching haughty models in beautiful dresses swirl past me, making notes, trying to make sense of it all; and then coming home at night, more or less taking my pearls off as I walked up the street, and going into a sort of Bedlam of spotty children, an untidy house and a meal to be cooked. The two halves of the picture hardly came together at all. But this is the kind of nightmare in which working wives and mothers quite often have to live, as many more women these days know.

It says a lot about Christopher Gorton that he was not deterred by such domestic chaos in pursuing our friendship. A very good relationship developed slowly between us and eventually we discussed marriage. Christopher was fifteen years older than me and worried that his heart attack a few years before made him an uncertain bet. I in turn was worried about him taking on three rather wild young children, though he was gentle and good with them. We married in 1952 at Hampstead Registry Office and it was a very happy occasion. Christopher somewhat foolishly gave the children cowboy outfits, which they insisted on wearing to the ceremony. I remember the calm and tolerant lady registrar saying, 'Posies and guns under the chairs, please,' since Christina had both hands full. A guest later commented that the party at my house was like a very pleasant children's party, and the children still remember taking advantage of their minimal supervision by drinking Pimm's No. 1.

We could not start our new family life under the same roof until we had found somewhere to live in Manchester and until I had sorted out my BBC work so that it could be handled by commuting to London. There was also the question of live-in domestic help. Before Christopher and I had finally decided to marry I had placed an advertisement in the *New Statesman*. I only got one reply, several weeks later, from a woman whom we came to call Miss Renee. Her first words to me on the telephone were, 'The thing I like most about this position is that there is no man in the house. I don't like men.' After I had broken the news about Christopher, she decided that she liked the sound of us anyway, so she accepted the job. Miss Renee then had to do what Alice had done in reverse, but as an Eastender she never really took to Manchester. However, she was immensely helpful over our move north and proved a splendid addition to the household for some time. She was Jewish and through her we all learnt a lot about Jewish ideas and customs. She transformed our Friday evening meal into the Shabat and organised it in style, with the boys wearing their school caps and Christina lighting the candles.

We moved to Manchester on 16 June 1953, two weeks after the coronation, which we watched on a little black and white television set in the crowded sitting-room of friends in Redington Road. Nicholas was much more excited by the news the day before that Edmund Hillary and Sherpa Tenzing (Tenzing Norgay) had conquered Everest. He had been following the ascent avidly in the newspaper; in fact it had finally convinced him that there was a point in learning to read. On the night before the move I took the children to hear Burl Ives in concert at the Festival Hall. The hall was packed and several times Burl asked the audience to shout out their favourite songs and he would sing what he heard. Christina, with rather odd taste for a six-year-old, was crazy about a particularly soulful number called *Grand Canyon Line*, about a bank robber on death row a few hours before his execution. She must have been the only one in the vast Festival Hall who wanted it, because she yelled herself hoarse and tearful trying to make Burl Ives hear. I took the children round the back afterwards and had a lovely reunion with Burl, whom I had last met in New York about ten years before. To her delight, Christina finally got her song, sung to her alone as she sat on Burl's knee. The press photographer there loved it too.

11 1953–59 – Rose Hill

My marriage to Christopher Gorton added yet another surname to a household already blessed with two. Miss Shapley now doubled up as Mrs Gorton and the children were Salt; all very clear to us, but endlessly confusing to schoolteachers and postmen!

Christopher Bellhouse Gorton was born in 1894, one of seven children, and fought in World War One. His father was an Anglican minister, a canon, and then an archdeacon in Hereford, but the family had lived largely in Lancashire. Christopher's two older brothers went to university and one, Neville Gorton, later became a flamboyant and much-loved bishop of Coventry. Their father died while Christopher was still at school and there had not been enough money for him to continue his education. He was always sorry about this and he certainly had the intellectual gifts and interests to have made good use of it. He got a position in a big Manchester textile firm, Tootal's, where he spent all his working life. He eventually became head of the department which made a beautiful fabric called 'Robia', which was a gossamer-thin voile with tiny tufts in different colours. Interestingly, it was the perfect material for saris and Christopher designed special sari lengths with borders for export to India. Robia was also very suitable for little girls' party dresses, as we discovered. With Tootal's Christopher got to travel and use his flair for languages, and he lived and worked at various times in both Paris and Buenos Aires. The Gortons were a large and interesting family and the children and I felt that we were lucky to gain such nice relatives in this way. One of Christopher's sisters was called Elgar, which fascinated my children, and through this they learnt all about the composer Edward Elgar, who was her godfather.

It intrigued friends that Christopher and I were so compatible, given that we had differing views in the fundamental areas of religion and politics. We did have our arguments, though the children only remember being truly alarmed over the Suez crisis!

But there was a strong attraction between us and many shared interests, including our love of good food and wine, and France. Christopher's affinity with France extended to his driving method, and there would be wails from the back seat as he lit a Gauloise with both hands, steering with his knees. His alarming style came into its own in France, though, where it seemed quite normal as we whizzed round the Arc de Triomphe sliding across lanes of traffic. Christopher was very handsome and extraordinarily like the French actor and singer Maurice Chevalier, especially, of course, in his summer straw boater. On our first family holiday in France, the children had helpless giggles when people in cafés and restaurants, after the initial double take, approached our table saying, 'Enchanté, Monsieur Chevalier.'

When I had first met Christopher he had been separated for some time, and he later got a divorce from his first wife, who was American and had returned to the United States. He had two daughters; Gay, the elder, was more or less independent, but Bridget was ten years younger and still at boarding school in England. She spent a lot of time in our household and was extremely good with Dan, Nicholas and Christina, who grew very fond of her.

Christopher and I did not immediately agree on where we should live in Manchester. He had been settled for some time in one of the leafy and spacious residential areas that had grown up around a north Cheshire village; a very desirable area in many ways, but not, I have to admit, desirable to me. Adults who commute to work and have scattered friends can probably live happily anywhere, but with children you are choosing a local community which is very important in their day-to-day lives. I still felt strong ties to Didsbury and the families we knew there, and in this matter I was grateful to Christopher for graciously giving in. So, Didsbury it was.

Didsbury is the southernmost suburb of Manchester, the last of the old villages on the road to London: Rusholme, Fallowfield, Withington, Didsbury. Across the Mersey lies Cheshire, or what was the edge of Cheshire until the creation of Greater Manchester. The name 'Didsbury' is Saxon, thought to have evolved from 'Dyddi's burgh', or a fortification built by Dyddi, presumably to repel the invading Norsemen. There is very little left of Didsbury's early history; no trace of the medieval village, a handful of late eighteenth-century or early nineteenth-century cottages, many good Victorian houses, and a great deal of between-the-wars development. Since my first move there in 1945 and later during my long residence from 1953, there has, of course, been considerable new building, not all well received by local residents. In the 1970s there were ambitious plans to demolish great swathes of artisans' cottages around the village main street and also moves by developers eager to buy into an area of splendid Edwardian half-timbered houses as they came up for sale. This led to what can only be described as a civic uprising, as residents banded together to retain the suburb's character by preserving and improving existing houses. Vigorous action by newly formed residents' groups succeeded in winning for Didsbury the protective umbrella of 'general improvement area' and, incidentally, enhanced its already strong sense of community.

A lot of the attractiveness of Didsbury lies in its proximity to the river and its abundance of trees, which are mostly mature and beautiful, some being known and prized individually. All this enhances the feeling of being much further than five miles from Manchester's centre and the industry which created the city's wealth. Didsbury also has two very special parks – the Old Parsonage, with its orchid house, and Fletcher Moss, which has an alpine garden on a south-facing slope. The Old Parsonage itself housed for a long time an attractive small art gallery, with some paintings by Turner and Augustus John and one tiny Constable sketch.

But it is, of course, people who create a neighbourhood, and during the sixty years I have known Didsbury it has always been blessed with a great variety of people of all income levels and occupations. It has never been exclusive or excluding and cannot be stereotyped as 'artistic' or 'executive' or whatever; these groups exist and a lot more besides. It has sometimes been called 'the Hampstead of the north', but residents of Didsbury do not feel the need for that kind of comparison – Didsbury is proud to be itself! It has had a sizeable Jewish community since the last century due to Sephardic settlement when the city was cotton king of the world. It has also always attracted teachers, journalists, writers, musicians and others in the entertainment world, including the BBC. However, it has never been a static or especially elderly community. This is partly due now to the large numbers of students in colleges established there, and housed in hostels and student lodgings. Several large Victorian houses, formerly homes of rich and powerful citizens of Manchester, have found new uses as colleges, student accommodation, hotels or restaurants. Didsbury has undergone many changes over the past few decades, but it has remained a real place, not just an area of land with a line drawn round it on a map. It has a past and a very lively present. If you believe in the 'genius loci', the spirit of a place, then the Didsburys of this country are well worth preserving.

The house that we bought in Didsbury was called Rose Hill and it was in Millgate Lane. I know I was equally attracted by the address as by the house itself. It was not beautiful but it had character, and though it might since have felt physically neglected at times, it surely felt the affection surrounding it and the happiness it brought to its residents. I lived at Rose Hill for twenty-eight years and still feel sad about leaving it.

The house was typical for that part of Manchester, one of the 'cotton barons' mansions' as we called them; only ours quickly became known as 'Shapley's Folly'. The previous owners had divided off for themselves the large orchard and stables, which they converted to their new house. But that still left the old house, surrounded by vegetable garden, tennis lawn, rose lawn, other little lawns and nooks and crannies, tall trees and wide borders of rhododendron bushes, mysterious outside 'offices' (but no garage), a long back drive and imposing wrought-iron front gates in a fish-scale pattern. The house itself was built in the white bricks so common in that part of the north, with the back section incongruously in red brick. It could only be described as Victorian gothic and was large and unmanageable with huge cellars and an infinity of dusty attics. It had high narrow ecclesiastical windows that let in lots of light, birthday cake cornices and elaborate centre mouldings, white as icing sugar, in the downstairs rooms. There were oriental-looking tiles let into bands on the top storey, absurd stone heads ornamenting the Norman porch with its dog-tooth decoration and another perched rakishly on the outside lavatory. These became known variously as Nero, Eleanor of Aquitaine, Richard Coeur de Lion and any other suitable historical figure the children learnt about. On one of the lawns there was a slightly less than lifesize statue of a naked girl sitting on a plinth, which the gardener claimed was of a girl with the unlikely name of Nubia who had lived there. A neighbour remarked unkindly that she looked just as though she had been caught sitting on the lavatory during an air-raid.

When we bought Rose Hill the only other bidder, so I always believed, was a friendly society who wanted it for offices. Many people in the neighbourhood heaved a sigh of relief when they heard that 'a family' was moving in. And move in we did, on that hot summer's day, coming up from London with dog, cat and Miss Renee, who had never been north of Watford and was overcome by height-sickness outside the Cat and Fiddle and prayed to be allowed to return to the flatlands of the south. She need not have worried; Rose Hill turned out to be only a few hundred yards from the Mersey and only a few feet above sea level.

At first the house was lived in quite normally. Six people shared twelve rooms, the children changed their bedrooms each night, climbed on to the roof to discover the view of the Derbyshire hills and set up camps in the farthest reaches of the garden. They, and most of the neighbourhood's children, spent that unbelievably hot first summer forming a club (the Kingston Klub, after one of the roads that bordered Rose Hill) in the smallest and dirtiest and dampest of all the cellars, with old car seats and one electric light bulb precariously rigged, and junk from other people's jumble sales. Parents wrung their hands as the sun shone outside, but the children stayed in the cellar. Everyone had an office; the youngest, a five-year-old, was assistant to the assistant secretary. Years later I asked the children what the club *did*. 'We just fought,' they said, after thinking it over, 'and the boys pulled the girls' hair.'

The children's club had one member who should have been ineligible on the grounds of species, but sheer force of personality made such a consideration irrelevant. Pierre's parentage was only half certain, the French poodle side; but just before his shaggy wool was clipped he was remarkably like an Old English sheepdog, so this is what we always assumed his other half to be. The specialness of pets is hardly a novel topic. But even today when two or three Didsbury residents of a certain vintage get together, Pierre's name can crop up. Barbara Woodhouse would have totally disapproved of the way he was brought up. He was undisciplined and alarmingly adventurous; sightings were reported from far afield. But first and foremost he was a home and family dog, happiest in front of a blazing fire, with talk flowing above his head and, often, cats and kittens snuggling up to him. When the children scattered to do different things he suffered agonies of indecision about whom he should monitor.

Pierre's home territory roughly corresponded to the round of our postman, Harold, because every morning bicycle and dog did the round together. Pierre's friendship with Harold stood him in good stead. One summer on the eve of our holiday we put him into kennels about five miles away. In the early hours of the

morning we got an irate telephone call to say that he had
demolished his pen and run away. At that very moment he
arrived back at Rose Hill in a frantic state with bleeding paws and
trailing a long rope behind him. We were leaving in a few hours
to catch the Dover ferry but no other kennel would take the
absconder. So Harold offered to feed him in the front porch and
keep an eye on him. As we set off down the drive Pierre sat
smiling in triumph.

Rose Hill had many official pets of several species, but
Christopher and I suspected unofficial ones at times. White mice
would emerge mysteriously from the cellars and frog, toad and
newt spawn somehow make the journey from the nearby stream
to a tank in our garden, only to metamorphose while we were
away on holiday. Twenty years later their descendants still lurked
in the garden. It was the perfect house for children, we decided,
though the row of bells in the kitchen – Morning Room, Library,
Master Bedroom, Nursery – suggested that the house was being
used rather differently from what was intended.

A running track and hurdles were set up on the tennis lawn,
and a game of cricket, punctuated by violent quarrels, was played
on the lawn in the holidays from dawn to dusk, winter and
summer, so it seemed – once in the snow by candlelight. I
remember one afternoon, as I was typing at a window, watching
children on every variety of tricycle and cycle slowly circling the
house, the speed never varying, a continuously changing frieze
against the sky and rhododendron bushes.

Rose Hill was made for parties, and we had them; garden parties,
tennis parties, cricket parties, bonfire parties. The most spectacular
was the 'West Indian' party, with all our friends and my BBC
colleagues and lots of people I had been doing programmes with
in Moss Side, including Brother Bernard, who was in charge of a
very lively Anglican church. On the day of the party my daily help
announced to me, 'There's a monk at the door with a van load
of beer.' Later the Moss Side contingent, with steel band, arrived
down Millgate Lane in a double-decker bus. We had invited the
neighbours anyway and warned the police about the noise. The
police came to check up on us and could not leave the music –
memories of Burl Ives's party in New York!

As the years went by the family began to draw in. The
blackcurrant bushes, the raspberry canes and the overgrown
chives of the vegetable garden went down before a bungalow and
other children. The beloved tennis lawn was sold and a house built

on it. No more cricket matches when the youngest player was four and the oldest sixty-four. No more fêtes for charity, no more hurdle races.

Eventually we could no longer ignore the problems, not least the expense, of trying to run a house meant for a large Victorian family and several live-in servants. We contemplated selling. I presented to the children the attractive prospect of a regular house, where we would not lose track of things or each other and dust would not accumulate. After all, their school compositions on 'My Favourite House' had often rather wistfully featured tiny, neat, warm story-book houses with everything in its place, a little square lawn at the front, and smoke coming out of the chimney. But the hold of Rose Hill was too strong for us all and we looked for ways to stay on. The only thing to do was to resume my career as a landlady.

Andy Pandy, our first lodger in Hampstead, had set some sort of precedent and we tried at Rose Hill to avoid what we thought might be 'dull' company. I would willingly drop a guinea on the rent to accommodate someone whom I thought was doing an interesting job – actors, writers, designers, working strange hours, throwing strange temperaments. We had them all.

George Hurst, the conductor of the BBC Northern Orchestra, who lived with us for some time, once conducted in front of the gramophone right through the score of the symphony for his next concert in the bay window of his ground-floor flat, watched (but he did not know it at the time) by a gaggle of fascinated children hiding in the rhododendron bushes. It was a very popular activity for the next few days: 'How much is that doggie in the window?' on the gramophone and a number five knitting needle. We had a Middle Eastern gynaecologist who must have had agoraphobia, because he worked inside a small cave that he had constructed out of books in a corner of the draughty sitting-room. We had an American lecturer, I remember, with a long bony New England face. He had an Arabic typewriter which interestingly worked backwards and about which he was not the least bit stuffy; it was the perfect aid to a child's convalescence after an illness. He was also learning to play the oboe. We thought he was coming on well, but once I heard a painter say to his mate, as they sweated over an elaborate cornice, 'Watch out for those snakes when you go past.'

For a time I had a big noticeboard in the kitchen. I was working and I thought that if I could train everybody to read the notices, life would be simpler. Then one day I came in unnoticed and heard the window cleaner say to my daily help, Auntie Phyll, an enormous lady with a fluffy yellow beret, weighed down with shopping, 'What are you reading that for, love? Do you think you're top of the form this week?' And they both roared with unkind laughter.

But that kitchen was quite a place. Everyone gathered in it for tea and biscuits in the middle of the morning, the lady who cleaned, any workmen who were around and the lodgers. It might be a beautiful young actress 'resting', or one of our medical students who had some reason for cutting morning lectures, but was able to totter down for the break in pyjamas and dressing-gown. There were some people who were actually working quite hard, but could be lured to the kitchen by Maureen, Auntie Phyll's small daughter. Maureen looked a bit peaky one day and was memorably described by her mother as 'bumfast'. She was all golden curls, bows and bangles and plastic handbag, and used to hammer on our doors with the words we had all been waiting for, 'Come along, auntie (or uncle), me mam's brewed up!'

All my family still have clear memories of this time. Looking back it mostly seems to have been summer, but obviously it could not have been. In any case the big old kitchen with its huge scrubbed sycamore table was pleasant enough in winter. We had an old boiler in the cellar which devoured anthracite and made the whole house throb like a ship's engine room. Our part-time 'boiler man', Joe Kirkham, came with the house; even he could not remember how long he had been keeping the boiler going but he seemed to be the only person who could control it. We were also lucky enough to have the continued gardening and odd-jobbing services of Frank Marlor, a lovely gentle man, really a gas worker, who became a long-standing friend and inseparable in my mind from my memories of Rose Hill.

The house's residents and helpers were, as is probably clear, a very heterogeneous crowd, and I suppose we wasted a lot of each other's time. But at least we were not shut away with no one to relieve the burden of loneliness. I did not pretend to be an efficient landlady, but I think I was kind, and if I could not mend a fuse I always kept candles and matches handy.

But you cannot be a landlady without meeting some very queer fish. People are not as easy to read as we like to think. I kept to myself any doubts I had, but the children had their own ways of summing things up. One once said about some new arrivals,

'They're awfully nice, Mummy, and we're pretty sure they're married, because she's got some silver-backed hairbrushes on the dressing-table.'

Our most bizarre brush with criminality came with a charming young man who had set up a company, complete with headed notepaper and fleet of sales cars, and a lavish personal lifestyle to match, including an Alsatian dog. It turned out that he had also set himself up with a completely bogus identity, family seat in the shires, Eton, Oxford and the Guards, all from observing his officers while in the army. I was unsuspecting and only alarmed by the number of female guests he was entertaining overnight, so I asked a male friend to have a quiet manly chat with him and suggest he might find another flat. The friend and I were then having a cup of tea, when we heard the tenant clatter down the stairs. We later heard from the police that he had gone to the airport and left the dog with someone to mind 'for a few minutes' while he hopped on an international flight, to be pursued by Interpol across the world. His cheque to me for the rent turned out to be the only one of hundreds which did *not* bounce, and a few days later I got a cheery postcard of the 'having a lovely time, wish you were here' variety!

Apart from any moral danger they might inadvertently have been exposed to, I know that the children were very fortunate. They learnt a great deal about human nature in a very lively way. Early on, they came to accept the fact that some lodgers preferred to dispense with their company entirely, while others enjoyed taking them for walks or showing them how to mend a puncture in a bicycle tyre. People were different, that was all.

By and large we greatly enjoyed our lodgers. I think we would have missed a lot in a small house just for us. At night lights always had to be left on for the journalist who caught the all-night bus back from town and would not want to come back to a dark house. Whatever time I went to bed, someone was up. Our actor, Robert Eddison, might be cooking himself his first proper meal of the day, delicious smells wafting out from under his door. A student would be brewing black coffee for a night's revision for an exam the next day. And maybe somebody just felt like playing the Goldberg Variations very quietly at 2 a.m.

For years we found that our lodgers never really left us. Some were careless about forwarding addresses and our hall table used to be littered with mail addressed to people who had left us years before. And people would turn up out of the blue; someone paying a sentimental visit to the university, or on holiday with a new partner. Our lodgers sometimes gave us headaches but they were never dull, and they did allow us to stay on at Rose Hill and share with others its generally agreed 'good vibes', as we learnt to say much later, and the still lovely, though shrinking, garden. Dan never forgot one of our early lodgers. He arranged to take the flat and as he left he said, 'By the way, I'm a chiropodist.' As the front door closed, Dan said, 'Isn't it funny ... I was sure he was English.'

My second marriage and our family's move from London to Manchester had clearly signalled a major change in my private life and the start of a new era. Professionally, though, these events had not meant a significant break. The BBC co-operated in my wish to continue with the commitments I had built up in London and I more or less commuted to work for about three years after our move north. It was a satisfactory arrangement, apart from my occasional weariness with early mornings, late nights, solitary stays in modest hotels and an over-familiarity with the train track between Manchester and London. I did a lot of work on those journeys and I still associate my programme ideas and scripts of that time with the rattle of trains. Fellow passengers sometimes stared at me, and not just because regular television appearances made my face familiar. I often had to rush to catch the train from London without removing the very heavy make-up and false eyelashes which early television demanded and looked distinctly blowsy!

This continuity in my work suited me and also made sense from the BBC's point of view, as experienced producers and presenters were quite valued then and could not be replaced overnight. Furthermore, and this simply will not be believed nowadays, people were not falling over themselves to work in television. Except presumably to the engineers developing it, the new medium just did not seem to be either particularly interesting or important. Its geographical expansion was slow and there were very few sets in private houses. By contrast radio had long proved itself to be a widely heard and powerful medium with a firm grip on the public's imagination and affection. Only the BBC's insistence on versatility and a general attitude of 'Oh well, I suppose I'll give it a go' led to a gradual building up of skills and interest. The turning point for the public, of course, was the coronation, a marketing exercise for television that might have

been dreamt up by an advertising agency. But more about my own
television work later.

I did a lot of interesting radio work in the 1950s, but not much
on the 'show biz' side. However, I do remember one item which
madly impressed my children and their friends, and indeed my
grown-up friends too. Danny Kaye came to Britain in May 1956
for his work with UNICEF and was due to speak to a public
meeting at Sheffield City Hall. I was asked to interview him live
immediately afterwards for the programme *At Home and Abroad*.
The occasion was carefully set up by the producer, who made it
clear in a letter to me that the focus was UNICEF and that 'the
main interest of the interviewer will undoubtedly be to hear the
work commented upon and explained by a man world famous
in a totally different sphere'. He added, 'Clearly if he cares to be
amusing this would be welcome, but of course the object of the
interview is a serious one.' I cautiously prepared detailed notes
and questions, but was apprehensive since I had heard that Danny
Kaye could do fearsome things to scripts. He exceeded my
expectations by not only deviating from the prearranged topics,
but also with a sweet smile taking my notes gently from my hand
and tearing them up into pieces as we started the interview.
Despite my terror I could not fail to respond to his incredible charm
and unexpected physical beauty; he had skin like roses and truly
golden hair.

My main radio work in the early 50s was by contrast rather
earnest and low key and mercifully free of the whims of star
guests. I was sometimes on the panel for *Questions and Answers*,
which was part of the BBC School Broadcasting Department series
Looking at Things. I also wrote many scripts for this series and took
part in some of the programmes. The scripts were very hard work,
often delving deep into completely new topics, but were
immensely satisfying to do. Also, there was always feedback from
the audience; sometimes a whole class and their teacher wrote in
to let you know their views, so one felt closely in touch across
the broadcasting medium.

In school broadcasting we always aimed to inform through an
entertaining approach, often part dramatisation, but the topics
were solid and practical. I wrote *Tables and Chairs, Curtains and
Covers, China and Glass, Parks and Gardens, Town and Village, The
Story of a Dress, The Story of a Tie, Arranging Your Own Room*, and
programmes on houses and ships and exhibitions. I used my
connection through Christopher with Tootal's to research the

programme on ties, which I also presented, and remember being rather impressed at how much mileage one could get out of such an unassuming topic. One teacher even wrote that the class was so interested that the children were genuinely surprised when the broadcast ended. I wonder if today one could render a class of children spellbound by a programme about a tie!

I always enjoyed as much as anything the chance that broadcasting gave me to do programmes on places, and particularly to exploit the riches of the north of England, which I already knew so well. In *An Ancient City* I wrote and narrated for schools a feature script on York, a sheer delight to do and well received by the listeners. Even my very solemn Lancastrian butcher in Didsbury, usually unmoved by my broadcasting work, waved a large meat chopper at me in his enthusiasm, saying, 'It were better than being there.'

I have visited many cathedrals in Britain and Europe, but my favourite has always remained Durham. Its position is stunning, perched upon an elevated rock and almost surrounded by the River Wear, with the old town clustered around it to one side and sheer cliffs down to the river on the other. It is generally thought to be the greatest piece of Norman architecture in Britain and, begun in 1093, took only forty years to build. For me it is a most powerful and beautiful example of the Romanesque, a simple, strong and masculine building.

Durham Cathedral, rather like Louisa M. Alcott's *Little Women*, is a personal enthusiasm which I managed to weave into my career quite a number of times over the years. I always felt lucky in handling interesting topics most of the time and passionately interesting ones (to me) every now and then. I first wrote and broadcast on Durham in 1938 in the series *Sermons in Stone*, then in 1941 did an item in *Children's Hour* and yet another programme for the Home Service in 1946. Five years later the schools series *Looking at Things* gave me the opportunity to write a dramatic feature script called *A Cathedral City*, and again it was especially satisfying to try to convey to young people the beauty and wonder of Durham and its cathedral.

The Durham programme encompassed a thousand years of history and hundreds of people. The next schools programme I did also focused on a particular place, but could not have been more different. It was *The Story of Saltaire*, for which I wrote a partly dramatised script. In this I could enjoy working on a topic that was both fascinating in its own right and also of close personal

interest, giving me an unforced opportunity to start telling three
of Sir Titus Salt's great-great-grandchildren something about him.

The programme covered Titus's birth in 1803 and early
childhood in an old stone house with walls three feet thick a few
miles away from Leeds. The family moved when Titus's father,
Daniel, became a farmer and then in 1822 moved again, to
Bradford, when Daniel Salt set up in business as a wool-stapler.
Titus was apprenticed to another firm to learn, from the beginning,
the processes by which raw wool is turned into woollen cloth.
He then went back into his father's business and later started up
on his own as a worsted manufacturer.

Bradford in the early nineteenth century was going through a
massive population explosion and great industrial and social
change; while fortunes were being made by the few people who
owned the machines, the others, the people who worked them,
were living in terrible conditions of overcrowding and squalor.
Titus became aware that the price of such industrial expansion
in the growing cities of the north was the health and well-being
of the workpeople. In my programme the young Titus questioned
the old Yorkshire saying 'Where there's muck there's brass', and
wondered whether people and machines could not exist together
in greater harmony.

The schoolchildren heard the story of how one day in a dock
warehouse at Liverpool Titus happened to see some dirty bales
of a strange wool that nobody else seemed interested in. The wool
came from South America, from an animal called the alpaca, a
close relative of the llama. He bought it up, took it back to
Bradford, and to everyone's surprise managed to spin and weave
it into a beautiful new cloth. Alpaca cloth immediately became
very fashionable and made a fortune for Titus Salt. It used to be
said of him that he made a thousand pounds before other people
were out of bed.

During these years Titus was playing an increasingly important
part in the affairs of Bradford, including helping to give the town
its first public park and concert hall. In the late 1840s he was
nearing the age when he might have retired to enjoy his wealth
and position. However, he started to turn over in his mind the
biggest of all his plans.

He found himself considering the idea of taking all his work-
people away from Bradford – noisy, smoky, crowded Bradford
– and building for them, not only a fine new mill, but also homes

to live in, a church, a school for their children, and places in which they could enjoy their leisure.

We're quite familiar with this idea today – perhaps some of you who are listening live in towns like Port Sunlight or Bournville where this has been done more recently – but when Titus Salt first spoke of his idea to the people round him, it was considered very advanced. However, Titus was nothing if not practical. He finally settled on a beautiful site by the river on the edge of the moors and hills for his town. It was still only three miles from Bradford and not only the river, but the railways and a canal, ran through it already. The new town was to be a business proposition from the beginning, there was to be nothing little or mean about the plan. The mill and the town around it were to be on a grand scale, and no expense was to be spared.

The new town was named 'Saltaire', after Titus himself and its setting on the River Aire, and the mill was indeed on a grand scale – 545 feet long, the exact length of St Paul's Cathedral. It was completed in time for Titus's fiftieth birthday in September 1853, and on that day a great banquet and opening ceremony were held.

The enormous shed where later the machines for combing the wool would be installed, was chosen for the occasion, and it must have been an amazing sight on the morning of the feast, the iron columns wreathed with laurel, and tables spread for over 3,000 guests. More than 2,000 of them were work-people from Titus Salt's mills in Bradford, who were to be brought over by the special train that he had chartered.

The catering, as one might expect, was in keeping with the scale of the mill and the guest list, including four hindquarters of beef, forty chines of beef, 120 legs of mutton, hams, pigeon pies, tongues, grouse and partridge, 320 plum puddings and 100 dishes of jellies. Many handsome speeches were made and the least flowery of all seems to have been by Titus himself:

I hope to draw around me a population that shall enjoy the beauties of the neighbourhood, and who shall be well-fed, contented and happy ... I have given instructions to my architects that nothing shall be spared to make the dwellings of my work-people a pattern to the country.

Sir Titus Salt died in 1876 and the Salt family, including my children's great-grandfather, Titus junior, continued to own the mill and run it with others. Titus junior died young in 1887 and in 1893 a syndicate of businessmen assumed control. The fortunes of the mill and the village fluctuated thereafter but Salt's (Saltaire) survived two world wars and several financial crises, finally ceasing trading in 1986. The empty mill was bought by a businessman and now houses a number of enterprises, including the 1853 Gallery, devoted almost exclusively to the works of the Bradford-born artist David Hockney. The village of Saltaire has always interested Victorian enthusiasts and town planning students but is now enjoying something of a tourist boom, along with Bradford generally.

Back in the 1950s, when Christopher and I were in Yorkshire we sometimes took our young Salts to Saltaire. All in all they saw a lot of the north of England, especially through family and friends, many of whom I made through my BBC work. Because they were growing up in Manchester, Christopher and I decided that we wanted the children to get to know another, unsuburban, part of Britain sufficiently well to feel that they had put down some rural roots. Though many non-Mancunians may turn their nose up at Manchester as a city, it is wonderfully placed for easy access to some of the most beautiful parts of Britain; north Wales, the Lake District, the Peak District and the rest of the glorious Pennine chain running northwards. We chose the southernmost dale of the Yorkshire Dales, Wharfedale. Several times we teetered on the verge of buying a cottage there, at a time when prices were quite reasonable, but never did. However, we did adopt the village of Buckden in Upper Wharfedale as 'our' village and its Buck Inn as our second home.

As with other enthusiasms, my feeling for this particular place happily spilled over into my professional life. In *Woman's Hour* I produced a talk on amateur drama in the Dales by Dick Gregson from Grassington, with whom I had worked in the 1930s in *Children's Hour*. I was also involved with a programme called *Coast and Country*, produced by my very dear colleague and friend in Manchester, Michael Barton. Among the programmes we did together was one on Wharfedale, in which I interviewed several people including Walter Flescher, a gamekeeper and well-known broadcaster of Burley-in-Wharfedale. This is how I introduced the programme in the *Radio Times*:

One Easter Monday a year or two ago we sat in the sun at Cam Houses and saw lambs being born. My children watched spellbound as the little creatures shrugged off their slippery sacs and lay panting on the turf. In no time at all, it seemed, they were trying out their rubbery legs and the air was filled with bleats. It seemed to me then that this was one of the most beautiful places in England. In those days there was not even a track to Cam; only the two stone farmhouses, possibly the loneliest in England, and the sweeping fells. But I hope that the two families who live at Cam will be able to take part in this programme because opposite those lonely doorsteps two rivers rise: the Ribble which turns west to become a Lancashire river, and the Wharfe which turns east to become, as some of us think, the most romantic and beautiful of all the rivers of Yorkshire. It has a long way to flow before it loses itself in the Ouse at Cawood, below Tadcaster, and the character of the dale changes every few miles. For me, Wharfedale will always mean these lonely upper reaches, silvery limestone and the greenest of turf, the curlew and tiny flowers in almost alpine profusion, and flocks of sheep pattering along the one narrow road by the river past the hamlets of Beckermonds and Yockenthwaite. For other listeners it will be other things: Barden Bridge or Bolton Abbey; or the Strid, that menacing spot where the river is forced hissing and bubbling through the narrow cleft between the rocks; or Wharfedale may be a favourite country inn and a dish of ham and eggs, or the more sophisticated pleasures of Ilkley on a bank holiday.

That early hope of mine with Christopher, that Dan, Nicholas and Christina would grow to regard Wharfedale as special, was fulfilled, though they have now travelled and lived all over the world. I still remember clearly one of our first Sunday mornings there as we sat in the little church at Hubberholme, just beyond Buckden, where the dale has become Langstrothdale. I thought then that if I were ever asked to show a visitor from overseas something of rural England in one day, I would bring them to that place. The church is very sturdy and light grey, with a rare medieval rood-loft of 1558, and has been in almost constant use since the time of the Norman conquest. It has rough pillars and the simplest kind of round-headed arches, a view of the steep green fell-side through the altar window, and on that Sunday there was an enormous bowl of meadow flowers on the altar. There were about eighteen people there; some in shorts and hobnailed boots, who had been walking on the fells and dropped down into the valley when they heard the vicar toll the bell, a few village people in their Sunday best, and a lot of children, who stared round and shuffled their feet and dropped their pennies for the collection at regular intervals through the service. I had told my children about the mice on the oak pews carved by Robert Thompson, Kilburn's famous 'Mouse Man', so they were happy discreetly feeling their way around finding mice. There was no one to play the harmonium, so some brave spirit started us off on the hymns and we just did our best. The air in the old stone building was so cold and damp that it struck right through to the marrow of your bones. So, afterwards we all followed the vicar across the bridge to the George Inn, owned then by the church, where he ordered hot coffee or cider for everybody. Hubberholme is a magical spot and one of Yorkshire's many famous sons, the writer J.B. Priestley, chose that his remains should lie there.

Dan has very particular memories of that holiday, because it was the week that England won back the Ashes in cricket. Wharfedale was at a fever-pitch of excitement, just like everywhere else. As you walked up the fells you could hear curlews and sheep bleating, as always, but there was another sound too. A man in a field turning his hay would stop to call out to you, 'What's the score now?' And down back in the village, a man on a ladder mending a cow shed roof would ask the same question of a little boy racing across to the village shop to get a loaf of bread for tea, and you can bet the little boy would know. In the Buck Inn nobody left the kitchen where the only radio set was. We got under the feet of the innkeeper's wife who was trying to get dinner ready, and village children kept poking their heads through the doors and listening for a moment and running off again to tell their mothers the latest news. The wife of a high church dignitary staying in the hotel, who had seemed very forbidding to us all, amazed us at tea by asking the latest score, and becoming overwhelmingly human when she heard it. And I shall always remember going for a walk with the children when the cheering was over and how they astonished the sheep with their happy singing, as we slithered and slipped down the almost vertical fellside, back to supper and bed.

12 1953–59 – *Something to Read*

I have always felt rather irritated by people who apologise for watching television; not just a particular piece of 'rubbish', but any television. This attitude is much less common now than it used to be, but it persists among the very high-minded. During my career I sometimes felt obliged to cloak even my recreational viewing with a 'keeping up professionally' label. This idea became a family joke as everyone put the case for their own 'professional' choices to help Mum in her work! I unashamedly love watching television, and as I have got older and spent a lot of time on my own it has become more and more important to me in feeling in touch with the world. Admittedly many of my own interests and tastes were formed early mostly by reading and doing things myself, like playing the piano. Perhaps children today do read less and are more passive in their recreation, but it does not have to be so. Television can entertain and inform and stimulate interests in a way unimaginable in my youth.

But television and radio are so different. Radio has always been very special to its practitioners and audience – you either love the imaginative, companionable and rather cosy feel of it or you do not – and I am content that my main BBC career lay there. But I am also glad that television emerged in time for me to have a good crack at it on both the performing and production sides. In the early days radio people sometimes had to be wooed or dragooned into the new medium, but many of us then enjoyed it immensely. The familiar and ordered, rather muted atmosphere of a radio studio gave way to a more cluttered and busy place, a much more technically complex operation, live transmission, theatrical make-up, strong lights (people occasionally fainted) and lines to be learnt. For some time performers did not even have the crudest prompts, then there were 'idiot cards' and later autocues, which enable people to read their full text while looking into the camera. Unfortunately I did not make it into the autocue era! Television also demanded of us a discipline and style of democratic team work which was very involving and appealing. The problems could be nerve-racking, but solving them and feeling that you had been part of a good programme was exhilarating. When I started we were all still learning and disaster lurked at every turn. But it was fun to be part of the pioneering stage of what has turned out to be such an overwhelming phenomenon.

I was a regular television performer in the early 1950s. In children's television, as well as the book readings for very young children, I also wrote scripts and performed in the series *People in Books*. In this we had young actors appearing as the characters in well-known books for older children. They dressed and acted fully in their parts but were interviewed by me as a modern reporter. Looking back on it now, this device seems to me rather imaginative and daring. I think I have only seen it since in Kermit the Frog's hilarious interviews with fairytale characters in *Sesame Street*. It was enjoyable to do, especially knowing as we did that the books featured were immensely popular with many of our viewers: *National Velvet, Swallows and Amazons, Masterman Ready, The Three Hostages, The Prisoner of Zenda, The Children of the New Forest, The Princess and Curdie, Five Children and It, Emil and the Detectives*.

My main television work then, though, was in women's programmes. When, during one of my many railway journeys between London and Manchester, I woke up after a short nap and met the steady stare of the woman in the opposite corner of the carriage, I knew I was for it. 'Ah,' she said, while I was struggling to collect my wits and looking, no doubt, as attractive as most people who have slept in trains, 'you're Olive Shapley, aren't you? I've been waiting to have a talk with you about the television.' This was our audience in person, and it had to be faced. For half an hour I listened to queries, criticism and, I must admit, a good deal of friendly approval; and it reinforced my impression of how important women's television programmes had already become to their viewers and how personal was the interest felt in them. Other programmes cast a wide net for their audience, but women's programmes, to be a success, had to be right on the target. And indeed they mostly were, because those working on them kept this fact firmly in front of them, under the most capable guidance of the editor, Doreen Stephens.

Three o'clock in the afternoon was the women's programme slot and I remember that Doreen had spent many weeks touring the country knocking on front doors and, over innumerable cups of tea, finding out what housewives, alone in their homes in the afternoon, really wanted from the BBC. It seemed that though they were not averse to general cultural items, such as the latest exhibition at the Tate Gallery, in reality such items were a long way from most daily lives. So home and self-improvement topics dominated, for example in the series *About the Home*. Occasionally the BBC was a little too clever for its own good in this direction, for instance with the diet sheets. After a series called *How to Get Slim*, 53,000 women wrote in for diet sheets. But another 3,000 wrote in to find out how to get fat! (A male producer, I recall, commented drily on the cussedness of women.) Then it was decided that no diet sheets might be issued because of the dangers of unsupervised slimming, and so 53,000 women had to have their stamps back. But still, it was nice to know that the viewers were really there. Women also wrote in their thousands in response to television's first keep-fit queen, Eileen Fowler.

Another member of that early band of television stalwarts was the cook Marguerite Patten. Her presentation style was so persuasive that I always felt that if, at the end of a recipe for Christmas cake, that nice, cosy voice had said, 'And now, just a *pinch* of gunpowder,' in would have gone my gunpowder without a moment's hesitation. Food presented special challenges to television. Recipes had to be presented slowly enough for them to be taken in, and not so slowly that the whole thing became boring. Also, photographing food was not easy. I remember watching an attempt to get a good picture of some innocent little biscuits. 'Tilt the plate this way, Bob. No, back again ...' Doyley on. Doyley off. And still the biscuits continued to look like flat, grey stones from some cold, cold beach.

I am married, 38, with 4 children aged 13, 9, 5 and 2. My husband is 41, a very good husband and father, except that he never wants to take me or the children out. Not even on Sunday afternoons in the summer does he think to come for a walk, unless I nag him into it ... I'm sure many wives face this problem. What does the panel advise?

This was a typical problem sent in by a viewer to *Family Affairs*, a regular item on women's television on which I chaired the panel for about a year. It was an interesting programme to do and seemed to touch a chord with the audience, since we were never short of problems or feedback about our discussions. Some of the issues raised forty years ago have since pretty well ceased to be issues; would a widow with a new male companion today be terrified lest their 'love-making get out of hand'? But it is still probably women who mostly detect family problems, worry about them and want to do something about them. And new issues have replaced the outmoded ones; one-parent families, stepfamilies, coming out as gay, AIDS.

Just before I started on *Family Affairs* I had appeared in another family-orientated television discussion, on *Panorama* (then only one year old) with Dilys Dimbleby, also a mother, and wife of *Panorama*'s presenter, Richard Dimbleby. The subject was corporal punishment and one newspaper described the programme as 'bristling with interest and topicality'. I remember that Dilys Dimbleby and I bristled in disagreement and no doubt, like all good topical broadcasting, initiated similarly heated discussions all round the country!

But it was my time as compère of the women's programme *Leisure and Pleasure* which largely gave rise to my fairly short-lived reputation as 'television's latest woman personality', as one newspaper put it in early 1954. This was certainly the television show of mine which lodged itself most firmly in the audience's mind for some time afterwards. I remember getting letters saying how interesting it was to see at last the face behind the voice (I had already been broadcasting for almost twenty years). But exposure of this kind held its terrors. Did you live up to expectations? What *were* the expectations? And for the first time one had to worry about clothes, make-up and hair. Not so many years ago I attended a reception at Broadcasting House for the dwindling band of us who had joined the BBC before 1935. Robert Dougall, the distinguished and popular newsreader, was also there and told me that throughout his career when he met his fans in the flesh they often told him he was too short! Television performers are doomed to disappoint.

Leisure and Pleasure was a magazine programme and it had a wider brief than the other women's programmes. It aimed to open a window on the world, an idea which was much more potent then than it is now. When I travelled about the country, particularly on my own turf in the north, I saw television aerials in lonely places, such as isolated villages and small hill farms. I was very conscious that inhabitants there depended almost entirely on television to bring them news of plays and new books, art shows and fashion, and to bring them, above all, people, all kinds of people, the famous and the not so famous, conversing, arguing, discussing.

The programme also had great success in stimulating new interests. I remember, for example, a series by the artist Mervyn Levy on painting pictures. It produced works of an extremely high standard from surprised and gratified housewives who had never before done anything more creative than bake a fine apple tart. One of the winners in the competition at the end of the series began to take art lessons afterwards and many others found a new and absorbing hobby. These developments mattered at a time when there were far fewer outlets of this sort for women outside the home than there are today. I once heard Doreen Stephens say that to her 'the measure of success of women's programmes is a constantly diminishing audience'. In fact she wanted her audience, instead of sitting in the dull apathy so dear to the imagination of television sceptics, to be so stimulated to new activities that they had no time to turn on their sets. A brave statement then, and just about unthinkable now! Those were idealistic and simple days.

There was no difficulty in persuading interesting people to join us on *Leisure and Pleasure* and of course almost all of them at that time were invited because of achievements elsewhere. It was only later that just being on television became a career in itself for many performers. I remember interviewing Violet Carson, nearing the end of her long first career and yet to flower again as Ena Sharples on *Coronation Street*. We met Joan Ingleby and Marie Hartley, distinguished chroniclers of Yorkshire life, and Pat Smythe, the show jumper. I remember a whole Christmas programme from Belle Vue Zoo in Manchester, where Gerald Iles presented an item on 'pets for presents'. Animals are always a risk on television and my announcing that day acquired a certain edge as I was eyed by a boa-constrictor about a foot away.

During all these early days of television the BBC, and of course ITV when it began in 1955, was slowly building up staff expertise in the new medium. I finally gave up my work in front of the camera, feeling too old to continue tackling with ease the ever-increasing complexity of television performance. But I was keen to turn my hand to producing. In 1959 I attended the second BBC television training course, along with a very interesting group of people, some of whom later rose to great heights. This was the first substantial course of this kind, the previous one having been more or less a pilot course for television training techniques.

The course lasted six weeks and was very intensive, including every aspect of television production. I loved it and enjoyed getting at last some solid backing to the rather 'seat of the pants' knowledge acquired by just doing television. We had lectures and practical work, and we all had to learn how to set up and operate microphones and cameras. At the end of the course each participant did an exercise, which we had to devise from scratch and organise, all within a tiny budget of course. I adapted a Dorothy Parker short story, which became a dialogue between a couple on a balcony in New England or somewhere. So I needed two actors. Despite being paid almost nothing, actors were delighted to appear in our modest little exercises, because they were such a good showcase, being seen by lots of producers in the businesss. I got in touch with a young man, Tony Warren, whom I had known as a boy actor for many years in Manchester. He and the woman were excellent in my piece, though he did point out to me tartly that he was about half her age!

That night Tony and I shared a carriage on the midnight train up to Manchester and sat up dozing, neither of us being able to afford a sleeper. At about Crewe, after a long period of silence, Tony suddenly woke me up saying, 'Olive, I've got this wonderful idea for a television series. I can see a little back street in Salford, with a pub at one end and a shop at the other, and all the lives of the people there, just ordinary things and ...' I looked at him blearily and said, 'Oh, Tony, how boring! Go back to sleep.' But Tony did not let his idea drop and soon after found himself in a job in Granada's Promotions Department. One thing led to another and on 9 December 1960 the first episode of *Coronation Street* appeared. Tony has never let me forget my error of judgement and for my birthday in 1986 gave me a copy of 'The Street's' twenty-five year celebration book, in which was written, 'For Olive who failed to see the point of *Coronation Street* on a railway train, on a dark wet night in the late 1950s.'

Back in Manchester after the television training course I got down to my new, if rather late, career as a television producer. The BBC had several scattered television and outside broadcast sites. One, a converted church in Plymouth Grove, still had a large notice visible above the altar, 'He That Hath Not Vision Shall Perish', much cherished in a world dominated by the studio

VISION sign. The main studio facility was another converted church, in Dickenson Road in Rusholme, which had one studio and very cramped make-up and other production facilities, with a canteen and a few poky little dressing-rooms. We coped well enough, though I do remember apologising sometimes to guests who clearly found the place not quite up to their expectations of the BBC. Nevertheless, out of that unpromising setting emerged over the years some extremely successful shows, such as *Top of the Pops*, and in some cases launching new television stars like Sooty, Harry Worth and Val Doonican.

In the first television show I ever produced (they were all live then) I made the mistake of including an animal. Disaster struck, but not in the usual predictable form of the creature relieving itself on camera all over the studio floor or grabbing the presenter's tie. It was a holiday programme and there was an item on pony trekking featuring Jonty Wilson, the blacksmith from Kirkby Lonsdale. I had been very keen to get everything right and had gone to some stables in Cheshire and carefully chosen a horse. A grey horse was what the cameraman said I had to have. So, I picked my grey horse and arranged that it should be sent in a loosebox, with handler, in plenty of time for rehearsal.

On the day of transmission the rehearsal wore on and there was no horse. Jonty Wilson was there all right, in his shiny riding boots and hacking jacket, and he rehearsed his part splendidly, slapping away at some odd piece of furniture that was standing in for the horse. Telephone calls to the stables only told us that the horse had been despatched at the time agreed upon. Then, at just about zero hour, the big doors at the end of the studio were flung open and a horse and rider wearily clattered up to the set. The loosebox had had a puncture and the poor girl in charge had ridden the last eight or nine miles through all the traffic. But after all that it was the wrong horse! This was a piebald, who looked simply terrible on camera, the dark very dark and the light very light, like a crazy map of the world. We all stood round shaking our heads and exclaiming, 'Look at him. Isn't he awful? Just the kind of horse we didn't want!' This was too much for one kind-hearted lady (the wife of another member of the cast). When the first item was well under way, she crept out to the canteen, got a handful of sugar lumps and fed them to the horse who was standing quietly in the nice cardboard stable we had mocked up for him. I shall never forget the noise his grateful munching made. It sounded like roof beams cracking. London rang up while the technical staff were still frantically trying to track down the sounds.

Books had always played a big part in my radio career, and book programmes of various kinds worked well on radio. However, television producers had so far been apprehensive. I was determined to do a successful television book programme, and thirty-five years later *Something to Read* is still the television work of which I am most proud. I did not set out to devise a critical programme in any narrow intellectual sense. I wanted it to do two things: to give viewers both the names of new books for their library and shopping lists, and the chance to take a long, uninterrupted look at authors who were in the news. The designer devised a very attractive set, like a sitting-room, and I had lots of ideas for books and authors. All I needed now was the most important element, the presenter.

I felt strongly that this innovative programme should not fall back on a well-known presenter, that we should break new ground and find fresh talent. I held auditions over two days and there were some promising people. However, on the second day a young man turned up who was clearly highly intelligent and knowledgeable, oozed confidence, communicated effortlessly through the camera, was very funny and never stopped talking. I knew instantly that this was the one. He was a *Guardian* journalist and his name was Brian Redhead. I had a fight, though, within the BBC to get him; one of the objections thrown up was the supposed incomprehensibility of his Geordie accent. Brian more than fulfilled my hopes in him and was central to the programme's success. I later enjoyed witnessing his long broadcasting career and now, like many other people, still find it hard to think of him as gone.

Brian Redhead's occasional co-presenters on *Something to Read* were Nancy Spain and Elizabeth Jane Howard and they worked very well as a team. They all reviewed books and we also had guest reviewers. Writers were invited on to the programme to talk about their own books or to discuss others', and we sometimes had a dramatised extract. The roll call looked interesting and varied then, and it still does. It included formidably successful women such as Monica Dickens, Penelope Mortimer and Katharine Whitehorn; toughish men, like John Braine, David Storey, Alan Sillitoe and William Cooper; Joan O'Donovan, full of fire; and Barbara Cartland and Denise Robins, voluble, splendid and behatted like birds of plumage. There was Susan Hill, still a teenager, explaining how she came to write such a good first book on a middle-aged marriage.

Elizabeth David talked about her cookery books, sitting at my own dining table, transported on to the set complete with tablecloth and fruit bowl. Arthur Marshall appeared, to poke the gentlest of fun at those odd birds of literature, Marie Corelli, Elinor Glyn and the doyenne of schoolgirl stories, Angela Brazil (he insisted on the pronunciation *Bra*zil). It is a curious experience to see a camera shake with laughter, but the cameras did this for Arthur Marshall. Many of the guests came back to my house before catching the midnight train home to London. I remember Arthur's delight in finding there my daughter and some friends, all blazers and pigtails, a real life scene from a Miss Brazil story.

The appearance of Yvonne Mitchell, a grand and gracious actress as well as an author, coincided with a minor fire in the studio during the final run-through. I remember her sitting on calmly in a great fur coat, talking to Brian about her new novel, while firemen trod over her with extinguishers, people shouted at each other and smoke hid everything from our view in the control room. But I dared not let them stop because we were checking the timing.

The journey north and inevitable hanging around at the Dickenson Road studio presented some special problems. One guest thoughtfully provided himself with a bottle of whisky and whiled away the time in his dressing-room drinking it. A few panicked telephone calls confirmed that the BBC might let itself in for rather more trouble by cancelling his appearance than by battling on, and this is where Brian Redhead really earned his keep. We propped the gentleman up in a chair with cushions and then Brian proceeded to both ask and answer his own questions at breakneck speed, without it being at all obvious that the guest's only contribution to the discussion about his book was the occasional nod and grunt, as I directed swift camera shots of him.

There were only two series of *Something to Read* but it was much enjoyed by those who worked on it, in front of and behind the camera. We had appreciative feedback from viewers, and their enthusiasm was shared by the studio crew, who as the captions rolled used to pounce on the books displayed on the set and piled up in boxes on the studio floor. When this first happened I got the idea for our subsequent closing shot (and in 1959 this was long before 'behind the scenes' shots became common): a slow pan round the darkening studio, with people picking up and examining the books, microphone cable or prop in hand. This summed up what I had wanted the programme to be.

I was always pleased for my children that I worked in television during their childhood and teenage years. The fun and interest that it brought into our household, not just my own work but programmes that they could go and watch live like *Top of the Pops*, went some way to compensate for their occasional benign neglect. Overall the family had a run of good luck during the 1950s, settled with Christopher very happily at Rose Hill. But then the children lost both their grandmothers within two years and we all felt sad that there was not one grandparent alive any more. My own mother's death affected me deeply. Apart from missing her gentle and loving personality, I discovered the shock of feeling orphaned, which somehow one does not expect to feel as an adult. And then we had another major blow.

In November 1959 Christopher was coming up to retirement from Tootal's on his sixty-fifth birthday, and we were both viewing it with some apprehension. He had a final weekend in Paris to say farewell to colleagues there and to stay with a close old friend. He had a very happy time with lots of good food and wine. But by the time he arrived back on Sunday night he was not feeling well and he stayed at home the next day. That evening the children and I went to buy a second-hand bicycle for Dan and Dan rode home. Nicholas, Christina and I went on to see a second-hand piano for Christina; she had joined the school guide troop that day and was still dressed in her new uniform. When we got back Dan was waiting for us anxiously at the front door and Christopher was upstairs in bed. He had collapsed on the sofa with a heart attack and Dan had called the doctor and our friend, Theo Chadwick, who was an anaesthetist. Christopher was already unconscious and he died about two hours later. We all felt devastated that his death was so sudden and we had not had a chance to say goodbye. That night Christina slept in Nicholas's bed because, as she told me years later, she was also very disturbed about sleeping with a dead body in the house. I had to wait till the next morning to get the undertaker.

Christopher's death was a great shock and we missed him dreadfully. We agreed, though, that he would have hated a long illness or being an invalid in any way. I was forty-nine and could not help but feel cheated by being widowed twice, after eight and seven years. But I had had the privilege and joy of two wonderful and desirable husbands, and had the children. Dan was sixteen,

Nicholas almost fourteen and Christina twelve; it was a tough time to lose a loving stepfather, who had put much effort into their sometimes demanding earlier years and had been really enjoying them as they matured. The children now had to mature even more as they coped with some adults' difficulty in handling their bereavement; an eye-opener indeed. We had a memorial service at St James's Church in Didsbury and chose Christopher's favourite music, including the 23rd Psalm. Nicholas remembers realising with amazement the strength of Christopher's wider role outside our family as we were faced on arriving by an overflowing church; there were Tootal's colleagues, friends and relatives, and boys from the Ancoats Lads' Club, where Christopher did voluntary work and to which he was devoted. We had lots of good things to remember – Christopher's warm voice and bright blue eyes, his sense of humour, his absentmindedness about which we used to tease him, his reading to us aloud by the fireside at night, our discoveries in Wharfedale. I was pleased that he had been able to begin to share his love and knowledge of Europe with us, and we had had two marvellous summer holidays in Brittany and Austria.

I find that families tend to be divided between those who keep and nurture their collective memories and those who are careless of their experiences as the years go by, getting out of them no particular pleasure in retrospect or even regarding them as positively morbid. Maybe I have felt an especial responsibility in maintaining my children's 'family history' because of their loss of two fathers. But as the four of us prepared to face the world again on our own, we all seemed to gain pleasure and amusement from our memories, however trivial, and strength for the future. I do believe that such shared consciousness is empowering rather than debilitating.

In most families it is the women who are the keepers of the family archives. For one thing, we are the story-tellers. You only have to listen to us talking to a friend on the telephone to know the truth of this. It seems to me that we have more of an eye, and an ear, than men have for the silly little things that make up a day. It was some time before it occurred to me that people should also try to write down some of their family history. I did not bother about this when my own children were growing up, but my grandchildren have convinced me that it must be done. 'That is a *family* joke,' my granddaughter Firoozeh has often said to me. 'Tell it to me again.' Each Christmas I think of getting it all together, massive Christmas cards in beautiful covers, but somehow it never gets done.

It is the little things that somehow thicken family life, and they disappear so soon. Of my own mother, and her large family living in south London at the end of the last century, I have just one or two memories. 'Smudgeley' as a name for the delicious goo at the bottom of a pie dish or casserole. That has survived for us. From one of my grandfathers I have his exercise books; 'Procrastination is the Thief of Time' written ten times in beautiful copper-plate. And I have my own father's Commonplace Book, compiled at the age of twenty-two, when serious-minded young men were going round London 'sermon-tasting' in the way the young go round pubs or clubs today. It consists of passages in, again, a beautiful script, from the books that interested him: *The Light of Asia, The Bhagavadgita, The Egyptian Book of the Dead*. These were much treasured for years, but had an added interest when my children's generation came back to the same kind of books and the same interest in the east.

For my mother's family and many other families at that time, it was sheer proximity and familiarity which glued them together. But these days roots are very quickly lost. Not many of us have children living just round the corner or in the same town, or even in the same country. So it takes a more conscious will to sustain a family history, but for me at least it has always been worth the effort.

13 1959–81 – The Rose Hill Trust

If asked to sum up the way my life has gone, I would say after a moment's reflection, 'Well, life has been both good and bad to me in rather extreme forms.' And when I think some more, I can see that various periods of my life have been dominated by quite serious runs of misfortune. That, at least, is how things might look objectively. But of course, we do not live our own lives objectively, which is no bad thing.

About a year after Christopher's death I began to realise that though I appeared to be coping well with my second widowhood, I was in reality sliding slowly into depression. But the momentum of work and busy family life masked my condition for many months. I did not get off the roundabout long enough even to assess things let alone take any steps to nurture my mental and physical health. Finally, after struggling for some weeks in the autumn of 1962, I had a nervous breakdown and was admitted to Cheadle Royal Hospital. It was a long and difficult climb out of the abyss, but by the middle of the following year I was back on an even keel. I was particularly helped by an unorthodox therapist called Eugene Halliday, to whom I was referred by an imaginative psychiatrist at the hospital. Along the way I learnt a lot about myself and the nature of endogenous depresssion. Knowledge in itself does not provide instant solutions to familiar problems when they crop up again, but it can give you some sort of armour with which to face the demons.

Just over a year later I collapsed dramatically again, but with pancreatitis. This condition was so unusual that the puzzled specialist dealing with my apparent daily heart attacks had not met it before, and it was eventually diagnosed by a junior doctor who was still referring to the textbooks. My relief at being diagnosed was tempered a bit by being told that pancreatitis was the almost exclusive preserve of 'elderly male inebriates'! I was interested to find myself anticipating ever more eagerly the morphine which alleviated the great pain, but was weaned off that and back to reasonable health.

All this demanded from the children resilience, a lot of common sense and co-operation among them as they juggled variously with running the house (and lodgers), school, exams and work, and worrying about me. They were not all based in the same place; Christina was at home, Nicholas at boarding school during term time and Dan working in London and already travelling around the world in his job. The BBC was patient and colleagues took up my baton at work. We were enormously helped by kind friends, many of whom were both emotionally supportive and very practical.

Thelma and Theo Chadwick, some of our oldest Didsbury friends, helped us over these difficult times, as did Mary and Brian Flowers. Mary was the elder daughter of Leonard and Bebie Behrens, from whom John and I had bought our house in The Beeches in 1945. She had two sons from her first marriage and was married to Brian Flowers (now Lord Flowers), who was then Langworthy Professor of Physics at Manchester University. The Behrens and Flowers households both lived at Netherby in Didsbury, where we all had many happy times. Mary and Brian were a tower of strength and Christina lived with them for some months in her O level year while I was still in hospital.

Eventually I resigned from the BBC staff and for the last nine years of my career, until the end of 1973, I worked on consecutive long-term contracts. Most of the work was in radio. I presented the northern edition of *Woman's Hour* for several years, from Manchester and Leeds, and contributed regularly to various topical and magazine programmes, such as *Home this Afternoon*, *Voice of the North* and *Talkabout*. I had occasional items on *The World at One* and *The World this Weekend* and appeared on *A Word in Edgeways*. The work was very varied, but my main interests continued to revolve around literary and social topics.

Woman's Hour never lost its daring edge when it came to delicate subjects, and I remember particularly an item on educating young people about venereal disease. The star was Dr Silver, consultant venereologist from the Bolton and Wigan area, who was a superb, enthusiastic communicator and very skilful with a mixed group of teenagers that I recorded in a youth club. Later I met him by chance on a train and we more or less carried on our

conversation about venereal disease where we had left off, to the
great interest of the other passengers.

Another *Woman's Hour* item entered the BBC Sound Archives
and has since assumed a radio career of its own, popping up
occasionally ever since. I introduced the item like this:

> I think this next item is going to make some of you very angry.
> But these young people have chosen, deliberately, to cohabit
> rather than marry, and they give their reasons. If their attitudes
> shock you, or even just irritate you, as they well may, it's
> perhaps worth remembering that today there are other young
> people, particularly in the big cities, who hold this same point
> of view.

In my discussion with the two young people – let us call them
A and S – A explained that he was good for S because he could
give her 'all the insecurity she needs'. I was not sure then whether
this statement was a slip of the tongue or a true reflection of the
situation, and I am still not sure! Of course this item, which had
quite an impact in 1967, has since become an increasingly quaint
piece of social history. However, we now know that the children
of such revolutionaries sometimes react against their parents'
views. The couple had a daughter, who has a close relationship
with them both, but after a recent radio airing of the interview
she wrote to me, 'I must admit I was absolutely shocked with the
things Mum said. They both sounded thoroughly irresponsible.
If I had that same attitude to life and kids everyone would
be horrified.'

The BBC continued to give me the chance to meet an enormous
variety of interesting people. On *Woman's Hour* we did the
occasional 'Portrait of a Listener' and this sometimes meant for
me summoning talents that I had discovered a long time ago. I
interviewed again Miranda Roberts, the Burnley housewife who
had responded so well to our new recording equipment before
the war. I also went back to the hospital at Scorton in Yorkshire,
which had featured in my documentary programme *Homeless
People*, and talked to staff and patients. The young monk there,
Brother Clement, who had been obsessed by radio when I visited
before the war, was now Abbé Raymond Thonn in the tiny village
of Aydoilles in the Vosges region of France. Raymond had managed
to keep his (Yorkshire accented) English in good shape back in

France by listening avidly to the BBC, including *Woman's Hour*, and he was a fascinating listener to interview.

In our 'Northern Guest of the Week' and other personality interview spots I remember the children's author William Mayne, Violet Carson, the Earl of Harewood, Thora Hird and Dora Bryan. I interviewed the Westmorland blacksmith, Jonty Wilson, who had appeared with the unfortunate piebald horse in that first television show I produced. I went to Downham, a little village near Clitheroe, to talk with Alan Barnes and Diane Holgate, local children who had appeared with Hayley Mills in Bryan Forbes's film *Whistle down the Wind*.

It was particularly pleasing to share on *Woman's Hour* the enormous success of Helen Bradley, the artist, who was also a delightful and easy interviewee. Born in 1900 into a middle-class family in a Lancashire village, she began to paint when she was over sixty to show her small grandchild what life was like when she was a child. She painted mainly with her hand and fingers and her pictures vividly depicted the Lancashire scene between 1903 and 1910. They echo the work of that other painter of the industrial north, L.S. Lowry, but with a unique style and charm of their own. Helen Bradley began exhibiting in 1966 and became equally famous in America. Her first book, *And Miss Carter Wore Pink*, was followed not long after my interview by *Miss Carter Came with Us*. One picture in this was of the scene in which a man shook the pink-clad Miss Carter at a suffragettes' meeting, causing her to faint in the middle of the road!

Probably the most outsize personality to appear was William Holt, the famous broadcaster and writer, who was based in, but by no means confined to, Todmorden, the Yorkshire Pennine town. I knew him as Willy Holt and he had had an extraordinary life. He began as a 'half timer' at the age of twelve in a shirt factory and then gained skill as a weaver. He was a soldier in World War One, taught English abroad and his many activities included politics and journalism. The first part of Willy's autobiography, *I Haven't Unpacked*, appeared in 1939 and *I Still Haven't Unpacked* in 1953. A couple of years after my interview with him, in 1964 at the age of sixty-six, Willy undertook a fifteen-month journey to Rome and back with his horse, Trigger, whom he had bought from a rag-and-bone merchant. They slept out every night, arousing great interest wherever they went, and Willy supported the two of them on paintings and sketches made and sold as they went. *Trigger in Europe* told the story of this remarkable journey.

One of my favourite authors has always been the French writer, Colette. She came at life from all angles, and it was a long and fascinating journey from her country childhood. She wrote of it all in her books, in which fact and fiction are inextricably mixed and presented in beautiful and original prose. She died in 1954 and was buried with the full military honours due to her as a Grand Officer of the Legion of Honour. For hours the people of Paris filed past her coffin in the courtyard of the Palais Royal, where her apartment was. I took the opportunity of the tenth anniversary of her death to suggest to the BBC that I go to Paris to interview for *Woman's Hour* Maurice Goudeket, her third husband. Monsieur Goudeket had been considerably younger than Colette, spoke excellent English and was charming and welcoming. In the apartment where he now lived the first things I noticed were some of Colette's famous paperweights on a table in the hall. The study walls were hung with portraits of her and a grey Persian kitten was a reminder of her love of cats. I was thrilled to make that visit and talk about Colette with her devoted partner.

Talkabout was a substantial magazine programme in the late 1960s, introduced from Manchester by Brian Trueman and occasionally Peter Wheeler. I did a number of serious features for it, produced by my colleague Hazel Lewthwaite. This is how I introduced, in the *Radio Times*, the feature *Something of a Handicap*:

A man who stammered badly once told me that having a stammer was like 'carrying around a bag of wet sand'. Unless you have stammered yourself or lived with a stammerer it is difficult to realise how much physical and mental energy has to be expended in overcoming this handicap.

Stammering children often meet ridicule from other children; school-leavers know that certain jobs are impossible for them and that interviews will be hazardous.

It seems amazing that some stammerers voluntarily go into performing before audiences, either live or in broadcasting, but two of my programme guests, J.H.B. Peel and Jonathan Miller, had done just that. Jonathan Miller explained that a 'performance' of any kind can help, from an assumed accent at the tube booking office to 'funny voices' in sketches in *Beyond the Fringe*. This device does not necessarily work indefinitely, though, if it is repeated in a set situation. Eventually *Beyond the Fringe* became for him a nightmare of jammings up and he left the cast several months before the end of their run. Some performers have actually exploited their stammer, like Patrick Campbell on the television show *Call My Bluff*. This, I have been assured by stammerers, is totally different from what they regard as insensitive and cruel mocking by non-stammerers. One reviewer wrote of my 'relaxed and understanding manner' in my programme on stammering. I did indeed bring to the subject many years of familiarity and acute interest and empathy, since both John Salt (author of the 'wet sand' quote) and my own three children were sufferers, to varying degrees at various times in their lives.

In the three series of *The Shapley File* I had the chance to take a close look at social issues, some timeless themes and some more topical ones. These programmes were immensely interesting and satisfying to do, and creative in that for each one I started with a blank slate. I had some initial ideas of my own, and I also researched the topics very thoroughly. But the major contributions came from people I knew personally or with whom I was put in touch by others. None was an 'expert', but in a low-key fashion they often had very original views and fascinating insights. Making these programmes proved to me yet again that in broadcasting I did not have to look beyond the ordinary to find the extraordinary.

For the first programme, *With Deepest Sympathy*, I drew on my own knowledge of bereavement to record the views of bereaved people and some of those who, by reason of their profession, are often called upon to help: a minister, a rabbi, a family lawyer, a doctor. The next programme, *Minus One*, grew out of the first and considered the situation of the family with only one parent through death or desertion, divorce or illegitimacy. Many of the issues explored in these programmes are now commonly aired and well understood, so that even I find it hard to remember that they were quite revolutionary in those days. The 'unmarried mother' has come full circle in the almost thirty years since this programme was broadcast. I looked then at both the social stigma and the emotional difficulties for a child not knowing its father. Since then the stigma has all but disappeared; but the emotional side, after perhaps being similarly disregarded, has re-emerged recently with this country's intense scrutiny of 'the family'.

Other *Shapley Files* looked at the children of immigrant families, at the faces of happiness and at voluntary social work in *The Do-Gooders*. In the final series I asked three questions: *What is a Home?*; *What is Loneliness?*; *What is Abroad?*

It has always seemed to me that children make 'homes' as naturally as they breathe; in trees, under tables, or by stretching a blanket across a clothes horse. Most of us carry on these activities in a rather more sophisticated way for the rest of our lives. For some women, especially, the urge to make a home is so powerful that they will get down to it on a one-night stay in a hotel bedroom, in a railway carriage or, as with one of the programme's participants, in a theatre dressing-room. I found people unwilling to admit that possessions played much part in this. 'People matter more than possessions' was a sentiment that they felt obliged to express. One young person looked back on a childhood home as a lost paradise, but two others thought of it as a prison to be escaped from as soon as possible.

I chose 'loneliness' as a theme because I saw it as perhaps the greatest problem of the 1960s, for all the social loosening up and newly discovered freedoms. Listeners might have already thought about the old person living alone and the bed-sitter dweller, but I found less obvious sufferers. There was the isolation of the Oxford student cut off from a working-class background and with no stake in the new one; the loneliness of deformity or disablement; the loneliness of mental illness; and the loneliness of being a creative writer. The final *Shapley File* took a look at 'abroad' and I discovered that it meant many different things. If you had always thought of Venice as a dream city rising from the waves of the lagoon, it might turn out to be exactly that, or it could end up as simply the place where your feet ached. Food featured prominently. For some abroad meant good, and different, food; but one couple just loaded the car boot with good English baked beans and reliable English tap water!

I was glad that I had one more opportunity in my career to be involved with television and it turned out to be great fun. I worked as a researcher on several series of *A Spoonful of Sugar*, produced by Nick Hunter, in which long-stay hospital patients had 'surprise' wishes fulfilled. This has become a standard entertainment formula, but it was quite novel then. The researchers used to go to the hospitals and, on the advice of the staff, talk to a number of likely participants. Some were spilling over with unfulfilled dreams and others needed a little encouragement. It was a delicate matter eliciting enough ideas to ensure a genuine surprise on the programme, and not showing when we thought something might be possible.

There was a major problem in the gaps between researching, and then recording and transmission. Anything could happen with patients over that time; they could deteriorate too much to be able to take part, or make a remarkable recovery and be discharged. They could also change their minds about appearing. However, the production schedule was not always the end of our troubles with some patients and I found myself looking back wistfully on the unpredictability of performing animals!

One elderly lady had led me to believe that her spoonful of sugar could only be provided by Isobel Baillie singing *I Know that My Redeemer Liveth*. So, we were very pleased to have that beautiful singer in the hospital ward waiting behind a curtain. The presenter and the lady got around to her favourite music and the moment had come. However, she now insisted that her favourite singer was Cliff Richard and she would not budge. Only after some gentle bullying was she finally persuaded to settle graciously for Isobel Baillie. The other production heart failure I recall was at a nursing home. I had found a quite voluble gentleman, but he did not seem to have any special requests. I finally put out feelers about long lost relatives, and discovered that he had a sister in Australia whom he had not seen for over half a lifetime. After some detective work she was tracked down and flown over at vast expense. I shall never forget his expressionless face when the curtain went back to reveal the surprise, and his flat voice saying, 'Ooh …'er?'

By the mid 60s Rose Hill was still humming along with lodgers and tenants. However, after twelve years its central role in my own family's life was coming to an end. Dan was independent and well into his career with BOAC (now BA), Nicholas was at art college and Christina about to go to university. My own day-to-day mothering role was therefore also finishing, and though I was very busy with my BBC work, it was not enough. I wanted to contribute substantially at last to a worthwhile social venture and felt the energy and enthusiasm to do it. I was not trained in social work, could not offer regular structured time and was not really a committee person. What I could offer, though, was some of myself and, crucially, Rose Hill.

Over the summer of 1965 I thought about my own future and that of Rose Hill. I went as far as putting the house on the market and watched disconsolately as couples wandered round, mostly declaring it full of character but unworkable. More depressing still, developers tramped over it and the grounds, estimating how many flats would fit on the cleared site. I knew what was the sensible thing to do, not least financially, but I just could not do it; I saw it as an act of murder. Rose Hill with its garden had been such a wonderful home to both my family and many other people, and an informal neighbourhood social centre. I felt that the price people often paid for privacy in apartment blocks and separate houses was a terrible loneliness. Houses like Rose Hill allowed people to lead private lives but within a feeling of community. My own experience as a single parent provided the inspiration for an idea. I discussed it with the children and was heartened by their support.

The 1960s was a time of liberation in so many ways, particularly sexual liberation, but social trends never move forward neatly in interlinking packages. So, although the illegitimacy rate was rising and adoption no longer the only option considered, the stigma of unmarried motherhood remained strong. This presented not only emotional, but also very real practical problems for single mothers and babies.

The 1965 report of the National Council for the Unmarried Mother and her Child said:

> There is almost no accommodation in this country for the unmarried mother who wishes to make a home for her child. Until adequate provision for flatlets has been made, many unmarried mothers will fail in their attempts to give their children a secure home. Moreover many responsible unmarried girls who have the capacity to care for their children may well have been forced to have them adopted because they realise that there is nowhere that they could live ... Pioneer experiments in providing flatlets seem a suitable field for voluntary effort.

At that time the illegitimacy rate in Manchester was very much higher than the national rate.

My idea became reality at astonishing speed, and for this I was grateful to a nucleus of enthusiastic and knowledgeable people. First I talked it over on the telephone with a friend who was a businessman and had already done sterling voluntary work in a different field. He paused for about half a minute and told me to meet him for lunch that day. He had with him a friend who was a senior social worker, and the three of us had a meeting that afternoon with the assistant medical officer of health at Manchester Town Hall. Within an hour the Rose Hill Trust for

Unsupported Mothers and Babies was born and it lasted for fourteen years.

Like any organisation, the Rose Hill Trust first needed to set up its structure. Trustees were appointed and friends recruited within the useful professions – a surveyor, an architect, an accountant and a solicitor. A case committee was formed with representatives from the Social Services Department and relevant voluntary agencies. A *Guardian* advertisement for voluntary helpers produced a marvellous response and a house committee got down to organising the house and ways of raising money. However, we strove to keep bureaucracy to a minimum and not to lose sight of the goal, which was to provide a home, where mothers and children felt welcome and safe but not over-scrutinised. The nursery became our showplace, but visitors met the residents or viewed their flats only by invitation.

We had worked out that if my family retreated into a smaller area of the house, it would probably divide into six one-roomed flatlets, leaving a big room for a nursery, with a laundry and drying-room in the basement. The first resident nurse was trained at the Princess Christian school and very important in setting up the nursery and establishing its standards. Later nurses, still carefully chosen but sometimes receiving training on the job, all had a small child themselves. This meant that at any one time six mothers and children were benefiting from the trust. The Public Health Department approved our plans and over the next year the flats were hewed out of the fabric of Rose Hill; walls were put up or knocked down, doorways created or blocked up, kitchen areas and bathrooms fitted, painting and furnishing done. There was never any doubt about the need for the accommodation and there was a constant flow of referrals to the case committee. The first residents were installed almost before we began and so the reconstruction was woven around comings and goings.

From the beginning we were clear that we were going to provide self-contained accommodation, not a hostel. Rose Hill was my home too, but I was away quite a lot and was in no sense a warden. This meant that we would have to let the rooms to girls who were responsible and who really desperately wanted to keep their babies. Not only that, but we could not take on people with serious problems, or those unable to get on reasonably well with others and be mutually supportive. Because we were a charity receiving public funds and much local support, we needed two basic rules: people had to start using the nursery within a reasonable time and men could not stay overnight. Through the careful work of the case committee and some on-the-spot ironing out of problems, Rose Hill largely managed to maintain an equilibrium and a positive and happy atmosphere. This is what allowed the residents, particularly the smallest ones, to flourish.

And flourish they did. The average stay was around two years; we had guidelines but they were flexible. This time enabled mothers to have a breather, recover from what were sometimes extremely sad or traumatic experiences surrounding the birth of their child, and take steps about their future. Some people resumed previous jobs or courses, and others surprised everyone, not least themselves, by embarking on further education and aiming for a different kind of life from that which might previously have been mapped out for them. In time residents established themselves on a financial footing sufficient to move out to a bigger flat or to share a flat with a friend. Some got married.

It seems melodramatic to put it this way, but the disastrous pregnancy turned out to be the cloud with a silver lining for some Rose Hill girls. One, who had left school very early many years before, resumed her education with some trepidation, but then carried on doggedly until she got an Open University degree. One of my uses as an older friend, when we discussed possibilities, was to provide encouragement and get practical advice. I also did not hesitate to pull any strings I could to open a door. Each term as my own privileged daughter went back to university, with her space to grow up and have fun, we were both very conscious of life's unfairness. But in time things came full circle with our early families. One Rose Hill baby ended up at my daughter's Oxford college. The ironies did not end there. Years later, Christina found herself being interviewed as a prospective adoptive parent and was asked about her attitude to relinquishing mothers. The social worker did not expect to hear that she had lived with many unmarried mothers, some of whom had rescued their babies from the 'jaws of adoption'!

The early Rose Hill Trust days were not all easy. We discovered that to some people the whole idea of helping unmarried mothers was anathema: 'They knew what they were doing, let them take the consequences.' Well, it became clear to us that some of our residents had *not* known the consequences, or had got pregnant the first (and sometimes only) time they had had sex. The popular image of the promiscuous fun-loving girl receded into myth, as the stories emerged. The amazing thing to me is that thirty years later young people can still be astonishingly ignorant about the basic facts and our society is still arguing about the value of sex education.

The Rose Hill fathers inevitably tended to lack identity or involvement, but the house in no way harboured a dislike of men. Not least, we had too many marvellous men working for the trust, raising money and being part of residents' new social lives. Clearly, not all our active supporters were paid up members of the sexual revolution; we were in fact a pretty solid and untrendy bunch. But people were moved by the children's right to grow up ideally with their parent and the women's courage and determination to create good and stable homes. The Rose Hill Trust changed people, both residents and helpers.

The trust went through various stages in its life cycle, as charities tend to, according to the commitments and energies of helpers and the characteristics of residents. We had some high-profile help; Thora Hird did a radio appeal and Godfrey Winn wrote an article in *Woman*. At the local level there were some memorable fund-raising events and working parties from clubs and schools. Residents always socialised within the house and during a particularly lively period we had lots of group activities, including art, yoga and cookery classes and concert parties.

The Honorary Secretary, Joan Livesey, saw the trust through from start to finish and was my permanent 'right-hand person'. For a long time the arrival every morning of Peter Burke, our postman, was the first big event of the nursery day. Peter, Mike Gould, our friendly neighbourhood policeman, and Frank Marlor, the gardener, were all embodiments of the saying 'over and above the call of duty'. They probably did not realise their significance to the children as caring and reliable male figures, but they were important. It must have seemed to Frank a very long time ago, when he first worked at Rose Hill long before our time, that he was reprimanded for hanging a hoe on a wrong nail in the garden shed. I wrote in one annual report:

> Times have certainly changed since then, but the shrubberies, paths and grassy slopes set out by some Victorian gardener still give great pleasure to our nursery children; they provide all the adventure that is needed at the age of two. It is delightful to see a line of very small children totter into a rhododendron bush and emerge half a minute later at the other end, still in line,

still tottering, and looking as pleased as though they had discovered the source of the Nile.

In the summer of 1973 we had a wonderful garden party, with games and music and dancing, to celebrate my own family's arrival at Rose Hill twenty years before. Many 'old girls' of the trust came with their children, and we had a birthday cake and sang 'Happy birthday, dear Rose Hill, happy birthday to you.'

By the beginning of 1979 the referrals were drying up and it was apparent that the trust was no longer filling a need. Since 1966 we had witnessed a revolution in family and social attitudes about unmarried mothers and services available to them, and places like Rose Hill had become only one of many options. That year I had a friend to stay who had worked with the Ockenden Venture and she thought that the house would be perfect for a reception centre for Vietnamese 'boat people'. The government had just made a major commitment to accept more Vietnamese refugees from Hong Kong and the Ockenden Venture was one of three main agencies involved in receiving and resettling them.

I got in touch with the Ockenden Venture and found out as much as I could about its work and its background. During the reception period families received medical check-ups, intensive English tuition and orientation to the country, and were helped to formulate their resettlement plans. The Rose Hill Trust was wound up and towards Christmas the first group of Vietnamese families moved in.

Those of us involved felt in retrospect that our efforts were worthwhile, but it was in many ways a disheartening time. Refugees mostly arrived still in a state of profound shock from their experiences, grateful though they were to be physically safe. There were medical problems to be addressed and, more significantly, enormous problems of adjustment – climate, food, language, English customs. The winter here brought surprises; some of the boys fell into the pond in Fletcher Moss Park because they would not believe me when I told them that the ice was fragile. We had a wonderful group of people working formally with the Vietnamese, such as the English teachers and the interpreter, Father Tien, a Vietnamese Catholic priest who had been in this country for eighteen years, and without whom the house simply could not have operated. We had dedicated volunteers, notably some of the local police led by Alec Harris, and members of the Jewish community, who told me that they understood only too well what being a refugee felt like. We got mountains of bedding, toys and clothes (huge men's suits for the tiny fine-boned Vietnamese), although my tactful efforts to stem the flow offended some.

However, what we did not really get was a general acceptance of or real interest in the newcomers. English people found the culture and language barrier as impenetrable as the Vietnamese did themselves and were at a loss as to how to cope with it. I understood this. I had to learn myself, with difficulty, but I discovered that the refugees responded to physical contact in place of the flow of conversation, and were happy just to sit in an English sitting-room and have a cup of tea. But there were deeper shocks too. After spending all day at Rose Hill encouraging the residents in their struggles with English, our English teachers used to meet a wave of dislike from passers-by as they came out of our gates. Through my close contact with these people sharing my house I had a sobering idea of the problems that lay ahead for them.

About twenty-five Vietnamese refugees in all came to Rose Hill from Hong Kong. I am still in touch with some of them, now scattered around the country, and the picture is by no means all gloomy, especially for the younger ones. One baby boy born from Rose Hill narrowly missed being registered as 'Olive', and Oliver, it seems, is growing up well.

By the end of 1980 I was beginning to feel too old to remain at the hub of a refugee reception centre. So, I waited until all the residents were settled and at last sold Rose Hill. I found a small terraced house in Stephens Terrace, right in the heart of Didsbury village, and moved there in January 1981. After a week of sleepless nights, I knew that I had made a mistake.

14 1981–92 – Stephens Terrace

Not long after my move from Rose Hill I asked a friend round to spend the evening with me. She is an art teacher and painter and as she was leaving she said, 'It is silly. I am going back to my dark empty house, you will bolt your door behind me, and we shall probably both switch on television to bring our rooms to some sort of life. If we were under the same roof, I might paint for an hour of two, you might write, and we could meet later and have a cup of coffee.' She was absolutely right and her remark encouraged me to think again about my own living arrangements.

My new house in Didsbury was in good condition and well decorated. It was warm, cosy, easy to run and within a few minutes' walk to shops, all the suburb's amenities and public transport into the city. Also there were clearly some nice neighbours. But of course I took some time to settle in there. All house moves are traumatic, particularly as you get older and have to shed a lot of possessions. Also I inevitably felt depressed about leaving Rose Hill, however much of a burden it had recently become. Nevertheless I felt instinctively that I had made the wrong decision in moving. The kind of life provided by Rose Hill, to which I had clung tenaciously for so long, did seem right for me. I now had plenty of time to think about why this should be so and speculate on whether my ideas on 'community living' might be shared by other people.

Many people live alone quite happily, but some feel hemmed in by a burden of loneliness and lack of stimulation. Furthermore, fighting the resulting depression takes a good deal of energy which could be used in other ways. Sitting on committees, attending lectures at adult education colleges, visiting country houses are good, but they are the trimmings, and it is the twenty-four-hour basis of life that needs to be right. When I made that house move, at seventy, I was in that period of life after retirement which is now much longer and healthier for many people than ever before, and when the days of sheltered housing with a warden on the end of a bell push still seem a long way off. I felt certain that there was a growing body of people in this country, men and women, retired or coming up to retirement, who would welcome some kind of community living. And yet there seemed to be no organisation tackling this problem in the way the Gray Panthers had done in America.

While I was still at Rose Hill I had put out feelers to people and organisations who might have been interested in using part of the house as an arts or community centre. There was quite a lot of interest in this idea, but funding was inevitably a problem. I had to have some sort of return from my only asset and most of the likely groups ran on a shoestring.

A few months after my move, in August 1981, the *Manchester Evening News* published an article floating my idea for community living and the response was dramatic. I got letters from people in very varied circumstances, who all felt willing to surrender some of their autonomy and privacy for a community ideal. Some people rang choked with tears because someone had actually put this down on paper. One woman wrote that her pleasant flat was 'safe and quiet – but so is the grave'. Two former residents of the Rose Hill Trust, just as lonely on their own with their teenage children as they had been when they first left the house, were also very keen to be involved. From these contacts emerged a woman who became my partner in this venture and we began to work actively to try to achieve our goal. She was also a widow with her own house, and between us we pursued a number of possible properties in our part of Manchester. Unfortunately, though, she eventually had to withdraw because of family difficulties.

During this period I prepared a 'statement' setting out my ideas, which was sent out to any person or organisation expressing the least interest in the idea. It briefly covered my own background, including the Rose Hill Trust, and went on:

With the active interest of one or two other people I am looking for a large house in this part of Manchester which could be made into five or six flatlets but with a common sitting-room or even kitchen.

I have approached a good many organisations and they find the idea good, but so far very little has been achieved. Older people are naturally cautious about committing themselves to a new way of life, and in many cases there are difficulties about selling a house and realising capital ...

The practical advantages of sharing a roof are clear; expense is one. There is also the question of security; many older people do not go out at night now because of a fear of mugging and of coming back to a dark, empty house; car owners could help non-car owners; pets become a possibilty again; holidays less difficult to take; the dangers of a fall, a heart attack or a stroke are very real to people living alone. Support and caring need only be minimal if that is the way some people want it, but they are not to be despised.

There are two extensions to the scheme which, I think, are worth considering. One is that we should try to reproduce a 'family' situation, with a wide age-range. This would mean that while some people could buy themselves into the scheme, others could only join in if they could pay rent. All the same, the dangers of 'ageism', the classifying of people by chronological age, would recede. The other idea is of having workshops in the house or of holding classes there. When I ran the home for mothers and babies, we had classes on cookery, painting, arts and crafts, yoga and so on, and this way the outside world came into the house. Unfortunately both these ideas remove us still further from any known category of organisation in this country.

There would be difficulties on the human side, I know. But having shared a home with other people for fifteen years I think some of us would find them easier than coping with the problems of loneliness.

Over the next two to three years there were articles in my local newspaper and *Prospero*, the magazine for retired BBC staff, radio interviews, and correspondence and meetings with interested individuals and organisations such as housing associations. Coincidentally Katharine Whitehorn wrote a splendid article in the *Observer* called 'Growing Old in Groups', which aroused a great deal of interest. She and I established contact, and my partner and I offered to be the focus for this interest. We then handled the correspondence Katharine Whitehorn had received, offering to put people in touch with each other in other parts of the country.

Sadly, despite all this activity and optimism, nothing got off the ground. Many people were interested, but no one was available with the right practical knowledge to push the idea through to a positive conclusion. The necessary elements just did not come together at the same time: the right people with the right skills and resources, the right property, the appropriate legal and bureacratic structure. Our failure lay partly in not fitting in to any existing organisational pattern, and not having the knowledge or energy to create a new one for ourselves. As time went on, I had to accept that I personally would probably not be a part of such a new venture. Nevertheless, I still believe strongly in the idea and would be delighted to learn that households along these lines have been established.

My association with Rose Hill ceased totally when I sold it. However, in 1984 I took the opportunity to have one last look over it before viewing it vicariously through the television screen. The house was between owners and was used for the filming of a television play, *December Flower*, which had a distinguished cast of Jean Simmons, Bryan Forbes, Mona Washbourne and Pat Heywood. There were brief outside shots but the interior scenes also were all done in the house. I and some of my family saw the play when it went out and experienced the odd sensation of seeing on the screen details of a place you know so well.

At the end of 1980 I attended a very happy occasion at the then Manchester Polytechnic, when I received an Honorary Fellowship for my radio work over the years. The group of six honoured that day included Reg Harris, the former world cycling champion, and a very special hero of mine, James Cameron, the journalist.

I received another honour on a more local level when a new kindergarten in Didsbury was named the Olive Shapley Kindergarten. The kindergarten was the brainchild of a Didsbury woman who had been on the BBC staff, Lyn Hunter. She and a partner gained the use of some beautiful premises, which were part of St Paul's Methodist Church Hall in Didsbury. Just before Christmas in 1981 the kindergarten was opened by Stuart Hall, the BBC television personality. It was a lovely event, with the newly enrolled pupils trying out all the equipment and activities, and somebody appearing as Father Christmas. It was an occasion for interested Didsbury and Manchester people to get together, among them Sir William Downward, the Lord Lieutenant of Greater Manchester. I had known Bill Downward for a long time and he was one of the nicest people I had ever met.

My connection with the BBC was quite strongly maintained one way and another over these last years in Didsbury, even apart from keeping up with old colleagues and socialising in the bar at New Broadcasting House. I was very pleased to be invited to become a member of the council of BBC Radio Manchester, and I served on it for three years. Local radio was one of the BBC innovations which had occurred towards the end of my career and it seemed to me the ideal in expressing a locality's unique personality and bringing broadcasting close to its audience and vice versa; a very long way indeed from John Reith's early lofty vision. I also continued to do some broadcasting myself, mostly interviews on my career for both network and local radio, and of course as time went by there were fewer and fewer of us around who had worked for the BBC before the war.

However, in 1985 I got the chance to do some more substantial work than responding to a guest interview. A radio series was produced in Manchester called *Classic Features*, in which four particularly interesting programmes were repeated: Stephen Potter's *Undergraduate Summer* from 1939; Jennifer Wayne's *A Week in Chalet Land* (1948); Denis Mitchell's *People Talking* (1958); and *Song of a Road*, which Charles Parker had produced in 1959 with songs and music by Ewan MacColl and Peggy Seeger. Alastair Wilson, the producer, asked me to introduce all the programmes, and write and broadcast the linking script for the first one. This was about the work of the 'Manchester group' in the 1930s of which I was a part, or, as the *Radio Times* put it, 'pink times and pinker programmes'. I described how 'we wanted to wrest John Reith's BBC from the grip of the stuffed shirts by taking the microphone out of the studio and into the country at large'. It was a most enjoyable opportunity to listen to some of those fascinating programmes again and hear the recorded voices of people I had known and worked with.

By the end of the 1980s I was finding it less easy to visit the BBC and keep up with friends that way. So, it was a surprise and a great honour to be told early in 1990 that the BBC was planning to host an eightieth birthday dinner for me. The dinner was held at New Broadcasting House. I had helped compile the guest list and it was such a pleasure to be surrounded by old friends and colleagues. These included Barney Colehan, Michael Barton, Trevor Hill, Stanley Williamson, Michael Green, Alfred Bradley, Gillian Hush, Don Haworth, Alastair Wilson, Bernice Coupe and John Reed. For several years I had been a devoted member of the BBC Philharmonic Club, including a period as a vice-president. So I was delighted that on this occasion we were entertained by a quartet of players from the BBC Philharmonic Orchestra. This had added poignancy for me, because just after the war my first husband, John Salt, had helped gather together the first nucleus of musicians which grew into this fine orchestra.

I have never considered myself particularly musical, though as a child I did achieve some competence on the piano. Nevertheless, for me, as for so many people, music has enormous evocative power and punctuates all of life's memories. *Desert Island Discs*, the radio programme devised and for many years presentd by Roy Plomley, is testimony to this. Some people might refuse an invitation to be the guest, but I imagine for reasons other than an inability to conjure up any musical memories. Towards the end of my BBC career I devised and broadcast some radio programmes for the BBC North Region *Talkabout* series which I called *Very Occasional Music*. For these I chose pieces of music that I loved and had particular associations with periods in my life. Later I also prepared and presented an entire programme on American folk music. My choices in these various programmes included some pieces that I have already mentioned, like *Omaha*, and pieces and performers from my 'American period': *The Skaters' Waltz* and *Sunny Side of the Street*, Pete Seeger, Leadbelly and Burl Ives. I cannot imagine what my wildly eclectic selection revealed about my personality, but I was grateful for the painstaking work of the BBC Gramophone Library in matching my memories.

15 1926–83 – Travel

In my childhood I did not belong to a travelling family. 'Abroad' was not something we envisaged for ourselves. Only rich families travelled abroad, we thought. Indeed I learnt many years later that when John Salt's family had gone to Switzerland in the summer, they took a nurse, a nursemaid, a governess, numerous trunks and the children's own cots.

I was sixteen before I left England and then I went with a Unitarian spinster, a member of our church, who took her nieces and myself to Le Petit Appeville, near Dieppe. It was a modest trip, but I can never be grateful enough for that modesty.

It began badly for me. I was discovered on the cross-channel steamer providently writing my postcard to my parents: 'We have arrived safely in France after a lovely voyage.' I was made to tear it up and scatter the pieces in the English Channel, and providence was not tempted. Immediately on arrival I had a leaflet thrust into my hand, which I proceeded to read. Our guide leapt at me. 'Do not read it, Olive, it may be something *indecent*!' she said, taking it away. I had had time to see that it was advertising a circus. But I was always very sensitive to rebuke and found it discouraging to have made two *faux pas* in the first few hours. However, the great adventure then began.

I remember that we consigned our luggage to a cart and walked along the cliffs to Le Petit Appeville; there was no money to spare on this holiday and this, I came to feel later, made it a valuable one. Gradually the narrow streets of Dieppe petered out and we walked along the clifftop and down into the valley where the tiny village lay. It was a dull, unexciting, completely typical Normandy village. We lodged with Madame le François, widow of the late mayor, in a biggish stone house a mile or two from the sea and half a mile from the main road. As we trudged into the courtyard, we passed the kitchen window, where Madame's daughter, Mademoiselle Marie, was making the 'potage' for our evening meal. We looked at the reckless piles of eggs and cream and sorrel, and the smell of the soup that later came out of the kitchen has never left me. For me no food in France, three-star restaurant or not, has ever tasted as good.

Everything about that holiday was strange and delightful; the routine, breakfast and *goûter* under the cherry tree, the path through the vegetable garden to the outside lavatory, the carefully planned outings. To Rouen by train, to Varengeville on our own feet. To the great Norman castle at Arques, to the chateau at Miromesnil where Guy de Maupassant was born. Ever the one to put my foot in it, I asked who Guy de Maupassant was. 'He skated on thin ice,' was the answer and I remember it to this day. We were a serious little party, intent on getting to know France, and all the time the sea thundered and the bees buzzed, the birds sang, there was the smell of apples and clover and at night the bats swooped round the tower of the little Romanesque church a few feet away from my bedroom window. That part of the world is as clear in my mind today as it was then, and I am deeply grateful that I first encountered France on my two aching feet and not from the back seat of my parents' motor car or from an aeroplane.

Although my father never left England, and was a moderate traveller even here, it was through him that I first knew the world. As well as his favourite *The Egyptian Book of the Dead*, H.G. Wells's *Outline of History* made my father and myself familiar with past civilisations. When I went to Persepolis I could have wept that he had never seen that place except through Wells's pictures. But, years and years too late, I came to value him. Through him I had pictured since I was ten years old the west door of the Norman church at Kilpeck in Herefordshire and when I finally saw it, I felt as if I was seeing it for us both. On our annual holiday at Deal in Kent my father and I would stand on the darkening promenade and look out to France. 'Cap Griz Nez,' he would say, as the flashing lights came on. But I believe he had no desire to go there. It was enough for him to realise that 'abroad' existed. It was enough that he could read about it in his books.

When my time came to travel independently, I did not for years make very much of my chances. For my generation, Paris was enough. Whenever we could scrape together the fare, it was to Paris we went, staying in dark little hotels on the Left Bank, spending all day in cafés over bitter Amer Picon or Noilly Cassis, putting the world to rights. I can still call up pictures of Paris at all times of the year, particularly in the winter when the ice was inches thick on the fountains of the Jardins de Luxembourg. There is nothing to say about the Paris of the 1930s that has not been said already and it still seems to me a good time to have been young. Everything we believed in so passionately seems to have been proved wrong, but the years of believing were good ones. Because our travels were so limited, we experienced them with intensity. Later on I met many more bored young people on the roads of India than I ever met in the cafés of the Left Bank.

One thing that I was determined my own children would have was itchy feet. Their education began early from my years in the BBC. Whenever possible I saved the best and most interesting jobs for the school holidays. This way they came to know England when they were quite young. 'Guess where we're going tomorrow?' I would say three days after Christmas. 'Mablethorpe!' It could have been Katmandu. We would set out on icy roads with minimal luggage and playing cards, Ludo, sketch pads and crayons for the dull parts, and while I interviewed a lady who, say, made unusual tea-cosies, the children would amuse themselves. 'How shall we go home?' I mused when my work was done. 'By the Roman wall,' someone would say. And so we covered the north of England, finding incredibly cheap lodgings for us all on my expenses and becoming familiar with byways, little lost churches, rivers and moors.

Later this enthusiasm was turned on the continent. I can think of nothing in my whole life which has given me more pleasure than packing the car at 3 a.m. and setting out with a carload of children for the south, seeing the dawn at Lichfield and the sun come up, getting the early morning boat at Dover, and setting our faces for the continent. I can think of no better gift one could give one's children, together with the ability and desire to draw on these memories in later life.

Nevertheless, I did not foresee that one of my children would repay this gift admirably by deciding to make his career in an airline. Dan's decision has worked extremely well for him, and, as his mother, I was for years entitled to concessionary fares. This was why one year my family sat around our dining table among the debris of a Christmas dinner working out 'Round the World ... Mum's Itinerary'. I then carried this same piece of paper around for two months of travel, while it got steadily grubbier and more creased, and I never deviated from it. It was studied solemnly at airports in Jamaica, Fiji, Hong Kong ... 'Ah yes, Mum's Itinerary'. That's a good emotive word – 'Mum'.

It was a memorable journey, and one of the aspects of it that I still remember most clearly was the variety of people I met. I discovered that if you travel alone, you *really* meet people. Accompanied by a husband or friend you are safe, and you need never leave that little territory you create for yourselves. But as a widow, on your own for two months, you have to put out feelers, lay yourself open. Waiting through the night in airport lounges, sitting by the roadside under a mango tree, walking through the gardens of a Japanese temple, you strike up close, almost intimate, relationships with people whose names you are never going to know. A good and interesting talk, a wave of the hand and you go your different ways.

Being London-born but a northern resident for a very long time, I discovered that these chance encounters could be peculiarly enriched if you came from the north of England. The best route from Hull to Carlisle, the beauties of Northumbria against those of Cumbria; with what passion I have discussed topics like these in different parts of the world. I remember sitting in the ruins of a Mongol fort in the desert outside Tehran and hearing a Yorkshireman telling of the exploits of the Brighouse Light Operatic Society. For a long time just living in Manchester was, as most travelling Mancunians know, an immediate introduction almost everywhere in the world. I have sat on the edge of a village well in India and seen the faces light up. 'Manchester United,' people would say, and there was always a knowledgeable one who added, 'Georgie Best, Bobby Charlton.'

One of my oddest experiences on my round-the-world trip was unexpectedly coming down on a strip of sandy beach in the New Hebrides (as it was called then) on a flight in a small aircraft between Fiji and the Solomon Islands. There were only four passengers, and conversation with the Dutch priest and the Japanese nun was clearly limited. The other passenger was a man who looked as though he was English.

'You're from England?' he said in a bored voice.

'From Manchester,' I replied.

'Oh,' he said, 'I taught at Manchester Grammar School. Where do you live?'

'Didsbury,' I said.

'Oh,' he said, 'I used to live in Didsbury ... before I went to Australia.'

Now, he remembered my road, but I *could not* remember his, so there, in the burning sands of the New Hebrides, he took out a twig and sketched out his corner of Didsbury. We were soon surrounded by a half-circle of naked children and mangy dogs. (I wish I could write 'men with bows and arrows' because they still had them in the New Hebrides, but it would not be strictly true.) And then we got back on our plane and never spoke again, but for me that was a very heart-warming episode, considering that we were in the Pacific and about as far from Didsbury, mile-wise, as you could get.

People at home were ready with dire prophecies before I went.

'You'll be bullied,' they said. Well, of course. If you go to a hotel alone and there is a rotten little table near the serving-doors, you will get it. 'And everyone will be served before you.' True of many countries, I found.

'You will be bored,' they said. Never, though sometimes one longed for news of England. Whenever I travelled I always took two kinds of book – books about the places I was going to visit and thrillers. (As a complete escape route in the middle of Sri Lanka, I know of nothing better than an ingenious murder in an English country house.) But, all the same, when you do come across a four-week old copy of the *Guardian Weekly*, you can hardly believe your luck. By the time I reached Katmandu I was beginning to feel a little cut off, and when I saw the news-seller putting out his wares under the banyan tree at night and spotted a three-year-old copy of *Woman* with a picture of a baby in a knitted vest on the cover, I almost burst into tears. But he would not let me buy it. He clutched it to him as though it were some rare manuscript.

'No, you may not buy,' he said but, seeing my face, 'you may sit down here and *look*.' Which I did and read every word of it.

'You will be lonely,' they said. A little, perhaps, but a curious fact emerged. I had imagined myself in hotel dining-rooms surrounded by happy, laughing families with children; and this, I felt, might be painful. But it never happened. People who travel considerable distances are either old or young, it seemed to me. The middle years do not allow this freedom to most people, concerned with jobs and families. And many of the elderly couples I encountered in Katmandu or Delhi or Tokyo had obviously said all they wanted to say to each other long ago. Meals were taken in silence and sometimes there was even a feeling of animosity. When I talked with them, it became clear that for some people, not all of course, this trip of a lifetime, saved up for, eagerly awaited, was now rather a bore. The best part would be showing those hundreds of slides to the neighbours.

With the very young it was different. Mostly they did not even *see* you. Sometimes they were very friendly. I stayed with some hippies in Katmandu, and for that invitation to come about you simply had to be on your own.

I also realised early on that one saw so much more alone. One day, again in Katmandu, I met a delightful American couple, both schoolteachers taking a year off. We found a lot to talk about, the London theatre, concerts, books. We were on a trip to Batghaon, one of the most beautiful cities of Nepal, but it was only when we got back that we realised that we had really seen very little. We agreed that we would limit ourselves to a polite nod if we met again.

One of the saddest things, travelling alone, was that there was no one to laugh with. Going round some of the beautiful Hindu temples in Katmandu with an elderly American couple, the name 'Krishna' was naturally woven into every sentence uttered by our earnest Nepalese guide. Finally the woman brightened and said, 'Oh, to think they have Hare Krishna groups in Katmandu, just like us!'

In the Solomon Islands I went to an evening lecture at the little Gulbenkian Museum. Some of the small English community were there, ladies in pinnies getting the tea and biscuits ready just like any Women's Institute here. The central aisle was flanked by statues of the old pagan gods of the Solomons, immense carved wooden figures with what I can only describe as very large 'appendages' almost meeting over the aisle. To spare our blushes, the ladies had thoughtfully hung damp tea-towels over them. They could not have made them more conspicuous. And I had no one to laugh with.

One of the closest friends I made on the journey round the world alone lived in Delhi. He was an Indian, a man in his sixties and he was deaf and dumb. He had been educated in England in the days when deaf children were not taught to speak. But he was a great communicator all the same. He worked in a tourist lodge as a kind of social secretary, which says a great deal for the imaginative thinking of the Indians who ran that lodge. So the spoken word is not always necessary and the written one will do. This man and I filled pages of rough paper – posters, backs of menus – and when I took my nine-year-old grandson to meet him on a later visit to Delhi, Aaron, no great one for writing, filled pages too. I looked up some of those scribbles later and one was all about the Wirral Peninsula. How odd! But people, and the bonds you make with them, are infinite in their variety.

A 'love of travel' has almost become a cliché for western people, to the point where to admit a strong preference for staying put at home might be considered rather odd. Foreign travel, however, means so many different things to different people, from a simple desire to relax every now and then in comfortable, undemanding surroundings in a warm climate to lengthy and serious low-cost treks off the beaten track in a dwindling range of unspoilt locations. I think, though, that almost everyone whose awareness extends beyond their own street harbours their own travel dream, their *Desert Island Discs* destination, whose fascination endures for them for whatever reason, be it the Galapagos Islands or Disneyland. The vast difference between the ordinary experience of my youth and that of today is that many more people now actually get to fulfil their dream.

For years I longed to go to the Himalayas and I did finally go, several times no less, and was not disappointed. My first visit was with my sons and we found that approaching the Himalayas from the south was just like tracing their appearance on a map of India as your eyes move northwards. This vast wall rises from the plains, so high that you cannot believe that there are mountains, not clouds, before you, the Sanskrit 'abode of snow'. Their sheer scale is hard for Europeans to encompass: 29,000 feet compared with Mont Blanc's 15,000 and Snowdon's modest 3,500. In other respects the scene is curiously familiar, with the streams, rock, rhododendrons and azaleas of the Lake District, and only the monkeys to strike a discordant note.

We went to Darjeeling, 'Queen of Hill Stations', founded by the British at the height of the Raj and still dominated by beautiful houses and trees. It is a fascinating town blending relics of the Raj, churches, shops, parks and pillar-boxes with a mixture of hill people, Tibetans, holy men, ponies and porters. The 'Everest' guest house fulfilled to perfection its expected role, providing comfort in the form of gas fires, hot-water bottles and morning tea in bed, with porridge and queen of puddings on the menu.

A major focus of this visit to the Himalayas, and one which I was to develop more closely during my two further visits, was the Tibetan community. This is partly centred on Sikkim, a small state wedged between Nepal and Bhutan, pushed by its maharajah into general western consciousness a few years before my first visit by his marriage to an American girl, Hope Cooke. Gangtok is the capital of Sikkim, a little like an American frontier town, and seven miles away, across a steep valley and paddy fields, is the Tibetan Buddhist monastery of Rumtek.

We spent three days in the guest house at Rumtek. The military police did not allow longer stays. It was rather like being transported back to the Middle Ages; sitting in the sun in the courtyard, with the monks chanting in the prayer-hall, cows and goats rooting about, little monks learning their lessons, and over all the smell of wood smoke from the kitchens.

Rumtek was fascinating enough in itself, but at that time it held an additional element of interest for me: Freda Bedi, with whom, together with Barbara Castle, I had been such close friends at Oxford. She had been born Freda Houlston, in Derbyshire, and now was K.T. Khechog Palmo, a Tibetan Buddhist nun.

Freda and I did all our talking in her room at the monastery where she had gone for a period of meditation; she was only allowed to leave this room when she went across the flat roof to see her guru. The room was cool and rather dark, with red walls, and windows opening on to the mountainside. There was a box bed in one corner, a mat for meditation, a table with Tibetan books wrapped up in cloth, a picture of the Dalai Lama, a vase of peacock feathers, a butter lamp. Freda's very few personal possessions included paper and a fountain pen and photographs of her children. She was looked after by a little Tibetan nun, called Pema, who never stopped smiling and making tea for us. Once, in sheer pleasure at having visitors, she struggled in with one of the monastery's peacocks in her arms and set it down among us on the floor.

In spite of Freda's shaven head, and the saffron and maroon robes of a nun, I found her very unchanged, with her still incredibly pale blue eyes. Dan and Nicholas thought I was tactless when I said several times, 'You haven't changed a bit.' But to me she had not. A few years later, when Freda was staying with me in Didsbury, we drove out into Derbyshire and made an unannounced visit to an elderly aunt. This lady opened the door on the rather unusual sight of a Buddhist nun and said, without batting an eyelid, 'Oh, hello, Freda, lovely to see you. Come in and have a cup of tea.'

When I first knew her at Oxford Freda was a very convinced Christian. On her marriage to Bedi, a Sikh from the Punjab, she went to live in India. People were very gloomy about their marriage but it was a great success, and they had three children, now grown up. Their son, Kabir, became an enormously successful film star, both in India and internationally. Freda and Bedi were very active in the fight for Indian independence, and Freda worked as a writer, a lecturer and a social worker. As the years went by she became more and more interested in Buddhism, found a teacher and began meditation. After about eight weeks, so she told me, she got her first flash of understanding, and from then on her life was changed. She became a Buddhist, but she went on leading a very busy life as the mother of a family, and in her work.

When the Dalai Lama and many of his people escaped to India from the Chinese in 1959, Freda's life took another turn. There were a great many monks in Tibet and about a quarter of the refugees were monks. When they took that appalling journey across the ice and snow they brought their culture and their long religious tradition with them. All this might have been in danger in exile. So, with the support of the Dalai Lama and the prime minister, Mr Nehru, Freda started up a school in Delhi for some of the younger lamas, the incarnate lamas, the ones into whom, the Buddhists believe, the soul of an earlier lama has passed. It was called the Young Lamas Home School.

Freda and I came out of her room at Rumtek and the setting could hardly have been further removed from her early one as a schoolgirl in Derbyshire. It was dark and the mists were swirling in. The courtyard was crowded with monks, and, up on the flat roof, among the fluttering prayer flags, the trumpets were being blown to announce the return of His Holiness, Karmapa, to the monastery.

When I saw Freda on my next visit to India she arranged for me to meet the Dalai Lama. I found him unpretentious and easy to talk to. He asked me, 'Tell me, what do you call Khechog Palmo?' I said, 'Well, I'm afraid I still call her Freda.' And the Dalai Lama said, 'I call her Mummy.' In 1977 I met Freda again in India, at the YMCA in Delhi, where we had a very happy reunion. But it turned out be our last, because Freda died very suddenly just a few weeks later, before I had returned to England.

I had for a long time been interested in Tibetans and their culture, even before Freda and I resumed active contact with each other. The Tibet Society and in particular the Tibetan Friendship Group enabled people like me to channel our interest into contributing in a small way to the welfare of Tibetan refugees in India. During the course of my activity I met through Freda a young man, Thupten Chophel, with whom I established an instant rapport and who became informally my foster son. Thupten's story was immensely sad, but typical among these 'forgotten' people. His family fled from their home in 1959 and his father and brothers were killed in the advance into India. His mother managed to carry him over the Himalayas, but then collapsed and died in the street. So, Thupten was looked after by the community, received an education and became a secretary in the small hill-station, Mussoorie, with the Tibetan Homes Foundation, which looked after refugee children. He married a nurse, who also worked with the foundation, and they had a family. I went to India for their wedding, but it was delayed because the time was not propitious. Nevertheless, while I was there they did have a party to celebrate their forthcoming marriage.

My visit to India in 1977 was very different from my previous ones. I went overland, a journey which soon after became almost impossible to take, across Europe to Istanbul, then through Turkey, Syria, Iraq, Iran, Baluchistan and Pakistan to India. After some time in India I took the road back, through Afghanistan and into Iran again. I was away four months, travelled 22,500 miles, and the entire journey cost £330. It was not exactly a package tour, but a COMEX, a 'Commonwealth Expedition' journey.

The idea of a Commonwealth Expedition was first conceived in 1963. It was the brainchild of Colonel Lionel Gregory, who had been with the Gurkha regiment and had had a lifelong love affair with India. The idea met with strong support from Mr Nehru and the Duke of Edinburgh. The journeys took place about every two years. The first eight were all overland to India and, having started in the universities, they came to involve about 2,000 young people from all walks of life. Local councils, the police and other service organisations, the public and private sectors were all represented. Involvement spread out from Britain to include other countries, such as Canada, Singapore, Australia and of course India itself. The philosophical base of COMEX was to focus attention on the Commonwealth and to reawaken among ordinary people something of the old relationships, eroded by time and neglect. This style of travel matched very closely my own preferred way. We travelled on very little money, staying in schools and convents rather than hotels. This ensured that we met ordinary Indian people rather than those with status and power. COMEX welcomed a sprinkling of older people too and felt that we had our uses in oiling the wheels of friendship and helping the group rub along together; I believe that we were also considered less complaining if things went wrong!

There were 280 of us on COMEX 8 in 1977 (the queen's jubilee year) and we travelled in eight big silver coaches. I travelled in the 'north-west of England' coach, and there was 'Somerset and Surrey', 'Singapore' and so on. The size of the party sounds horrendous, but it turned out surprisingly manageable. We also lost each other constantly and often deliberately. The itinerary was ingeniously worked out to include various points where coaches had to meet up, but with a lot of flexibility in between. This meant that a coach or smaller groups or individuals could go off and do their 'own thing' for several days at a time.

We passed through every kind of countryside – deserts, mountains, forests, endless little villages and towns – but the variety of human life encountered on that trip seemed endless too. First, there were all the people of the countries we passed through, and the ones I remember most vividly were the nomads of Baluchistan. They were travelling, as their people must have been doing for centuries, from one oasis to the next. With the camel train, the women were muffled up to the eyes in black, the men and boys were on foot herding the animals along, and there was always one camel with a nest of rugs on its back carrying the lambs, the chickens, the babies, all those too young to walk. We learnt very early that these people did not want to be photographed, spoken to, even noticed. On this kind of travel you learn very quickly to be aware of local prejudices and ways in which you might give offence. You learn that the women in your party must be very decently covered in Muslim countries, that you do not use your left hand for eating in India, and, if you stay in a village overnight, you do not refuse a beautiful meal spread out on the floor on spotless newspaper because you are fairly sure that this represents that family's stock of food for quite a few days.

In India, especially, it is very easy to meet people. I had a tooth filled in Poona.

'What do I owe you?' I asked the young dentist.

'My fee,' he said, 'is that you bring some friends and come to tea with me this afternoon.' We went, and he had called in his music teacher and, while we sipped mango juice, they settled down cross-legged on rugs and played a beautiful afternoon raga on sitar and tabla.

We wrote our names and addresses on many grubby slips of paper and they came home to roost. Some years later I had a letter from India, from Trivandrum.

'I am the second cousin of the car park attendant on Kovalam Beach,' it read. 'My cousin was very kind to you.' He was; he extricated me from a very difficult argument with a taxi-driver. 'I would like to bring my family to England. Will you please arrange.' I sent a very carefully thought-out, but regretful reply.

And then there is Indian curiosity. You are never offended by a complete stranger in a bus or train asking you if you are married, what kind of job you do, how much you earn. During a later visit to Simla, an elderly Indian in dhoti and wild turban came up to me and said, 'I have been watching you walking on the Mall. Tell me *exactly* how old you are, and if your teeth are all your own!' You can only answer truthfully.

On our overland trip it was only in India that one could be certain of finding people who spoke English, and I find that snapshots are invaluable in these other, difficult circumstances. Photographs of your family, your house, your pets are studied carefully, and sometimes must be handed over. School photos of your children grinning and almost toothless at the age of seven form an immediate bond. Once on that journey my dog-eared snaps really proved invaluable. We were coming through the desert from Baghdad to the Iranian frontier, we arrived in the middle of the night, all 280 of us, and were not welcome. While the more formal proceedings were under way, a man on our coach had an idea.

'Get your snaps out, Olive,' he said.

I got them out. I have an Iranian daughter-in-law and I knew the words for grandmother in Farsi, the language of Iran. These were indeed the only words I knew.

'Mama Bozoorg,' I said, pointing to myself, and there were the snaps of that part of my family.

'Firoozeh! Jamshid!' I said, pointing and producing very honoured Persian names. Guns went down, we were allowed in the compound, and some of the men began a game of football with the guards.

Another way in which this large, heterogeneous crowd of people on COMEX made friends was through our work. When we stayed for a few days in a town the teachers would go off to look at the schools, the nurses to the hospitals, the police cadets to the jails, and I always went to the radio stations. There was very little television at that time on our route. Immediately I felt at home and could communicate without the need for words. Radio stations sometimes seemed to me the most international of all institutions. In Baghdad I heard a news bulletin being read in an entirely strange tongue but with the authentic rhythm of a BBC newsreader (that man had probably been to London for some training). In Kabul I was invited to a phone-in programme. The whole programme was in Pushtu, of course, of which I do not understand one word, but when a particularly insistent voice came on, I knew they were thinking, 'We've got a right one here.' BBC Radio Manchester seemed very near at times like that!

It was not only the people in the countries we went through who brought the journey alive, but also one's travelling companions. The age range was something like seventeen to sixty-seven, which was the age I reached in Ootacamund. The variety of jobs and backgrounds was also enormous. We spent long hours in those non-air-conditioned coaches, and tempers could easily become frayed. Our north-west England coach, carrying thirty-eight of us, was usually fairly untidy, but although we argued a great deal, we did not quarrel. The greatest source of irritation, I suppose, was other people's possessions. Our original luggage was minimal, but because everyone wanted to buy presents for their mothers in the bazaars and souks, we rapidly began to look like a junk shop.

Because we were a large party, oddly enough, we had considerable privacy. You did not have to be a good companion all the time. You could, if you wanted to, take two days off, sit by a window and look at the landscape, unbothered. There was no question of being anti-social, as there were plenty of people to talk to each other. In fact, you were never lonely, a very happy experience for many of us, but you had privacy. A perfect situation.

I think, too, that for many of us on that trip there was a great sense of freedom, as about 90 per cent of our ordinary lives fell away. No radio, no television, no telephones, no old friends, no daily routine. I came back feeling very fresh, not stale any more. You learnt to be tolerant of other people, and you had time to know yourself better. You certainly felt yourself changing. I remember that in Bangalore, in south India, the whole party had joined up again and were staying in the local sports stadium. Luxury! We actually had showers and yards and yards of airy, clean concrete stands to sleep on. The first night we were there the man next to me sat up in his sleeping-bag in the middle of the night and said, 'Good Heavens, a rat has just run over me!' I do not like rats at all, but I heard myself say, in a schoolmistressy voice, 'Do you mind. Some of us want to sleep!'

I went on two other COMEX trips. Neither of them went overland because of the volatile political and military situation in several countries to the west of India. COMEX 9 in 1979 travelled within India entirely by train; from the Nilgiri Hills to the Himalayas, from the Bay of Bengal to the Arabian Sea. Since the Indian railways and train stations were built by the British, you have the odd sensation of alighting at, say, Hyderabad and being rather surprised that you are not at, say, Tunbridge Wells. The final expedition in which I participated, COMEX 11 in 1983, was smaller than previous ones with the British contingent being multi-racial, entirely Manchester-based and organised by George Brew, an energetic lecturer at Manchester Polytechnic.

By contrast my visit to India in 1982 was in a very small party, just me and my nine-year-old grandson. 'I don't see why it shouldn't work,' said his father. 'There's only sixty-two years between you.' Aaron and I had an eight-hour journey by bus from Delhi to Mussoorie, where we stayed with Thupten's family. Our very modest luggage was parked at our feet. 'This is *travelling*, Aaron,' I said smugly as the thirsty day wore on and we passed through a succession of Indian villages, women at the wells, old men asleep on charpoys, the heads of water buffaloes rearing up out of ponds. This was a phrase he was to turn back on me many times later when some minor disaster struck.

In Simla we stayed in a very cheap, draughty hotel on one of the town's many peaks. From our huge double bed Aaron and I could see the snow mountains to the north. Outside the hotel door was a lady with snakes in a rough basket, and monkeys swung from every tree. At night, wrapped in our blankets against the cold, I read Enid Blyton to him. We met Granada Television, filming scenes for *The Jewel in the Crown*, their adaptation of Paul Scott's *Raj Quartet*. I admit it was good to sit around in the lounge of their hotel and hear shop talk again and compare local pubs with one of the technicians who lived in Didsbury.

I suppose we made an odd couple, this elderly woman and the small innocent-looking boy. Sometimes I wondered what memories Aaron would bring back with him. For a time he could not stop talking about Baljee's, the restaurant in Simla where 'our' waiter always unfurled a white cloth for us and showed him how to make water-lilies out of starched linen napkins; so British Raj.

But when I telephoned his mother soon after our return, she said, 'He and his friend are making a beautiful little shrine to the Buddha in the barn.'

Aaron also taught me a great deal about myself. 'You are all right, Olive,' he said, 'but you *do* panic.' He was the easiest and most unfussy of travelling companions. After a terrible night in Delhi airport trying unsuccessfully to get a flight home, we returned to the YMCA to gather our forces. My nerve snapped. 'Shut up, Aaron,' I said. 'Stop fooling about. Sit down and keep quiet and we'll make a list of all the things we have to do to get ourselves back to England.' He sat down on the bed and said slowly, 'Yes, and at the top put "Get back our sense of humour".'

I look back on all my travels with great interest and pleasure. But I think that I am like many travellers, in that I have always felt most deeply of all for my own home, and I have been lucky to spend a great deal of my life in homes which I love.

16 1992–96 – Postscript

Didsbury was my home for almost forty years and for much of those last years I was able to enjoy it to the full. I went into Manchester, to the BBC, to courses at the adult education college, to concerts and shops. I continued to see old friends and made some lovely new ones centred on one of the local pubs. We were a disparate lot, of varying ages and backgrounds, but all preferred meeting in a warm and friendly atmosphere to sitting at home for hours on our own. My 'community living' idea had not borne fruit, but I made efforts to link up with others who lived alone. I also travelled regularly for much of that time, to India and even further afield to see Dan and Christina; Dan had various overseas postings with British Airways and Christina was living in Australia.

Nicholas has lived for many years in mid Wales and has made a very good life there with his family. He knew that the Mid Wales Housing Association was building some new 'sheltered' flats in Llanidloes, his nearest town, and suggested that I might apply to live there. So, in 1992 I finally left Didsbury and moved to a beautiful new complex, tucked in among the Welsh hills and right on the River Severn. I am not very mobile and am conscious of the loss of control over aspects of life that I used to take for granted. It is a difficult part of old age but one with which you somehow have to come to terms. I have contact with old friends through telephone calls, letters and some visits, and have made some new friends. My books and mementos of my life, work and travels continue to give me enormous pleasure. Writing this book also, with all the looking back over scripts and articles, letters, notes and photographs that it has entailed, has given me a chance to reflect on my life and recognise some themes.

In the early 1950s I wrote a newspaper article which I called 'Strawberries and Cream'. In it I ranged over household budgeting and the way women tackled it. Those were still fairly austere days after the war and also a time when there was a much clearer demarcation between men's and women's family roles than there is today. I wrote of the impact that the war had had on people's lives and how people were having to accept that some of their aspirations were probably not going to be achieved.

> That being so, one has to make the best of what is left, and it is here that women sail into their own. They may prefer to leave the larger decisions to husbands, pontifically working out figures on the backs of envelopes, but only a woman knows the day-to-day things which give character and vigour to a family.
>
> She knows that if, in the cause of economy, *all* inessential and frivolous things are thrown overboard, it will be very hard to get them back again, or even to want them back. Women are usually excellent at keeping their foot in the door so that it doesn't quite shut. Semolina is fine for ten days, but it must be strawberries and cream on the eleventh; and strawberries and cream served with a flourish and on the best plates.

I went on to list the extravagances that lifted my own life – the odd new book and glass of sherry, some good clothes for all the family, and what we would now call 'time out' for myself. I also speculated on what others' choices might be, and some of these certainly date the article!

> A new hat every spring, a permanent wave twice a year, enough hot baths and time to take them, a really good cup of coffee once or twice a day, a bottle of French perfume at Christmas, a matinee every month, a sitter-in on the nights when the Parish Council meets, Saturday morning ballet classes for a rather solid little daughter.
>
> If all these things sound very small and unimportant, I can only say that everyday life takes its colour from them. You can't grieve for ever about a house or a car or a holiday you never had, but you can be steadily worn down by the kind of daily life which has no highlights, no pleasant tastes and smells, no entirely indefensible extravagances. I am quite sure that you must keep your eye unwaveringly on the strawberries and cream while you stir the semolina.

This attitude to daily life was something that John and I had shared and it lay behind one of his very last remarks to me about the children: 'promise that you won't let their lives be drab'. I did my best to bring them up in the way that he and I had envisaged doing together, to encourage them to enjoy life, to make them easy in many different surroundings and so interested in people and places and ideas that boredom is unthinkable.

What I strove for was tricky in some ways, because there were competing strands; the comfort and security of 'roots' and a sense of belonging, combined with the unpredictability and fluidity of new experiences. I think in many ways my children have been lucky compared to both John and me. From our totally different backgrounds we both had to fight hard and sometimes painfully to pull up our roots so that we could refashion ourselves in our own way. The issue of class in English society was acute when we were young. I wanted to make my children classless, because it seemed to me one of the kindest, most helpful things an English parent could do for a child. To be brought up within the strangling, stifling confines of one class in English society seemed to me to be a great deprivation.

John and I met on a little island, a no-man's-land between our two families, our two ways of growing up, our two classes. He was one of the children that I had so envied; nannied, protected, living behind the noble gates and charming walls of an English country house. There was travel abroad as a child, surrounded by luggage and servants, the whole paraphernalia of the upper-class English family abroad. And yet, of it all, the greatest thing he remembered was when, as a little boy, urged by his governess, he went shyly to the porter of a Swiss hotel and brought out with great difficulty the magic, untried, perhaps meaningless words, 'Un timbre de poste, s'il vous plaît.' And he found that they worked, that they did indeed produce, with no look of surprise, as though it were the most natural thing in the world – a postage stamp! This he never forgot and, apologising, often asked to tell again. All those years of stuffy travel, carefully nurtured in a charmingly gilded cage, and this was the greatest memory of all. It proved to be a door for him in his battle to escape, so that he could return and relate to his family and background on his own terms. John remained a loyal and dutiful son of his family, but he felt intensely the need to establish his own, new, kind of life.

A few years later than John, I began to fight my battle, to escape from the much more stifling (it always seemed to me) cage of a lower middle-class child's background. I had the kindest, best and most tolerant of parents, but my longing to escape was as compulsive as if they had been ogres who kept me chained up in a cellar. It was only later that I came to appreciate fully not only my parents' admirable qualities of character but also their interests and enthusiasms. I have written already of my father's interests, but my mother also was remarkable, as I came to realise. As well as having a wonderful sense of humour, she maintained a constant curiosity in the world around her. She would walk down suburban streets at night and stand on tiptoe to peer over privet hedges, delighted at the glimpse, completely uncensorious, of other people's lives. She also loved riding on the tops of buses or trams; the New York 'el' was made for her. Her formal education had ended early, but she continued to educate herself and develop interests through her reading. She had extraordinarily wide tastes and I, as well as both John and Christopher, had a lot of pleasure choosing books for her as presents.

Parents tend to be over-anxious about their children and 'culture'. The first stirrings of a child towards culture have to be respected, but too much watering is as fatal as too little. You do not want to be given *Alice in Wonderland* when you have barely stopped tearing pages out of your books. If you enjoy *Jane Eyre* in your adolescence, you do not want the collected works of Charlotte Brontë to be eagerly bought for you. You do not want to be taken to art galleries too soon. Most of all, you want to make some of the discoveries for yourself. Parents find it extremely hard to hold back, but tastes are best passed on by enthusiasm that children know to be genuine. I have always admired the attitude of Colette's mother, Sido, who kept the twenty or so volumes of Saint-Simon by her bed, and only thought it odd that her eight-year-old daughter did not share her enjoyment. But her daughter never forgot her mother's genuine admiration for the author; the fact of such devotion remained and worked its own spell. Children need to discover their own enthusiasms, but they will respect anything that raises the emotional temperature of a parent.

On our family holidays in France I used to take the children on detours to go through Colette's home village of Saint-Sauveur-en-Puisaye in Burgundy. We sometimes spent a night in the little hotel on the crazily sloping square, and made the ritual tour to look at the school, rebuilt since Colette's day, and the church, where Sido's dog barked at the elevation of the Host during Mass to the annoyance of the priest. We walked along the sandy paths and by the muddy pools of that not particularly beautiful countryside. The tour always ended at the flat, sun-bleached house with the stone steps going up to the door, shuttered and barred against intruders and curious sight-seers; the house had a plaque on it, 'Ici Colette est née.' To me the whole village was steeped in memories of Colette's books and to go there was the most overwhelming experience. It was in no sense a literary shrine, like Haworth or Dove Cottage, and this made it all the more overpowering.

This question of literary pilgrimages is a mystery to me. If you are affected by them, then nothing else will bring a place alive. I always knew I would be happy never to see whole areas of the world's surface because I could not relate them to a writer, because they had not won for me permanent life through memories and burning love or hate of some writer. The intrinsic beauty of a place can mean very little. Grasmere is lovely, and I used to read and re-read *The Prelude*, but because of, to me, the basic unattractiveness of Wordsworth's character, I could pass through Grasmere ten times a year and never stop to look at Dove Cottage or the churchyard. If I did stop, it was the memory of Dorothy that drew me.

I have, though, always had a love affair with William Hazlitt. He was one of the authors that examinations could not kill. At school I once hit a girl over the head with the leg of a broken chair because she insisted that Charles Lamb was a better writer. Everything about Hazlitt, from his beautiful, cutting style to his romantic looks to his unhappy life, had seemed to me the height of romanticism. I would not have thought of trying to pass this on to my children. However, one summer we were proceeding towards Shrewsbury on our way to Pembrokeshire. 'Proceeding' is the word, because I was for the first time driving a car with a caravan attached and was finding it a frightening experience. Suddenly I saw a name on a signpost – Wem. This was where Hazlitt spent much of his childhood. I let out a shout, turned the car, went into a hedge, tried to back, and got into a hopeless jam across the main road. Christopher said, 'Have you gone mad?' and the children cringed in the back seat as traffic began to pile up on either side of us. In a cloud of disapproval, we eventually disentangled ourselves and made our way to Wem. There we looked at the little low house where Hazlitt's family had lived, and his father's Unitarian chapel. We bought hot bread and fresh pork brawn and sat in a green, misty early-morning field and ate our totally indigestible breakfast. 'Who was Hazlitt?' the children asked. So I told them and quoted what I could remember of *On Going a Journey* to an awed family. I do not know whether any of them has read a word of Hazlitt since, but my enthusiasm did register with them. The fact that grown-up people can be potty and behave irresponsibly about dead authors is quite a useful lesson to learn, and they all still remember the hot bread! Hazlitt would have approved.

I always felt lucky that there was a large cultural overlap between my private and professional interests. Clearly this is not the fate of everyone and indeed in times when just having a job is fortunate in itself, having an enjoyable job seems a luxury and a privilege.

I was never ambitious within the BBC. I must also say honestly that I did not consciously experience any disadvantage as a woman in my working life. I am well aware of frustrations that women today may feel as they reach the perceived 'glass ceiling'. However, I suppose like many women of my generation I set for myself certain limitations. I enjoyed broadcasting and programme making and did not feel drawn to, or indeed suitably talented for, high administrative office. I saw my work more in terms of 'making a living' rather than a 'having a career' with the progression that that implies. I think I would have felt the same even if I had had the support of a husband throughout my children's upbringing, but as it was, there were compromises to be made in order to be a 'good enough' parent. But the flexibility that my BBC work often allowed helped me in my family life. Also, much more positively, we all *enjoyed* my work – the people, the places and the endless variety of interesting topics. As a mother I mostly did not feel disapproval for choosing to work; widowhood was respectable and professional aspirations acknowledged. But I could only do it by having live-in help, a 'wife' in effect, and for many periods during the children's growing up I was lucky to be able to do that.

From my observations of younger women today doing the same balancing act, sometimes with a co-operative partner and sometimes not, or with no partner at all, I am tempted to say that things have actually got more difficult for many working women, especially mothers. Expectations about everything are higher: better education, more demanding work, longer hours. And on top of all this, more perfect children, though fewer. It is certainly wonderful now that more girls and women have real options in life, which is such a different situation from when I was young. Over the years I have talked with many girls at school speech days and relished for them their delicious freedom and choices. But choices can also mean compromises for those who see themselves as 'all-rounders'. I think that women still cannot have it all, or rather, cannot do it all perfectly! The world of work, however, could certainly become more 'family friendly' for both women and men – part-time permanent jobs, flexible hours, work-based childcare. In practice, notwithstanding politicians' rhetoric, children and family life are still undervalued.

A few years ago on a visit to Sydney to see Christina and her family, I had lunch in a restaurant with a very old friend, Neil Hutchison. Neil had been a BBC colleague in Manchester in the 1930s and had gone to Australia after the war to work for the Australian Broadcasting Commission. Within minutes we were reminiscing about our work in the pioneering broadcasting days, remembering the excitements and giggling over the disasters. The young waitress was so intrigued by our animated conversation that she could not resist asking us what it was all about; she clearly found it hard to imagine that fifty years ago even existed, let alone that people could still have fun remembering it! That is what I mean by having the luck to do a job that I loved and that gave me a whole way of life. My feeling was summed up for me perfectly by a conversation I once had with Aaron, my grandson, when he was very small. He told me that he dreamt of being a deep-sea diver. 'The only thing I don't understand, Olive,' he said, 'is, do I pay them or do they pay me?'

References

Dovovan, Paul, 1992, *The Radio Companion*, London, Haper Collins.

Grevatt, Wallace, 1988, *BBC Children's Hour: A Celebration of Those Magical Years*, Lewes, Sussex, The Book Guild.

Hartley, Ian, 1987, *2ZY to NBH: An Informal History of the BBC in Manchester and the North West*, Timperley, Altrincham, Cheshire, Willow Publishing.

Kingsley, Hilary and Tibballs, Geoff, 1990, *Box of Delights: The Golden Years of Television*, London, Papermac.

Pickles, Wilfred, 1949, *Between You and Me*, London, Werner Laurie.

Scannell, Paddy and Cardiff, David, 1991, *A Social History of British Broadcasting: Volume One, 1922–1939*, Oxford, Blackwell.

Other Written Sources

Files at the BBC Written Archives Centre, Caversham.
Olive Shapley's personal papers.

Index

Note: Olive Shapley's own radio and television programmes are in bold italics.

About the Home, 158
Alcott, Louisa M, 9, 86, 131, 150
Alice (Pye), 109, 117, 120, 125, 136
All Your Own, 135
America, 78–108
American Boys Calling Home, 94
American folk music, 104–5
An Ancient City, 150
Andrews, Bowker, 60
Andy Pandy, 133–4, 145
At Home and Abroad, 149
Aunt Alie, 2–3
'Auntie Annie', 16
Auntie Phyll, 146

Bacup, 68
Baillie, Isobel, 175
Barbirolli, Sir John, 59
Barnes, Alan, 171
Barton, Michael, 153, 186
BBC (British Broadcasting Corporation)
  Alexandra Palace Television Studios, 135
  BBC European Service, 73
  BBC Local Radio, 186
  BBC Radio Manchester, 186
  Broadcasting House, London, 38, 74–5
  Broadcasting House, Manchester, 45
  Dickenson Road Television Studio, Manchester, 162
  Lime Grove Television Studios, 135
  New Broadcasting House, Manchester, 186
  New York Office, 77, 80–2, 91
  Plymouth Grove Outside Broadcast Unit, Manchester, 161–2
  School Broadcasting Department, 149–53
  Talks Department, 65–6
BBC Philharmonic Club, 186–7
BBC Philharmonic Orchestra (BBC Northern Orchestra), 34, 58, 59, 186–7
Bedi, Freda (Houlston), 25–6, 29, 195–6
Beecham, Sir Thomas, 58–9
Beeches, The, Didsbury, 109
Behrens, Leonard and Bebie, 108, 169
Behrens, Mary (Flowers), 108, 169
Behrens, Ruth, 108
Belfast, 78
Belle Vue, Manchester, 59
Bell, Mary Hayley, 44
Betjeman, John, 132
Betts, Barbara (Castle), 23–7, 29, 72, 195
Betts, Jimmie, 24
Beyond the Fringe, 172–3

Bill and Ben (Flowerpot Men),
    134, 136
Bird, Maria, 133
Birmingham, 73–4
Bombed Out, 71
Boyd, Donald, 53, 67, 72, 89,
    109
Bradford, 64, 151, 152, 153
Bradley, Alfred, 186
Bradley, Helen, 171
Braine, John, 163
Bridson, D G (Geoffrey), 36–7,
    46, 49, 89
    Coal, 37, 46
    Cotton, 37
    Harry Hopeful, 37
    Steel, 37, 49
    Wool, 37
**Broadcasting with the Lid
    Off**, 51
Brock, Dr (Dame) Dorothy,
    18–21, 70, 126
Brontë family, 55–6
Brontë Parsonage Museum,
    55–6
Brother Bernard, 144
Brother Clement (Abbé
    Raymond Thonn), 53,
    170–1
Brown, Jardine, 65
Bryan, Dora, 171
Buckden, 153
Buck Inn, Buckden, 153, 155
Burgess Hill School, 133
Burke, Peter, 179
Burley-in-Wharfedale, 153

Call My Bluff, 173
Cam Houses, 154
Cameron, James, 185
Campbell, Patrick, 173
Canal Journey, 50, 51
Cansdale, George, 133
Cardiff, David, 48, 51, 56–7
Carson, Violet, 43, 160, 171
Cartland, Barbara, 163

Castle, Barbara (Baroness Castle
    of Blackburn), 23–7, 29,
    72, 195
Castle, Ted, 72
Cathedral City, A, 150
Cavalcanti, Alberto, 57
Chadwick, Thelma, 169
Chadwick, Theo, 165, 169
Charge of the Heavy Brigade,
    64–5
Child Comes Home, A, 110–5
Children in Wartime, 76
Children's Hour, 33, 34, 40–5,
    82–8, 94, 99–101, 108, 135,
    150, 153
    Derek McCulloch ('Uncle
    Mac'), 34, 82–3
    First Attempts, 135
    Fortnightly Newsletter
    (from America), 82–8, 94,
    99–101, 108
    Franklyn Kelsey's serials,
    40–1
    Out With Romany, 45
    Toytown, 40
    Young Artists, 43–4
    Your Own Ideas, 44
Chophel, Thupten, 196–7
Churchill, Odette, 134
Classic Features, 186
Classic Soil, The, 54, 66
Coast and Country, 153–4
Coatman, John, 117
Colehan, Barney, 43, 186
Colette, 172, 206–7
Collins, Norman, 124
COMEX (Commonwealth
    Expedition), 197–201
Communism, 28–9
Conversations in America,
    97
Cooke, Alistair, 80, 81, 83–4,
    91, 97
Cooper, William, 163
Coronation (Elizabeth II), 138,
    148–9
Coronation Street, 161
Coupe, Bernice, 186

Craghead, County Durham, 53
Critics, The, 61
Crossley family, 64
Curzon, Clifford, 59

Dalai Lama, 196
Dangers of Being Human, The, 66
Darjeeling, 194
David, Elizabeth, 164
Davis, Elmer, 106
Dear Kay, 97
December Flower, 185
D-Day landings, 105–6
Dehn, Harold, 45
Delhi, 193–4
Desert Island Discs, 187
Dickens, Monica, 163
Didsbury, 109, 140–2, 203
Dimbleby, Dilys, 159
Dimbleby, Richard, 133, 159
Dobson, Mabel, 80, 96, 97, 98
Doonican, Val, 162
Dors, Diana, 133
Dougall, Robert, 159
Downward, Sir William, 185
Dramatic control panel (radio), 48–9
Duckham, Alexander, 32–3
Dulwich, 17
Dulwich Picture Gallery, 17–8
Durham, 150

Eason, Ursula, 78
Eddison, Robert, 147
Elgar, Edward, 139
Emmerson, Mr, 53
Emmerson, Mrs ('Mrs Armstrong'), 53, 75, 89
Ervine, St John, 20
Evans, Dame Edith, 126–7
Evens, Reverend G. Bramwell, 45
Eyam, 46–7
Eyewitness – 'New York At War' parade, 95

Family Affairs, 158–9
'Family history', 166–7

Father Tien, 180
Fields, Gracie, 60
First Attempts (Children's Hour), 135
First Steps in Learning, 4–8
First World War, 3–4
Flescher, Walter, 153
Flowers, Mary, 108, 169
Flowers, Professor Brian (Lord Flowers), 169
Focus on Fashion, 137
Forbes, Bryan, 171, 185
Formby, George, 73
Fortnightly Newsletter (from America) *(Children's Hour)*, 82–8, 94, 99–101, 108
Fowler, Eileen, 158
Free Trade Hall, Manchester, 59
Friern School, 4
From the Children, 71

Gambell, Doris, 40, 43
George Inn, Chollerford, 58–9
Ghosh, Jhoti, 72
Good Housekeeping (magazine), 71
Good Old Days, The, 43
Gorton, Bridget, 140
Gorton, Christopher Bellhouse (second husband), 117–8, 137–8, 139–40, 149, 153, 154, 165–6, 168, 206, 207
Gorton, Gay, 140
Gorton, Neville, 139
Goudeket, Maurice, 172
Gould, Mike, 179
GPO Film Unit, 57
Grasmere, 207
Grassington, 153
Green, Michael, 186
Gregson, Dick, 42, 153
Gregory, Colonel Lionel, 197
Grenfell, Joyce, 133
Griffiths, Joan, 125
Guthrie, Woody, 104

Haley, William, 106
Halifax, Earl of, 106

Hall, Henry, 43
Hall, Stuart, 185
Hallé Orchestra, 38, 45, 58, 59, 67
Halliday, Eugene, 168
Hampstead, 71–2, 133
Harding, Archie, 36, 37, 51, 54, 66
Harewood, Earl of, 171
Harold (postman), 143–4
Harris, Alec, 180
Harris, Reg, 185
Harrisson, Tom, 56
Hart, Adam, 136
Hart, Christina *see* Salt, Christina
Hartley, Marie, 160
Hartnell, William, 127–8
Have a Go (initially *Have a Go, Joe*), 43
Haworth, 55–6
Haworth, Don, 186
Hazlitt, William, 207–8
Health for the Nation, 57
Heywood, Pat, 185
Hibberd, Stuart, 34
Hill, Susan, 163–4
Hill, Trevor, 186
Himalayas, 326
Hird, Thora, 171, 179
Hockney, David, 153
Holgate, Diane, 171
Hollingworth, 67
Holt, William, 171
Homeless People, 52–3, 57
Home This Afternoon, 169
Hopewell, Harry, 45
Hotel Splendide, 53–4
Houlston, Freda (Bedi), 25–6, 129, 195–6
Howard, Elizabeth Jane, 163
Hubberholme, 154–5
Hudson, Harry, 43
Hunter, Lyn, 185
Hunter, Nick, 174
Hurst, George, 145
Hush, Gillian, 186
Hutchison, Neil, 209
Hyde, 23, 24, 25

Iles, Gerald, 160
India, 193–9, 200–2
Ingleby, Joan, 160
Ives, Burl, 104–5, 138, 187

Jack Hardy's Little Orchestra, 45
Jackson, T. Leslie ('Jacko'), 44
    Call My Bluff, 44
    This is Your Life, 44
    What's my Line?, 44
Jazz, 27

Katmandu, 192–3
Kaye, Danny, 149
Kelly, Charles, 45
Kelsey, Franklyn (*Children's Hour* serials), 40–1
    The Children of the Sun, 40–1
    The Island in the Mist, 40–1
Kennedy, Frances, 21
Kirkham, Joe, 146
Kirkwood, Pat, 44, 73
Knight, Eric, 42
    Never Come Monday (radio play), 42
Kris, Ernst and Marianne, 72, 89, 101, 118–9

Langstrothdale, 154
Laughton, Charles, 54
Laughton, Tom, 54
Leadbelly, 104–5, 187
Leisure and Pleasure, 159–60
Le Petit Appeville, Normandy, 188–9
Levy, Mervyn, 160
Levy, Muriel, 43
Lewthwaite, Hazel, 172
Lingstrom, Freda, 70, 72, 133
Listener, 50
Listen with Mother, 127
Little Women, 9, 83, 86, 131–2, 150
Littlewood, Joan, 54–5, 66
Livesey, Joan, 179
Llanidloes, 203
Lodgers, 133–4, 145–8
Lomax, John and Alan, 105
London County Council, 3

Looking at Things, 149–50
£.s.d.: A Study in Shopping, 36, 49–50
Lum, Mrs, 70, 77, 89
Lynn, Vera, 126

Mabel (Dobson), 80, 96, 97, 98
MacColl, Ewan (Jimmie Miller), 54, 55, 186
McCulloch, Derek ('Uncle Mac'), 34, 82–3
McMillan, Margaret, 31
McMillan, Rachel, 31
McMillan, Rachel, Training College, 31–3
Madge, Charles, 56
Malleson, Joan, 27
Manchester, 33, 34, 40, 51, 57–62, 72
Manchester College, Oxford, 29
Manchester Evening News, 183
Manchester Guardian, 79
Manchester Polytechnic, 185
Marles-les-Mines, 53
Marlor, Frank, 146, 179
Marshall, Arthur, 164
Marshall, George, 78
Mary Datchelor Girls' School, The, 18–22
Mass Observation, 56
Matthews, Thomas, 38, 59–60
Mayne, William, 171
Mead, Margaret, 126
Meet the Ackermans, 97
Michelmore, Cliff, 135
Miller, Jimmie (Ewan MacColl), 54, 55, 186
Miller, Jonathan, 172–3
Mills, Hayley, 171
Mills, John, 44
Miners' Wives, 53, 75
Miners' Wives (Postscript), 75–6
Miss Renee, 138, 143
Mitchell, Yvonne, 164
Mobile recording unit (radio), 48–9

Modern Woman (magazine), 132–3
More, Kenneth, 131
Morris, Noel, 45
Mortimer, Penelope, 163
Music, 4, 19, 187
Jazz, 27

National Council for the Unmarried Mother and her Child, The, 176
New Books and Old Books, 131–2
Newcastle, 51, 58
Newsom, John, 30–1
Newton, Eric, 61–2
New York, 78–9, 80, 82, 84–5, 87–8, 92–3, 94–7, 98
New York Speaks to London, 95–6
New York Times, 106
Night Journey, 51–2
North of England, 24–5, 38–9, 40, 57, 60–1, 72, 150

Observer, 184
Ockenden Venture, The, 180
O'Donovan, Joan, 163
Olive Shapley Kindergarten, The, 185
Olive Shapley Tells a Story, 135–6
Out with Romany (*Children's Hour*), 45
Oxford University, 21–2, 23–30

Panorama, 159
Paris, 27–8, 189–90
Patten, Marguerite, 158
Pearson, Neil, 177
Peckham, 2, 9, 10, 11
Peel, J. H. B, 172
Pelletier, Rooney, 76
People in Books, 157
Pickles, Mabel, 41
Pickles, Wilfred, 41–3, 49, 54, 117
Pierre (dog), 143–4
Plague at Eyam, 47

Politics, 27–9
Porter, David, 40, 46, 89
Pougnet, Jean, 20
Priestley, J B, 155
Prospero (BBC retired staff
    magazine), 184
Pye, Alice, 109, 117, 120, 125,
    136

Questions and Answers, 149
Quiet House at Haworth,
    The, 55–6

Raby, Frances, 35–6, 89
Rachel McMillan Training
    College, The, 31–3
Radhakrishnan, Sarvepalli, 29
Radio Daily (New York), 106
Radio documentaries, 48–57
Radio Times, 83, 153–4, 172
Rankin, Molly, 131
Ratter, Magnus Cluness, 10–1
Redhead, Brian, 163–4
Reed, Henry, 43
Reed, John, 186
Reimann, Louis Ferdinand
    Augustus Emil
    (grandfather), 3
Reith, Sir John, 37–8, 186
Richard, Cliff, 175
Richardson, Ralph, 57
Rickman, John, 72, 115–6, 121
Roberts, Miranda, 63, 170
Robeson, Paul, 103–4
Robins, Denise, 163
Rochdale, 60
Rockefeller Centre, New York,
    80
Rogerson, Haydn and Mamie,
    38, 67
Roosevelt, Eleanor, 86–7, 104,
    126
Roosevelt, President, 85, 95
Rose Hill (house), 142–5, 175–6,
    180, 182, 183, 185
Rose Hill Trust, The, 175–80,
    183
Rumtek, 195–6

Rusholme Repertory Company,
    44

St Hugh's College, Oxford, 23
Salt, Aaron, 193–4, 201–2, 209
Salt (Hart), Christina, 60, 61,
    115, 133, 140, 154, 165,
    173, 175, 178, 203, 204–5,
    209
Salt, Dan, 60, 101–3, 107, 108,
    109, 115–6, 133, 140, 148,
    154, 155, 165, 173, 175,
    190, 203, 204–5
Salt, Daniel, 151
Salt, Firoozeh, 166
Salt, John Scarlett Alexander
    (first husband), 42–3,
    64–123, 188, 204–5, 206
    background and early years,
    64–5, 204–5
    father, 64
    mother and sisters, 64, 90,
    115, 119, 122, 165
    childhood travel, 188
    Army, 65
    BBC career, 65–6, 68, 73, 77,
    81–2, 105–6, 108, 110
    thoughts on America, 78–9,
    88–9, 90–3, 106–7
    ill health, 103, 107–8,
    109–10, 115
    death, 115–23
Salt, Nicholas, 110, 133, 140,
    154, 165, 173, 175, 203,
    204–5
Salt, Sir Titus, 64, 150–3
Salt, Titus Junior, 153
Saltaire, 64, 150–3
Sargent, Dr Malcolm, 59
Scannell, Paddy, 48, 51, 56–7
Scarborough, 53
Scarlett, General, 64–5
Schubert, Paul and Topse,
    89–90, 92, 96
Second World War
    Outbreak, 67–8
    Evacuation, 68–9
    Blitz, 68–9, 73–5
Seeger, Peggy, 186

Seeger, Pete, 104, 187
Sermons in Stone, 150
Shapley, Bill (brother), 3–4, 7, 15
Shapley File, The, 173–4
Shapley, Francis (grandfather), 2, 167
Shapley, Frank (brother), 3–4
Shapley (Reimann), Kate Sophie (mother), 2, 3, 9, 12, 13, 40, 120, 165, 167, 205–6
Shapley, Olive Mary
  Shapley family (see separate entries)
  birth, 9
  childhood, 2–8, 9–17
  Unitarian Church, 10–1, 29
  adolescence, 18–22
  primary school, 4–8
  secondary school, 18–22
  first broadcast heard, 21
  Oxford University, 21–2, 23–30
  sex, 24, 26–7, 39
  Worker's Education Association (WEA) lecturer, 30–1
  nursery teacher training, 31–3
  recruitment to the BBC, 33
  Children's Hour, 33, 34, 40–5, 82–8, 94, 99–101, 108, 135, 150, 153
  abortion, 39–40
  radio documentaries, 48–57
  radio drama, 46–7
  first marriage (John Salt), 64, 66–7
  miscarriages, 72
  nervous breakdowns, 101–2, 168
  childbirth, 101–3, 110, 115
  children (see separate entries under Salt)
  America, 78–108
  John's death, 115–23
  Woman's Hour, 27, 124–31, 169–72
  television, 134–6, 148–9, 156–65, 174–5
  second marriage (Christopher Gorton), 137–8
  Christopher's death, 165–6
  The Rose Hill Trust, 175–80, 183
  'community living', 182–5
  Honorary Fellowship, Manchester Polytechnic, 185
  The Olive Shapley Kindergarten, 185
  BBC eightieth birthday dinner, 186–7
  travel, 188–202
  culture, 206–7
  literary pilgrimages, 207–8
  thoughts on BBC career, 208
Shapley, William Gilbert (father), 2, 3, 16–7, 66, 167, 189, 205–6
Sillitoe, Alan, 163
Silver, Dr, 169–70
Sikkim, 194–5
Simla, 199, 201
Simmons, Jean, 185
Smith, Herbert, 117
Smythe, Pat, 160
Solomon Islands, 193
Something of a Handicap, 172–3
Something to Read, 163–5
Sooty, 162
Spain, Nancy, 163
Spoonful of Sugar, A, 174–5
Stephens, Doreen, 157, 160
Stephens Terrace, 181
Stockport, 62
Storey, David, 163
Story of Little Black Quibba, The, 136
Story of Little Black Sambo, The, 136
Story of Saltaire, The, 150–2
Strawberries and Cream, 203–4

Tagore, Rabindranath, 10, 29

Talkabout, 129, 169, 172–4, 187
Television, 134–6, 148–9,
   156–65, 174–5
Terry, Sonny, 104
Thanksgiving Day, 85, 96
Theatre Workshop, 54
They Speak for Themselves,
   56–7
Thompson, Robert ('Mouse
   Man'), 155
Thompson, T., 46
Thonn, Abbé Raymond
   (Brother Clement), 53,
   170–1
Thorp Arch, 64, 115, 119
Tibetan Buddhism, 16, 195–6
Tibetans, 194–7
Todmorden, 171
Tootal's, 139, 149
Top of the Pops, 162, 165
To Travel Hopefully, 129–30
Toytown (*Children's Hour*), 40
Travel, 188–202
Trueman, Brian, 135, 172

Uncle Ernest, 16
Unitarian Church, 10–1, 29

Very Occasional Music, 187
Vietnamese 'boat people',
   180–1
Voice of the North, 169

Warren, Tony, 161
**Wartime Thanksgiving Day,
   A**, 96
Washbourne, Mona, 185
We Have Been Evacuated, 68
Wellington, Lindsay, 77, 81,
   105
Wharfedale, 153–5
Wharfe, River, 64
Wheeler, Peter, 135. 172
Wheldon, Huw, 135

Whistle Down the Wind, 171
Whitehorne, Katharine, 163,
   184
White House, The, 86
White, Josh, 104
Whitworth, Robin, 46
Williams, John, 135
Williams, Stephen, 43
Williamson, Stanley, 186
Wilson, Alastair, 186
Wilson, Jonty, 162, 171
Wilton, Connecticut, 89, 96
Wilton, Wiltshire, 96
Winn, Godfrey, 179
Wolfe, Thomas, 98
Woman (magazine), 179
Woman's Hour, 27, 124–31,
   169–72
   Daily Serial, 130–1
   Northern Edition, 169–72
World Goes By, The, 96–7
Women in Europe, 76–7
Women in Wartime, 69–70,
   76
Women of Today, 134
Women's television
   programmes, 157–60
Word in Edgeways, A, 169
Wordsworth, Dorothy, 207
Wordsworth, William, 207
World At One, The, 169
World This Weekend, The, 169
World War One (see First World
   War)
World War Two (see Second
   World War)
Worth, Harry, 162

York, 150
Young Shoreditch, 132
Young Artists (*Children's*),
   43–4
Your Own Ideas (*Children's
   Hour*), 44